Personal Accounts of Events, Travels, and Everyday Life in America

Personal Accounts of Events, Travels, and Everyday Life in America

An Annotated Bibliography

COMPILED BY

E. Richard McKinstry

A Winterthur Book

1997

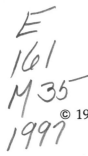

FIRST EDITION

Library of Congress Cataloging-in-Publication Data

Personal accounts of events, travels, and everyday life in America : an annotated bibliography / compiled by E. Richard McKinstry. — 1st ed.
— (A Winterthur book)
Includes bibliographical references and index.
ISBN 0-912724-39-0
1. United States—Description and travel—Bibliography—Catalogs. 2. United States—Social life and customs—Bibliography—Catalogs. 3. American diaries—Bibliography—Catalogs. 4. Travelers' writings, American—Bibliography—Catalogs. 5. Winterthur Library—Catalogs. I. McKinstry, E. Richard.
Z1236.P47   1997
[E161]
016.973—dc21   97-10832
                                                              CIP

Manufactured in the United States of America

Contents

Preface

The organization of this volume is quite simple. Following the customary introductory front matter is an annotated bibliography of ninety-four manuscript personal accounts in the Winterthur Library acquired by the Joseph Downs Collection of Manuscripts and Printed Ephemera through 1989. Each bibliographic entry includes a description of the item under consideration, mentioning the account's author or subject and his or her life dates, title, date, length in number of pages or volumes, illustrative material, and height in centimeters. Brief essays describe the contents of the manuscripts and often include references to related works.

Immediately following the manuscript accounts is a bibliography of 406 published travel narratives held in the Printed Book and Periodical Collection at Winterthur. Because the titles of the volumes regularly detail the itinerary of the author, annotation was thought unnecessary; however, bibliographies in which some of the narratives have been recorded are furnished. A short-title list of those bibliographies cited appears after the entries.

Indexes play a major part in the efficient use of any bibliography or guide. To enhance the usefulness of *Personal Accounts*, three indexes are included. The first is a chronological index to the manuscripts. This index records the year, the keeper of the diary or other personal account or the title of the account, and the entry number of the item. The second is a comprehensive index to the manuscripts. Numbers in the index refer to the numbers assigned to the personal account, from M1 to M94. The third index refers to geographical places mentioned in the titles of the published travel narratives.

It is worth noting some standard sources that were consulted to identify the individuals who kept or who were mentioned in the personal accounts, to verify geographical locations, and to pinpoint historical events. The most informative biographical works were the *Dictionary of American Biography*, the standard in the field for sketches of important American figures, and for background on Englishmen, the *Dictionary of National Biography*, a superb multivolume compilation from Oxford University Press. Offering briefer entries than its cousin, the *DAB*, is *Who Was Who in America*. For nineteenth-century people, *The National Cyclopedia of American Biography*, a thirteen-volume source published from 1892 to 1906 by James T. White and Company of New York, was most valuable. Census indexes and city directories furnished limited but important information for identifying residents of a particular location. Because there are many manuscript personal accounts in the collection by personages in the world of art or by people who discuss artists, two standard sources were illuminating: *The New-York Historical Society's Dictionary of Artists in America, 1564–1860*, compiled by George C. Groce and David H. Wallace and published in New Haven, Connecticut, by Yale University Press in 1957, and *Who Was Who in American Art*, edited by Peter Falk and issued by Sound View Press, Madison, Connecticut, 1985.

Many personal accounts in the Downs collection are travel narratives. For geographical locations in the United States, the *American Guide Series*, prepared by members of the Federal Writer's Project of the Works Progress Administration, offered needed identification. Gazetteers, especially the hefty 2,478-page *Lippincott's Gazetteer of the World*, published in 1880 in Philadelphia by J. B. Lippincott and Company, were useful. The nineteenth-century Baedeker guidebooks of Europe were edifying for that part of the globe. Finally, the *Atlas of the World*, published by the National Geographic Society in Washington, D.C., 1975, helped identify itineraries of both ships and travelers.

Historical events occurring in the United States are outlined in the *Encyclopedia of American History*, edited by Richard B. Morris and Jeffrey B. Morris and published in 1976 by Harper and Row, New York. Happenings elsewhere are summarized in *An Encyclopedia of World History*, compiled and edited by William L. Langer and issued by Houghton Mifflin Company of Boston, 1972.

Finally, because many diarists mention reading material in an abbreviated fashion, some bibliographical verification had to be undertaken. Databases of both OCLC and RLIN were consulted to identify authors and titles of books and periodicals that diary keepers remembered in their passages.

Acknowledgments

This volume is the third in a series of bibliographies published to describe the holdings of the Winterthur Library. Like its predecessors, *Trade Catalogues at Winterthur: A Guide to the Literature of Merchandising, 1750 to 1980*, published in 1984, and *The Edward Deming Andrews Memorial Shaker Collection*, issued three years later, this volume focuses on just one aspect of an incredibly varied collection of research material.

While one name appears on the title page of *Personal Accounts*, many other individuals contributed to its production. Katharine Martinez, former director of the library, always voiced her support and encouragement. Working in an environment that promotes and appreciates research projects such as *Personal Accounts* has made my work much easier and enjoyable. Other library staff members who have contributed to such an environment are Eleanor McD. Thompson, librarian of the Printed Book and Periodical Collection, and Kurt A. Bodling and Heather A. Clewell, formerly of the Joseph Downs Collection of Manuscripts and Printed Ephemera. I would be remiss if I did not mention the names of two former Downs collection librarians, Beatrice K. Taylor and Barbara M. Adams, who worked with the materials described herein as our immediate predecessors. Indeed, many diaries and other types of manuscripts included in this volume were acquired during Taylor's tenure as Downs collection librarian; to her, everyone owes a great deal of gratitude.

A special word of thanks is due to Maja Teufer, who volunteered many hours of her time to compile the initial draft of the bibliography of travel narratives. Her painstaking efforts in recording the entries are greatly appreciated. Without her excellent assistance, this volume would have been delayed for several months. Former colleague Don C. Skemer, curator of manuscripts at Princeton University Library, read the manuscript and made useful comments.

Finally, a word of appreciation is due Winterthur's Publications Division, especially Susan Randolph, whose editorial expertise was most welcome and appreciated. This is the third time that I have worked with the folks in Publications on a book-length project and the third time that I have gladly recorded my thanks for their many contributions.

Introduction

The Joseph Downs Collection of Manuscripts and Printed Ephemera is a rich, special collection for the study of domestic life, objects associated with the daily activities of our forebears, art, and the concerns of an increasingly mobile and multifaceted American population. Its resources include a variety of primary research materials, including sketchbooks, design books, architectural drawings, advertising literature of all kinds, fabric swatch books, greeting cards, business records of craftsmen and businesses, and even children's toys, games, and paper dolls. In addition, an important portion of the Downs collection focuses on personal accounts in the forms of diaries, travel accounts, journals, commonplace books, and memoirs. The Printed Book and Periodical Collection—featuring rare books—complements the holdings of these original sources with thousands of published works, especially travel narratives. This descriptive bibliography details the nature and contents of the holdings of personal accounts in the Winterthur Library, particularly manuscript diaries and printed travel accounts.

Although the words *journal* and *diary* are commonly used interchangeably, in reality they are two very different literary forms.[1] Individuals write journals as one way to focus on their internal concerns and ideas rather than to record external events that they see and that are beyond their control. On the other hand, because the chief purpose of the diary is to chronicle external events, they serve as an important way for people to react to their observations and surroundings. Having this distinction, however, does not necessarily mean that a manuscript fits neatly under the definition of journal or diary. In fact, Samuel Johnson equated journals and diaries in his dictionary when he wrote that a diary is "an account of the transactions, accidents and observations of every day; a journal." Steven E. Kagle, a modern prolific writer on the history of the diary, notes that "while

[1] For the difference between journals and diaries, see Steven E. Kagle, *American Diary Literature, 1620–1799* (Boston: Twayne Publishing, 1979), p. 16.

many of the best colonial diaries adhered to relatively simple
forms with limited motives, the diaries of the early nineteenth
century were more likely to mix elements of the diary of external
incident with those of the introspective journal."[2] It is thus customary for personal accounts such as the ones described in this
volume to combine the attributes of both a journal and a diary.
The reader will notice quickly, however, that each manuscript
has a dominant direction.

The diary constitutes the largest segment of personal
accounts of Americans in the Downs collection. Originating with
early explorers and colonists, it is one of the oldest forms of writing in the country. The Puritans of New England kept diaries for
spiritual reasons. Later, diaries dealt with such topics as love
and courtship, war, and distinctive historical events. Although
the most common diary is the one that records a specific activity,
some writers kept diaries that transcended particular incidents.[3]
These so-called life diaries are, unfortunately, few and far
between.

Over the years, diaries have been kept by prominent and
ordinary people alike. George Washington chronicled his life at
Mount Vernon, Robert E. Lee sketched his military exploits as a
colonel in the Second United States Cavalry in Texas, and
Increase Mather commented about life in colonial America.
While these accounts are important because they represent figures significant in the history of the United States, they are less
useful for historians studying the activities of American society
at large. Not everyone oversaw the activities of a plantation like
Washington, not everyone was a soldier like Lee, and not everyone could offer the keen insights of Mather. Instead, the diaries
kept by such folks as Florence Ashmore Cowles, who discussed
her life in postbellum Petersburg, Virginia; John W. Kinsey, a

---

[2] Thomas Mallon, *A Book of One's Own: People and Their Diaries* (New York:
Ticknor and Fields, 1984), p. [1]; Steven E. Kagle, *Early Nineteenth-Century American Diary Literature* (Boston: Twayne Publishing, 1986), p. 4.
[3] Kagle, *Early Literature*, p. 3.

traveler who maintained a journal of his trip from Lowell, Massachusetts, to Chicago in 1850; and Harrison Vandegrift, a Civil War soldier who wrote about his experiences in 1863 and 1864, are more meaningful.

People keep diaries for many reasons.[4] Children and teenagers are encouraged to write as a way to instill discipline, and sometimes they continue the practice into adulthood. For example, fifteen-year-old Martha Vail was given a diary as a Christmas present in 1892 by her mother, another diarist. In it Martha faithfully recorded her concerns and the events of her young life in Somers Center, New York.

Some individuals maintain diaries in their youth so that in old age they can relive past experiences and so their descendants can better understand the pattern of life generations before their own. David Clapp, a printer, writing when he was twenty-five years old, summed it up: "The pleasure of recording the incidents and a description of the scenes I witnessed; and the anticipated satisfaction of perusing the record at some future time, and thus again living in those incidents and gazing upon those scenes have been my principal objects; not perhaps unaccompanied however, with the belief or the hope that other eyes—eyes of affection and of friendship—may likewise glide over these rude sketches and either bless Heaven that the writer still lives to enjoy with them the perusal, or drop one tear to the memory of the deceased."[5]

Individuals often keep diaries because of their sense of history, believing that what they are observing and writing will be important to future generations. John Fanning Watson, a resi-

---

[4] On the reasons for keeping diaries and their common contents, see Arthur Ponsonby, *English Diaries from the Sixteenth to the Twentieth Century with an Introduction on Diary Writing* (London: Methuen; New York: Doran, 1922), pp. 6–25.

[5] David Clapp travel journal (entry M17), 2:2–3, Joseph Downs Collection of Manuscripts and Printed Ephemera, Winterthur Library (hereafter in this introduction, works of individually named diarists are located in the Downs collection).

dent of Philadelphia in the nineteenth century and an author of
some renown, kept volumes of diaries that focused on important
events of his day. His mother, Lucy, encouraged him at an early
age to be conscious of history by her own activities as the Watson family genealogist and as a chronicler of her own mid eigh-
teenth-century New England youth. John Vaughan's sense of
history took a slightly different tack but was equally earnest.
Vaughan lived in Wilmington, Delaware, in 1802 during a severe
yellow fever epidemic. A physician, he was interested in chart-
ing the spread of the disease and recording the activities taken
to alleviate it. Vaughan's reason for maintaining his diary was to
better understand the cause and spread of yellow fever and to
consider a cure so that succeeding generations could be protected from the affliction. A different example of a diarist with a
sense of history is represented in the writings of Joseph Richardson. His volume, entitled "Garden Book," was important
because it served as a personal record of one growing season
and facilitated his planning of subsequent annual planting
schedules.

A diary—a journal actually—serves as a confidential repository for the writer's own thoughts. Florence Ashmore Cowles
wrote emotionally about the affection that she had for her husband, Will, and about the animosity between her and her
mother-in-law. Of Will, she said, "to make Will unhappy for one
minute is to me the most terrible thing in the world."[6] Of Will's
mother, she commented that she was frequently in bad humor
and unnecessarily critical; she added that Will did not realize
how unkind his mother could be. Florence's diary is a splendid
example of how an individual who is generally self-conscious
could privately unburden herself and then undoubtedly feel better for having done so. Another such individual was Walter
Mason Oddie, an artist whose painting style is categorized in the
early Hudson River school style. Oddie constantly complained

---

[6] Florence Ashmore Cowles diary (entry M22), p. 47.

about not having enough money and once wrote, "I shall know no peace of mind until I am once more free from the turmoils of debt—and stand independent of the world as far as relates to obligation."[7]

Diary keeping furnishes a special way to broaden a person's education. Individuals taking what we call the grand tour of Europe often kept a daily record of their journey for future reference. The thoroughness of some observations suggests that guidebooks, rather than personal scrutiny, may actually have served as the source of the commentary.

Legal matters inspired the writing of entire diaries and accounted for lengthy passages in more general journals. In 1876 the recently widowed Lavinia M. Hoagland had to resort to legal maneuvers to claim her husband's estate since he had died without having signed a will. Because Hoagland's financial affairs were complicated and because Lavinia was challenged by attorneys in New York and members of her husband's family in New Jersey, it would not be unreasonable to conclude that she kept her diary as a form of self-protection in case she had to remember how events had transpired. William Thorn, the operator of a sawmill in upstate New York, wrote about his courtroom experiences as a way to vent his anger. In 1805 he said that he was not fond of lawsuits and added that he could recall many instances when he chose to lose money rather than bring an adversary to court.

Finally, diaries were maintained to furnish their keepers with information that they might need to review in subsequent years. Artist Edwin Whitefield, a native of Great Britain, traveled to the midwest during the 1850s and 1860s to explore and promote land development. His diaries include textual descriptions of what he saw and sketches of the scenery. In 1888 Whitefield remarked that he hoped to return to England to interest his fellow countrymen in investing in Minnesota. While in England, he

---

[7] Walter Mason Oddie, "Private Notes &c."(entry M67), 1:[159].

undoubtedly hoped to rely on his records of the trips that he had taken decades earlier to refresh his memory. In a similar vein, an unidentified New Yorker journeyed to present-day West Virginia in 1839 to examine an area for his own settlement or speculation along the Coal River. His diary furnished a permanent annal of the trip.

The contents of diaries are as varied as their keepers. Artists write about their special endeavors, travelers comment about what they see, and inventors note their thoughts for new products. Although writers concentrate on disparate topics, common threads appear from diary to diary. For some reason, nearly everyone comments about the weather. That is understandable in some instances, for weather is incredibly important for ocean voyages and for timing garden plantings. At other times, it is trivial, perhaps merely serving as a consistent way to open diary passages.

Another common topic among diarists is health, either personal, familial, or of friends. Food and drink are often singled out as well. When they are encountered, royalty and celebrities engender habitual comment. Family and personal milestones, including births, marriages, deaths, and birthdays, are more often than not mentioned in diaries. And an individual's reading habits often come to the fore.

Personal accounts—diaries specifically—are valuable sources for historians. They often are the only immediate record of events, people, or special occasions. Harrison Vandegrift's account of his military exploits before the Civil War battle at Gettysburg, for example, is important for its detail of a little-known but potentially meaningful encounter with Jeb Stuart's troops. Benjamin Johnson's description of his encounter with an inebriated Thomas Paine is illuminating for its characterization. In addition, diaries tend to offer a degree of candidness that other writings cannot approach because their keepers have not always allowed for the possibility that other eyes will review their words. A summary of the events of the Centennial Exhibition years after the fact, for instance, lacks the straightforward and sincere commentary that recent visitor E. S. Marsh provided in his manuscript. Arguably, diaries are the most truthful source for the historian because their immediacy and their details—perhaps frivolous—allow for a break from the rigors sometimes associated with the reading of historical accounts.

This introduction has concentrated on diaries and journals. In addition to these two forms of personal accounts, the Downs collection includes commonplace books and memoirs. The commonplace book is an intriguing source; its contents usually represent the activities and thoughts of individuals through the words and art of others. For all intents and purposes, what makes up a commonplace book is whatever its compiler deems important enough to keep and record: perhaps copies of poetry by Walter Scott, an essay by a religious figure, a watercolor by Audubon, a fond wish from a friend, even legal forms. In short, commonplace books are records of influence.[8] They tell today's reader what people, readings, and events had an impact on individuals generations ago. Although perhaps unrevealing singly, when considered with others of the same period, commonplace books uncover much that was important to individuals in any given period.

Just as commonplace books are useful for studying groups of individuals, memoirs are important for gaining an understanding of the lives of individuals. Written by the subjects themselves, often at an advanced age, memoirs tell people's stories from the perspective of time. Although such an approach can lend context to the account, it also allows for the possibility of misrepresentation because of either poor memory or an effort to sanitize unpleasant episodes.

The collection of personal accounts in the Downs collection ranges from commonplace books of teenagers to Civil War diaries, from a diary of a female prison guard to a European travel

[8] Mallon, *Book of One's Own*, p. 120.

narrative of a Quaker on a mission to heal a rift in a Quaker community in France, from a journal kept by a Bucks County, Pennsylvania, farmer to a log of a supercargo on an ocean voyage to the Orient, from an account of a taxidermist traveling through Panama to the recollections in memoir form of a septuagenarian known for his connections in the world of Boston politics and art. Each in its own way describes a portion of the American experience, and each complements the others in its contribution to the understanding of our nation's past.

It is best if the reader of any personal account separate its contents into two parts: primary material that reveals themes and secondary material that provides a background and context to what is judged important. In writing the descriptions of the material in the Downs collection, these overall themes have been extracted and discussed.

Manuscripts

M1   Adams, Charles E., b. 1856.
[Diary]. 1886–91.
4 v.: ill.; 21 cm.
Charles Adams worked chiefly as a woodcarver in New England
during the time that he kept this diary. On October 7, 1885, as
he recalled five months later, John W. Ayres, a cabinetmaker
from Salem, Massachusetts, hired him to work on the renovation
of the Loring-Emmerton house in Salem. Adams contributed
carvings on moldings, a cap for a bay window that required a
design in the form of a basket of fruit, capitals on pilasters that
were to be situated between the double doors of the parlor, a
panel that would go above a French window, and decorative elements for a clock. Adams commented on visits made to Ayres's
shop by George Emmerton, the current owner of the Loring-
Emmerton house, and Emmerton's architect, Arthur Little. On
February 3, 1886, Little "could not seem to think where the little
capitols that [he was] cutting were to go," although on February 12 Little admitted that he liked them. On March 6 Ayres let
Adams go because most of the work that had been contracted
for was finally completed.
   Adams next found employment in Providence, Rhode
Island, where he was hired by a man named Brown and later by
the firm of Morlock and Bayer. He worked on various projects,
including a board—perhaps a sign—for Providence Coal Company, a capital for the Barnaby Building, columns for the firm of
French and McKenzie, a ceiling molding for Peabody's and Sons,
a sign reading "Town Hall," and a mahogany table for Potter
and Company. When his employment ended at Providence in
mid September, Adams moved to Boston to look for
employment.
   During the six years that Adams worked throughout New
England and kept his diary, he would gravitate to Boston after
each of his jobs ended. Some of his family resided there, and he
struck up a friendship with Jennie Gookin that was very important to him. In addition, Adams wanted to pursue his education
in art, so he enrolled in a Boston school run by George Hartnell
Bartlett, a fairly well known teacher of drawing. At school
Adams worked on exercises dealing with light and shading, geo-

metrical patterns, and charcoal and attended lectures by Bartlett on historic ornament. Boston had many stores that sold artists' supplies, so Adams found many places to purchase the materials that he needed for his class as well as for some other work that he did, including modeling objects in clay and casting figures in plaster. At leisure, Adams enjoyed watching baseball; Boston's team made it possible for him to pursue this diversion. He also became a frequent bicycle rider and relied on Pope Manufacturing Company for supplies for his "wheel."

Wherever Adams worked, he was involved in the labor-union movement. In Providence, for instance, he went to a lecture on labor by Henry George. He always kept his carvers union dues paid and even noted in his diary when a death assessment had to be collected by the union. When it was necessary to act as a unit, the carvers did not hesitate. On April 8, 1887, the union met in Boston to appoint a committee "to see James Wemyss and see if they could not settle their trouble without a strike." In July 1890 the executive committee of the carvers union petitioned to reduce working hours from fifty-four to fifty per week and was instrumental in sending $300 to fellow carvers in Grand Rapids, Michigan, to help support them while they were on strike. Elected a shop representative at one point, Adams had to find out why some workers were not receiving the 3¢ raise that had been negotiated with their employers. Implying that he might have served as treasurer, Adams noted on June 25, 1890, that he "straightened out the accounts for the union." Adams also attended social events sponsored by the carvers union.

Adams admired the work of others in his profession but was critical if a co-worker's carving was below standard. He commented favorably on the work of Luigi Frullini, an Italian artisan known in the late nineteenth century for his excellent carving of objects in Renaissance style. In autumn 1887 Adams had the opportunity to examine a sideboard that Frullini had carved, and he tried to sketch the front panel "as near as [he] could remember." Adams was chagrined when the sideboard left the shop in which he was working at the time.

Although Adams earned his living as a woodcarver from

1886 through 1891, he was also actively engaged in architectural design. An interest in this field is manifested in his walks through towns and cities to study exterior architectural carving details on well-known houses and buildings. While he was employed in Salem on the Loring-Emmerton House, he had an opportunity to study interior architecture as well. In July 1888, while he was between carving jobs, Adams traveled to Portsmouth, New Hampshire, and Kittery, Maine, where he helped his Uncle Henry draft plans for a private house in Kittery, two area high schools, and a courthouse.

M2   Andrews, Joseph, 1806–73.
Journal of Joseph Andrews. 1835–36.
[145] p.; 21 cm.
In May 1835 Joseph Andrews left the United States for London to further his education in engraving. Although he had been apprenticed at sixteen and had operated a successful business that at one time employed fourteen engravers, Andrews believed that his knowledge of the craft was still incomplete. His choice of destination is not surprising; it was in London that other American painters and artists had received training for decades. Andrews made a tolerable but not entirely pleasant thirty-five-day crossing of the Atlantic on the *Hollander*. He passed the time reading Shakespeare, Sir Walter Scott, the Bible, and Emanuel Swedenborg, whose followers had established the New Jerusalem Church to which Andrews belonged.

Andrews's London friends and contacts made him feel welcome. On June 29, 1835, Andrews called on William Edward West to ask if he might engrave one of his paintings. Andrews was given *The Dutch Girl* and told that another of West's paintings, *Annette Delarbre*, owned by B. Wiggin, might also be available. On July 8 he engaged Joseph Goodyear for six months to oversee his engraving work. An acquaintance persuaded Andrews that it was necessary for him to understand the form of the human skeleton in order to enhance his skills as an engraver, so he purchased John Flaxman's recently published *Anatomical Studies of the Bones and Muscles for the Use of Artists* and studied it in detail. To further his knowledge of the human form even more, Andrews visited a surgeon named Baleman who had a four-month-old fetus "showing the process of the formation of the bones. It is one of the most wonderful things that I have ever seen."

Andrews devoted many hours to the study of engraving but still managed to travel around London and record his thoughts about the city and its people. He was enthusiastic about the River Thames and the buildings along its northern and southern banks. He felt comfortable on Oxford Street and enjoyed the atmosphere of Hyde Park. He wrote, however, "The crowds of people one meets in the frequented parts of London are astonishing and a great proportion of them unpleasant to the sight and numbers loathsome from filth and natural & accidental deformity."

As a member of London's community of artists, Andrews felt compelled to remark about copyright issues, classical and modern artists, and his contemporaries. According to Andrews, in England the copyright of a painting was retained by the artist. Writing of this, he invoked the names of two royals: "The Duke of Bedford & Lord Egremont two of the greatest collectors of modern art had set their faces against this practice of paying the Painters for the privilege of engraving from pictures out of their possession." On the relative merits of classical and modern artists, Andrews commented: "It requires much deep study and a highly cultivated taste to appreciate or feel the beauties of the first class, while subjects of the latter address themselves immediately to the feelings of almost every one from their interest." Andrews was favorably impressed with George Cruikshank and felt that he had made an excellent choice when he asked Joseph Goodyear to be his mentor, but he believed that the engravings of Joseph Goodall were less than satisfactory: "His work although preeminently beautiful as to effect was as to style of Engraving in some parts rotten."

Andrews finished his studies in London in March 1836 after having engraved both of West's paintings. He then went to Paris and engraved a portrait of Benjamin Franklin. Andrews left for Boston and home on July 23, 1836. His journal ends on August 5 while he was still at sea.

Andrews's journal has been transcribed and is available in typescript form at Winterthur. In addition, see Nancy Carlson Schrock, "Joseph Andrews, Engraver: A Swedenborgian Justification," in *Winterthur Portfolio 12*, ed. Ian M. G. Quimby (Charlottesville: University Press of Virginia, 1977), pp. 165–82.

M3   The Arthur diary from Jany. 2nd, 1804 to Dec. 31st, 1805: the history of a farm on the Hudson River near Fishkill, N. York. 1805. [218] p.; 20 cm.
Kept by an unnamed member of the Arthur family, this journal describes the routine of a farm in early nineteenth-century upstate New York. Its owner, perhaps John Arthur, the only member of the Arthur family whose name appears in the 1800 census from Dutchess County, where Fishkill is located, records such activities as harvesting rye and corn, haying, boarding other people's cattle and horses, selling farm goods in nearby villages as well as in New York City, maintaining equipment, and marketing fruit and milk. Arthur includes payments made to hired hands and carefully notes money both invested in and realized on his products.

Arthur was a member of an organization called the Franklin Union Society and served as a warden of a local church, probably Episcopal. Despite the relatively late date of this diary, Arthur was probably engaged in trading slaves. On October 6, 1804, he sold Cato for $250 to Major Prevost, and on April 15, 1805, he entered into an agreement with Lewis Stebbins to buy Betty for $90. Arthur mentions on March 13, 1805, almost in passing: "This day sold Farm to William Tabor for fifteen thousand Dollars payable half 1st May 1806, the remainder in 3 equal payments on the 1st May 1807, 1808, & 1810 with Interest."

M4   Bachman, Mary Eliza, 1818–41.
The friendly repository and keepsake of Mary Eliza Bachman, 1835. 1831–36, 1839.
[127] p.: ill. (some col.); 21 cm.
Mary Eliza Bachman was a young girl of thirteen when she began to keep this personal keepsake and twenty-one when she last wrote in it. Although she dated the volume 1835, it contains

entries from several years between 1831 and 1839. On its pages
Eliza copied poetry, including "Eliza's Search after Happiness,"
"Friendship," "What Is Charity," and "The First Kiss of Love."
In addition, Eliza asked her friends to write and draw in her
book.

Apart from recording the personal thoughts of a teenager
and young adult, this small volume is important for its connection with John James Audubon and his *Birds of America*. Eliza
was the daughter of John Bachman, a Lutheran clergyman and
noted naturalist from Charleston, South Carolina. Bachman and
Audubon met for the first time in mid October 1831 when Audubon was looking for a place to lodge in Charleston while he studied the birds of the area. Bachman invited Audubon to stay with
him, and all soon became good friends. Audubon described the
Bachmans in a letter to his wife dated October 23, 1831: "An ami-
able Wife and Sister-in-Law, Two fine young Daughters and 3
paires more of Cherubs all of whom I already look upon as if
brought up among them." Audubon's favorable working conditions contributed to the successful completion of many bird studies. In another letter to his wife, Audubon wrote: "I am
positively busy—I have drawn 9 Birds since here which make 5
Drawings when finished—Mr. Bachman is more kind every day,
and as I hope my letter of last Sunday (this day week) has
reached thee I will not repeat any more the generous conduct
which he has assumed towards us all."

If Audubon had referred to his companions by name, he
would have written about George Lehman and Edward A.
Leitner. Lehman traveled with Audubon and was responsible for
drawing many background settings for *Birds of America*. While
residing with the Bachman family, Eliza asked Lehman to contribute something to her keepsake book, and he responded by
painting a watercolor of Charleston that featured Castle Pinck-
ney, a local landmark. When *Birds* was published, this view was
used as the background of the plate depicting the long-billed
curlew.

Leitner, a native of Stuttgart, was a botanist who had originally come to Charleston in 1830. In 1832 he advertised in the
Charleston *Courier* that he hoped to give instruction in botany at

the local medical college. Among the people who offered references concerning his botanical knowledge was the Reverend Bachman. Eliza asked Leitner to contribute to her book as well. His drawing shows a European village scene, probably something recalled from his childhood. In 1838 at the age of twenty-six, Leitner was killed by Seminoles during a collecting trip to Florida. A third illustration of note in this manuscript has been attributed to Audubon's son John. It is dated October 15, 1833, and shows a Carolina wren.

In early 1839 Audubon's other son, Victor, visited the Bachmans for the first time. Since his brother had married Eliza's sister, Maria, Victor probably was going to Charleston to meet his brother's new in-laws. While there, however, he and Eliza fell in love, and the couple was married on December 4, 1839. Their marriage was to be short lived, however, for Eliza contracted tuberculosis and died in 1841.

Some illustrations in this manuscript were reproduced in *Audubon: The Charleston Connection*, edited by Albert E. Sanders and Warren Ripley and published by the Charleston Museum to coincide with an exhibition held September 8 to November 17, 1985. The quotations from Audubon in this entry are from a two-volume work, *Letters of John James Audubon, 1826–1840*, edited by Howard Corning and published in Boston by the Club of Odd Volumes in 1930.

M5   Bell, Abraham, b. 1813.
[Diary]. 1867, 1869, 1872–73, 1876–78, 1880–84, 1886–89, 1891–92.
18 v.; 13–16 cm.
Abraham Bell was involved in mercantile affairs in New York City during the first half of the nineteenth century. His family firm had trading contacts in Belfast, Dublin, Liverpool, and London as well as in the United States. The ships that the firm sent out contained various cargoes, including cotton, potash, turpentine, and tobacco. Returning vessels held such items as textiles, Irish whiskey, earthenware, watches, and glassware. By the time Bell started keeping these diaries, he was retired from his successful business and had many leisure hours to fill.

Bell had homes in Yonkers, New York, and Narragansett
Pier, Rhode Island. During the winter months he regularly visited Green Cove Springs, along the St. John's River south of Jacksonville, Florida. At Green Cove Springs, Bell whiled away the
hours playing quoits and tenpins, fishing, walking, and taking
part in croquet matches. He must have been serious about his
croquet, for at times he supervised the rolling of the grounds by
local workmen. Bell was careful in choosing his partners and
ruled out any more matches with at least one individual: "This
will probably be the last of my Croquet playing with Warren, he
is so dictatorial & overbearing that I lose all interest in the
game."

Probably because of his business success, Bell was
acquainted with several important political figures. In 1872,
while visiting with Rhode Island governor William Sprague, himself a former merchant, Horace Greeley called. That same year
Bell met Supreme Court chief justice Salmon P. Chase, Sprague's
then father-in-law, on a boat bound for Newport. And Bell
wrote of driving out of Newport in the company of a General
Sherman, presumably William Tecumseh Sherman.

Although there are eighteen volumes of Bell's diaries in the
collection, they unfortunately reveal little about their keeper.
Most of the entries reflect a routine life with predictable activities
and few surprises. A typical entry, written on September 9,
1873, when Bell was sixty, reads: "Light Clouds . . . Wind North-
erly. Thermo. @ 7 am. 55° @ 12 m. 67° N. East. Sent Charley to
Wakefield [Rhode Island] to get the horse, Prince, shod,
remained in the house all morning. Wrote to H. K. Dillard, Mr.
Purdon called, Drove to Wakefield with [wife] Rebecca. Called at
Sheldons to buy a mattress. Recd. letters from J. H. Coates &
A. Bell, stopped at J. C. Dillons." When Bell did offer comments
about what he was doing, they were generally negative. He
attended the presidential inauguration of Ulysses S. Grant in
March 1869 and instead of commenting about the significance of
the event complained about conditions: "The streets were so wet
& muddy that we did not get out of the carriage, returned to
Alexa. about 3 pm. tired and hungry." His comments about the
1876 Centennial International Exhibition in Philadelphia were

similarly negative: "The roads were so muddy in the neighbor-
hood of the Centennial grounds that it was rather unpleasant
walking about there."

Papers relating to Bell's business career are located at the
State University of New York at Albany, the New-York Historical Society, and Harvard Business School's Baker Library.

M6 Bell, John G., 1812–89.
[Diary]. 1849–50.
[71] p.; 13 cm.

John Bell kept this diary for a little more than one year while he
traveled from his home at 289 Broadway, New York City, to Panama, on to California, and back to Panama. The 1849/50 New
York directory lists Bell as a taxidermist, and a later issue refers
to him as a naturalist. His last appearance in the directory series
is 1886, when he is still listed as a taxidermist. Bell took his year-
long journey chiefly to acquire specimens of birds that he had
not yet encountered in his profession. The above record of pages
in this diary does not include the many blank leaves at the end
of the volume.

Bell left New York on a steamship on March 1, 1849, and
arrived at the Chagres River in Panama twelve days later. He
and his party headed up the Chagres with native-born guides,
and en route Bell commented, "I shall always number the time I
spent on the Chagres River among the happyest hours of my
life, such a variety of flowers & trees and enormous leaves &
such beautiful vines . . . I never saw before." On this part of his
journey, Bell slept in the huts of the natives, whom he characterized as being polite and attentive but very fond of money.
Because the luggage that held his guns had not been transported
upriver with him, Bell had to be content with only watching
birds for a time. When his luggage finally arrived, Bell "went to
work in earnest collecting birds." He continued: "I go out every
morning at 5 oclock & return at 9 to breakfast, then prepare my
birds. We then dine at 4 and sometimes I go out after dinner
shooting."

Although Bell primarily was concerned with shooting and
studying birds, he took time to travel throughout the country-

side and to write about some of the things that he saw. Bell visited an ancient settlement that he called Old Panama. He noted that the women there were generally neatly dressed, except for their footwear, and that native Spaniards continued to dress as he had imagined they would back home. The children were all naked. Many of the residents enjoyed cockfights, and the local priests were known to bet heavily on them. The streets were well paved with hard stones, the houses contained much mahogany, but "all seem[ed] to be going to ruin." Before Bell left Old Panama, he visited the remnants of what may have been an old city lookout or wall and took a brick from its tower and some mortar from one of its arches as souvenirs.

On May 18, Bell left Panama on the steamer *Panama* for San Francisco and arrived there on June 5. Although Bell had most of his trip ahead of him, his diary was mostly completed upon his departure for California. Bell still wrote about birds and even listed those he saw around San Francisco, but he seemed more interested in other matters, including a side trip to see where gold had just been discovered. Exactly one year after leaving New York, Bell headed back. His diary ends on March 28, 1850, while he was traveling once again along the Chagres.

M7   Bixby, Sarah.
Journal. [Ca. 1850].
[121] p.; 13 cm.
Sometime during the mid nineteenth century, Sarah Bixby, a young schoolteacher, kept this diary to coincide with her first teaching position. Her journal documents five months of rural American life more than a century ago.

Bixby's hometown was Mayville, New York. Located on the northern end of Chautaqua Lake in the western part of the state, at midcentury it was a small village of about five hundred people. Bixby taught in a one-room schoolhouse near Mayville. As a teacher, she was concerned with the number of children left in her charge—attendance varied from seven to eighteen on any given day. Out of school, she read biographies, embroidered, quilted, made bonnets, enjoyed walks, and delighted in picking wild berries. Although not a party-goer, she frequently had friends to visit and seemed to be happiest when with them. Bixby regularly recorded weather conditions and was pleased to have her daguerreotype taken on May 10. When school was dismissed on September 9, her school money, presumably for the term, amounted to $18.67.

Dating this diary is difficult because there are few revealing comments about current events or noteworthy people. Since Bixby recorded her church attendance on Sundays, a perpetual calendar reveals that her diary could have been written in either 1845, 1851, or 1862.

M8   Bogert, Mrs. James.
Diary of a western tour. 1839.
[31] p.; 21 cm.
This short travel narrative begins on June 6 and ends on July 13, 1839. Mrs. James Bogert writes about her family's round-trip to Niagara Falls from their home at 46 Bleeker Street, New York. Recording an itinerary that took them to Albany, then to Utica, Syracuse, Auburn, Geneva, Rochester, and finally Niagara, the diarist writes of little except their modes of transportation (she disliked the railroad and fast carriages), friends met along the way, and hotel accommodations. Of the sight of the falls from the Canadian side, she said: "No description can do justice to this mighty rush of Waters—it inspires me with reverential feelings of awe—and while I gaze in silent wonder, contemplating its foaming Surges, an Echo proclaims to my listening Ear—how boundless—boundless, is Eternity!"

The Bogerts visited the falls and Canada during a time of anti-British sentiment. About one and a half years earlier the *Caroline*, a small American steamboat, had been set afire and then adrift by a party of Canadian militia. Some of its crew had been killed. The so-called Caroline Affair touched off a strong anti-Canadian sentiment that would last for several years and, judging from her diary, that was shared by Bogert. She wrote: "Being on British ground, which I predict will not always belong to them, at least if a War should occur, I hope the Americans will claim and subdue Canada." Perhaps reacting to her sense of patriotism, at a gift shop she bought, along with other purchases, a piece of what was purported to be part of the wreck of the *Caroline*.

M9   Bradbury, Gotham, b. 1790.
          Gotham Bradbury's journal. 1881–83.
          190 p.; 27 cm.
          The keeper of this diary, called Captain Bradbury, presumably as a result of his military rank and not because he was a sailor, was ninety years old when he began to write in this volume. He was born in Chesterville, Maine, and later resided in Farmington, a fairly prosperous neighboring community. For most of his life he labored as a farmer, although in 1811 he worked in Bath, Maine, for a shipbuilding firm. Bradbury had six daughters, two sons (one of whom died in 1874), and two wives. His older sister, Jenny, was ninety-two in 1880. His father was a joiner and carpenter and later a farmer.

For someone aged ninety, Bradbury was quite active. He mended fences, made wooden spoons for cooking, split hardwood for his heating stove, gardened, and repaired household items. An inveterate reader, Bradbury subscribed to numerous publications, including *Harper's Monthly*, *Atlantic Monthly*, *Scribner's Monthly*, the *Golden Rule* (a religious journal from Boston), and at least four newspapers. He delighted in writing letters to friends and boasted in his diary on August 21, 1882, that he had written to 3,912 of them since March 1, 1854. Bradbury smoked a pipe (preferring the Vanity Fair tobacco brand), walked with a cane, suffered from what he termed *palpitations*, liked to lend his bass voice to choirs, and detested cats to the degree that on July 25, 1881, he recorded that he had "killed a couple of our useless cats."

Bradbury lived at a time when many things in the United States were undergoing change, including medical treatments, political ideas, religious thoughts, and ways of communicating. On January 26, 1881, the local physician, Dr. Douglass, brought his "electric machine" to the house to treat Bradbury's daughter's bad wrist. Bradbury wrote: "All our family took shocks and [then we] gave the cats electricity which caused them to jump smartly." One year later Bradbury recalled this event and commented that his arm had not been free from pain since his treatment. Bradbury was a life-long Republican and had no use for political corruption or the Greenback Party, which was in decline as he was keeping this diary. He reacted predictably when President Garfield was killed, saying that he thought the assassin, Charles Guiteau, deserved to be hanged. He did not like Roscoe Conkling, a New York politician, presumably because of the feud between Conkling and James Blaine, Maine's famous Republican leader and presidential candidate of 1884. Robert Ingersoll, the noted attorney and agnostic, did not gain favor with Bradbury either. He accused Ingersoll of demoralizing the youth of the nation. Bradbury wrote derisively about séances: "As far as my observation has been, but a very few persons of strong intellectual powers of mind have embraced these pretended spiritual manifestations."

Finally, Bradbury related his first experience with a telephone: "I was at West Farmington to day and while in a store where the merchant kept a *telephone*—I heard a woman's voice. The man said it was his wife that lived seventy-five rods from where we were. The man put his face near a little box or hole in the wall and said—'I am so busy now that I cannot talk with you.' I had previously heard and read about the telephone but had never until at this time witnessed the operation."

M10 Breese, John M.
Journal of a voyage from Newport to the East Indies in the Mount Hope. 1802–3.
[147] p.; 32 cm.
The voyage that is recorded in this manuscript took place between September 8, 1802, and April 29, 1803. It was made by the trading ship *Mount Hope* to transport sugar, coffee, cotton, saltpeter, and flour between Newport, Rhode Island, and the Isle de France, now called Mauritius, located in the Indian Ocean. The title chosen for John Breese's journal appears as a heading only on the pages that describe events on the trip to the East Indies. The headings used for the rest of the manuscript vary.

The information supplied by Breese about the voyage is routine, suggesting that the trip was uneventful. He commented about the latitudinal and longitudinal position of the ship, wind directions, miles traveled each day, weather conditions, course direction, necessary repairs to the ship, encounters with other vessels on the way, and progress in loading and unloading at the dock. Almost invariably, in order to fill in the blank spaces of the pages, Breese penned random thoughts, quoted well-known writers, including William Shakespeare and Henry Fielding, or commented about people. He was particularly opinionated about the Irish and women. Breese used the pages at the back of the volume as a commonplace book, writing essays, anecdotes, extracts from periodicals of the day, and poetry.

M11   Bridgman, Sarah E.
[Commonplace book]. 1830–32, 1835.
[122] p.; 23 cm.
The only specific information about the keeper of this volume is recorded on the front page: "S. Bridgman, 105 Hudson St., New York." New York City directories for the decade of the 1830s, however, do not include any references to a member of the Bridgman family at that address. Entries dated 1835 in this book are from Delaware and southeastern Pennsylvania, suggesting that if Sarah had lived in New York at one time, she probably moved after a few years.

   This commonplace book contains prose and poetry from such authors as Lord Byron, Robert Burns, Sir Walter Scott, William Cowper, Alexander Pope, and Harriet Beecher Stowe. Toward the back of the volume are several kinds of plant materials pressed between the leaves. One caption notes that a plant had been taken from the spot where American and British forces had battled during the revolutionary war in Chadds Ford, Pennsylvania.

M12   Brinton, Mary C.
[Commonplace book]. 1826–29.
[180] p.; 20 cm.
According to a note inside the front cover of this book, "Mary C. Brinton was mother of Clement Stocker Phillips—her youngest

son—my father—P. P. P. May 12, 1960. She married Clement Stocker Phillips & thei[r] son, my father, was named after him. She must have been romantic."

The pages of this commonplace book contain both poetry and prose on a variety of topics. Cited sources include Lord Byron, Vivian Grey, Hannah More, *Bracebridge Hall*, and the *Christian Observer*. One selection is in French, "Sermon sur le Jugement dernier," par Massillon, and many of the writings are of a religious nature. Two of the compositions are headed "Germantown," suggesting that Brinton may have lived in this Philadelphia suburb.

M13   Brown, T. Stewart, b. 1838.
[Diary]. 1863–65.
3 v.; 16–18 cm.
In 1863 T. Stewart Brown worked with his father making and selling trunks and valises in Philadelphia. The relationship between father and son was not as good as it might have been, for on April 9, Brown wrote: "Had a talk with Father about matters & things. Could not agree and will see the trunk business to ____ if I can make any opening elsewhere." For the time being, however, there was nothing else for Brown to do to make his living.

The Civil War interrupted his work in the family business. On June 27, he was mustered into the service for what he thought would be ninety days, doubtlessly as a result of the recently passed Conscription Act. Brown was first stationed at Camp Prevost in Pennsylvania and then marched a short distance to Carlisle, where he and his fellow soldiers were shelled by a battery of Confederate troops. Brown was mustered out of the army early on August 1. He returned to Philadelphia and rejoined his father in the trunk business. On November 12, 1863, he married Lizzie Wonderly, the twenty-three-year-old daughter of Jacob S. Wonderly, a merchant who sold combs, brushes, and fancy goods.

During 1864 and 1865, Brown led a quiet family life with his wife in Philadelphia. He lived with his in-laws and continued to work with his father, although business was usually "dull." He

attended the opera, went to the opening of the Sanitary Fair in
1864, and had his photograph taken. Although Brown did not
serve any more time as a soldier, he commented on the progress
of the war. On May 8, 1865, for example, he wrote: "Great excitement about the war news—which are favorable." At this time
the Battle of the Wilderness was taking place in Virginia. And on
June 7, he learned of the death of a friend, Harry Marchant, presumably lost during the fighting in Virginia. On election day
Brown "voted Clean Union for Old Abe." On April 3, 1865, he
heard about the capture of Petersburg and Richmond, Virginia,
and wrote: "city perfectly wild with excitement." A son was
born to the Browns on February 20, 1865, and they named him
Edgar. On September 9, 1864, Brown was elected secretary of
Consolidated Oil Company and served in that capacity until the
following February. He left Philadelphia after these volumes of
his diary were written, moving to New York City, where he
worked in the coal business.

M14   Burdick, Horace Robbins, 1844–1942.
[Diary]. 1914–17, 1928, 1930, 1933, 1934.
5 v.; 17–20 cm.
H. R. Burdick was born in East Killingly, Connecticut, and was a
resident of Malden, Massachusetts, for most of his adult life. He
studied at the Lowell Institute and later at the Boston Museum
of Art, where he was a pupil of artists George Hollingsworth,
William Rimmer, and E. O. Grundmann. Burdick was best
known as a restorer of paintings and a portraitist who worked in
oil and crayon. He was a member of the Boston Art Club, and
his works were shown at Fanueil Hall; the Berkshire, Massachusetts, courthouse; the New London, Connecticut, city hall; and
the Massachusetts Supreme Court building. Burdick's daughter,
Doris, born in 1898, was an artist in her own right, concentrating
on illustration and silhouettes.

Burdick's diary reveals that he was a very active conservator
of paintings for people in the city of Boston and its environs. In
1914, for example, he retouched spots in a portrait of Daniel
Webster by Gilbert Stuart and twenty years later, at the age of
ninety, did some reframing. Most of his activities as a conserva-

tor focused on retouching, varnishing, and cleaning. The repetitiveness of such work prompted him to remark in 1914 that he was "sick of varnishing painting." Burdick never gave up seeking work; in January 1934, he applied for a job at the Isabella Stewart Gardner Museum in Boston.

There are many references in these manuscripts to Burdick's career as a painter. He experimented with several media. In 1933, for instance, he remarked that he "painted in opaque water color on old yellow paper with fair success"; in 1914 he tried painting postcards "with little success"; and again in 1914 he tried to retouch a chromolithograph. Burdick worked in monochrome, did miniatures, used wax colors, and painted portraits from photographs of his subjects. In 1915 Elisa Currier expressed an interest in taking painting lessons from him. Burdick delivered talks on painting throughout his life and was an inveterate reader of historical and technical publications on art. Among the items that he read were works on the practice of drawing, on English pastel and watercolor painters, Samuel Isham's *History of American Painting*, Charles Lewis Hind's *Education of an Artist*, a biography of Whistler, and books about landscape painting by modern Dutch artists. In addition, Burdick attended numerous lectures and exhibitions of American and foreign artists at such places as the Fogg Museum, the Metropolitan Museum of Art, and the Vose Gallery.

Although Burdick's diaries are the focus of this description, the Downs collection also has a daybook that he maintained from 1869 to 1885 in which he recorded his professional activities. Two pictures of paintings by Burdick—a portrait of Calvin Coolidge and *The Madonna of the Apostles*—and two sketches have been laid in it.

M15   Burgess, Frances, b. 1844.
[Diary]. 1864–65.
2 v.; 13 cm.
These volumes chronicle the activities of a young woman who resided in Cortland County, New York. Frances Burgess's daily routine was not remarkable for women of her time. She spent many hours occupied with work around the house, including

cleaning, sewing, cooking, and washing. She was a regular
churchgoer, attended lectures on temperance, and played the
melodian and the piano. In July 1864, Burgess remarked that
"three more terms is only necessary for me to take before being
capable of teaching." There is no evidence, however, that she
ever finished her training. Burgess was a regular reader of books
on how to live a proper life. Among those she read were *Mary
Moreton: or, The Broken Promise, a True Story of American Life*, by
Timothy Shay Arthur, an author of books on manners, temperance, and Christian life, and *Moral Heroism: or, The Trials and
Triumphs of the Great and Good*, published by the American
Sunday-School Union.

It would not be unreasonable to conclude that her friendship
Although Burgess lived in a relatively isolated part of New
York State, she was able to keep up with events of the Civil
War. On August 3, 1864, she wrote that it "does seem hard to
see them [the soldiers] go south to leave dear friends at home,
still *dear brothers* you are going in a good cause, do not feel very
well tonight." When Lee surrendered, she was jubilant: "There
is hardly one copperhead in our place, all are *strong Union*. 'We
have killed the *Bear*.'" Of President Lincoln's assassination, she
noted that it was a sad and gloomy day. She recorded when
John Wilkes Booth was caught, wrote about the capture of Jefferson Davis, and confided to her diary on April 29, 1865: "Have
not done much today. Could but think of the death of 'Lincoln'
all day." She implied that she dreaded practicing a piece of
music, "Children of the Battlefield," because it reminded her of
the war.

It would not be unreasonable to conclude that her friendship
with Albert F. Smith, a soldier, helped in some measure to prompt
her interest in the war. On April 25, 1864, she wrote that news had
reached her that an important battle was imminent and that she
"had a real *crying fit* in my room all to myself." The battle that she
anticipated took place in Virginia from May 5 to 12 between forces
lead by generals Grant and Lee. Known as the Battle of the Wilderness, the Union's Army of the Potomac suffered about 30,000 casu-
alties, counting among them the wounded Smith, who had been
shot in the left arm. "How glad I was to hear he was no worse
off," Burgess wrote. Smith recovered in a hospital in Washington,

D.C., and then returned home, where Burgess saw as much of him as possible. Unfortunately, something in her behavior with Albert led her parents to scold her regularly, and with these rebukes Frances's diary ends.

M16   Butler, William Colflesh, b. 1859.
Diary of Wm. C. Butler. 1880–81, 1916.
[184] p.; 20 cm.
William Colflesh Butler was a resident of Philadelphia whose ambition was to become a painter with either a signmaking firm or an ornamental painting business. He hoped to find a position painting railway cars and remarked on April 9, 1880, that at the Pennsylvania Railroad Company "they do the finest kind of decorative painting on those Pullman Cars, that is just what I want to get at." Butler discovered one month later, however, that there were no openings at the company. Hoping to improve his skills, he took painting lessons from E. S. Haley and also worked at his father's wheelwright shop decorating wheels. On September 16, Butler struck out on his own. He ordered business cards that read: "Wm. C. Butler, Sign and Decorative Painter, S. E. Corner 39th and Spr. Garden Sts. West Philadelphia. Artistic Painting in all its Branches." Unfortunately, Butler found little work. He remarked, however, that he had been commissioned to do a sign for Bradley and Callaghan, storekeepers, that his uncle had asked him for a sign, and that he had a thirteen-foot sign to letter in gold. Early in 1881, Butler gave up his own shop and did work for others, including Lengerts Wagon Shop.
     During summer 1881, Butler's family rented a place on Massachusetts Avenue in Atlantic City, New Jersey, to run as a boarding house. Butler kept up with his painting by decorating shells to sell through the vacation season. His interest in botany came to the forefront when he went to the local Government Life Saving Station in Atlantic City to gather different kinds of seeds for his uncle's nursery in Germantown, a Philadelphia suburb. Butler's uncle, the husband of his mother's sister, was Thomas Meehan, a botanist, horticulturist, and author. A native of Scotland, Meehan had worked at Kew Gardens in London

and Bartram's Garden in Philadelphia. He was a member of the Academy of Natural Sciences of Philadelphia, the American Association for the Advancement of Science, and the American Philosophical Society. Meehan served on the State Board of Agriculture of Pennsylvania as its botanist and in 1882 was elected a member of the Philadelphia Common Council, where he was instrumental in establishing many small parks throughout Philadelphia. Butler remarked in his diary several times about the activities of his uncle and mentioned that on July 10, 1881, he and his wife, Butler's Aunt Kate, came to spend the day in Atlantic City.

When Butler returned to Philadelphia from Atlantic City at the end of the summer, he found employment in a furniture factory, located at the corner of Powelton and State streets, whose proprietor was George Smith. In December, after having been laid off, he found work as a filler for the Hale and Kilburn Manufacturing Company. Apparently Butler abandoned his professional interest in art, for a 1904 Philadelphia city directory lists him as a finisher for an unidentified furniture manufactory.

In 1916, at the end of his diary, Butler wrote biographical sketches about his parents, who by that time had both died.

M17   Clapp, David, 1806–93.
        [Travel journal]. 1831–43.
        4 v.; 17 cm.
        David Clapp was born in Dorchester, Massachusetts. He received his education locally and when he was thirteen years old got his first job, working as a tanner. After Clapp's schooling was finished in 1822, he became an apprentice at John Cotton's printing shop in Boston. By this time Clapp had already begun to record his activities and thoughts regularly in a journal. February 6, 1827, was Clapp's "freedom day," as he called it, the last day of his apprenticeship. He continued working with Cotton for pay until 1831, when he struck out on his own in a short-lived partnership with Henry Hull. From 1831 until 1892, when he retired, Clapp was a busy printer who enjoyed an excellent reputation. Among many other items, he printed volumes of

the Boston city directory, the *New England Historical and Genea-logical Register*, and the *Boston Medical and Surgical Journal*. Clapp was a member of the Massachusetts Charitable Mechanic Associa-tion, the New-England Historic Genealogical Society, Saint Mat-thew's Church, and the Boston Old School Boys Association. He married Mary Elizabeth Tucker in 1835, and they had six children.

David Clapp's travel journals, except for one passing refer-ence, have nothing to do with his profession. Rather, they include observations and stories about his trips from Boston to New York City, Washington, D.C., and Niagara Falls. On keep-ing journals, he wrote: "The pleasure of recording the incidents and a description of the scenes I witnessed; and the anticipated satisfaction of perusing the record at some future time, and thus again living in those incidents and gazing upon those scenes have been my principal objects; not perhaps unaccompanied however, with the belief or the hope that other eyes—eyes of affection and of friendship—may likewise glide over these rude sketches and either bless Heaven that the writer still lives to enjoy with them the perusal, or drop one tear to the memory of the deceased."

Volumes 1 and 2 of Clapp's journals were kept during the second half of 1831 and cover his visit to New York City. He traveled there with his business partner, Hull, on a boat called the *Boston*. His first trip by water, Clapp, perhaps in his enthusi-asm, wrote at length about what he encountered on board: enter-tainment by a black band, difficulties trying to sleep, strangers, the approach to New York's harbor, and meals. In New York Clapp stayed at the Franklin Hotel and visited Peale's Museum, where a snake commanded particular interest; the Castle Garden at the Battery; many churches; the Market; and what he called the large Methodist printing establishment.

Volume 3, written in 1841, describes a trip to Washington, D.C., and features a tally of expenses at the end. A seasoned traveler by this time, Clapp's comments are generally matter-of-fact and lack the enthusiasm that marked his words about his trip to New York a decade earlier. Clapp does reveal himself, however, after visiting the chamber of the House of Representatives: "There was very little dignity manifested by the members, most of them being engaged in writing or reading newspapers."

Volume 4 is an engaging account of Clapp and his wife's trip to Niagara Falls. They went by rail, changing trains frequently because of the many short lines throughout New York State, befriended a foreign clergyman and his wife on the way, and finally found themselves in uncomfortable quarters at Niagara Falls in a temperance hotel. Clapp writes about the falls with awe, remarking that it was truly one of God's wonders.

A lengthy obituary on Clapp, featuring his portrait, appeared in *New-England Historical and Genealogical Register* (vol. 48, no. 2 [April 1894]: 145–56).

M18   Clarke, Thomas Benedict, 1848–1931.
A memorandum book descriptive of a collection of oil paintings belonging to Thomas B. Clarke (representing American art from 1860 to 1881). 1872–81.
[152] p.; 20 cm.
Thomas Benedict Clarke was born in New York City in 1848, the son of an educator who founded the Mount Washington Collegiate Institute in New York. Although Clarke graduated from his father's school, he did not continue his education. Rather, he turned to the business world and entered into a partnership in a lace, collar, and linen concern. After quickly achieving financial success, he began to purchase European art, favoring works of Italian, French, and German salon painters. He soon gave up collecting European art, however, because he thought it was too expensive to accumulate and turned his attention to American paintings. Clarke became an avid collector and sometimes bought works directly from an artist. He befriended George Inness and by century's end had thirty-nine of his works. In addition, Clarke served as Inness's manager. Clarke was also partial to the pictures of Winslow Homer, owning at one time fifteen of his oils and sixteen of his watercolors. Clarke was constantly upgrading his collection and selling for profit. He even opened his own gallery, the Art House, for this purpose.

In 1899 Clarke sold 373 of his paintings at auction for $235,000, realizing a 60 percent to 70 percent profit over his original purchase prices. Before his death, Clarke had amassed impressive collections in other areas, including Chinese porcelain, seventeenth- and eighteenth-century English furniture, American portraits, and textiles. He lent many of his art objects to museums for exhibition.

This memorandum book is composed of several sections. One contains a list of the American paintings that Clarke owned in 1872, usually identified by a short title, with their costs expressed in a letter code, a few of their dimensions, and a sale price if disposed of. A second section lists paintings that Clarke lent to galleries in 1879 for exhibition. A third section was written in 1881 to provide a fresh list of Clarke's holdings and where they were located. Two pages list "commissions out," and other pages list pictures bought for other people and their prices. Finally, Clarke includes a brief list of old porcelain in his collection.

This manuscript might be used profitably with *The Private Collection of Thomas B. Clarke of New York, Exhibited at American Art Gallery, New York, Dec. 28, 1883 to Jan. 12, 1884,* a fifty-page descriptive catalogue of the highlights of Clarke's collection. It was printed by Studio Press and contains an introduction by Sylvester R. Koehler, a nineteenth-century art historian.

M19 Cogdell, John Stevens, 1778–1847.
[Diary]. 1808, 1825.
2 v.: ill.; 22 cm.
John Cogdell, a sculptor, painter, lawyer, and banker, was born in South Carolina and graduated from the College of Charleston. When he was about seventeen he began to study law, and in 1799 he was admitted to the bar. In June 1800, he and his brother Richard traveled to Europe, and John's appetite for art was whetted. Upon his return to America, Cogdell settled in Charleston and began his career as a lawyer. In 1810 he began the first of his four consecutive terms as a member of the South Carolina House of Representatives. In 1818 Cogdell was

appointed comptroller general of South Carolina, and from 1832
until his death in 1847, he served as president of the Bank of
South Carolina. Despite the requirements of his professional life,
Cogdell found time to be quite active in painting and clay modeling. His talent in art elicited encouragement from prominent artists of the day, including Washington Allston and Gilbert Stuart.
Cogdell's works were exhibited at the Boston Athenaeum, the
National Academy of Design, the Charleston Library Society,
and the Pennsylvania Academy of the Fine Arts.

These volumes cover trips that Cogdell made to northern
cities in 1808 and 1825. They form part of a larger collection of
Cogdell material at Winterthur that includes four other manuscript volumes containing copies of letters that he either wrote
or received in 1816 and from 1829 to 1841. They record another
trip that Cogdell made to the north in 1816 and offer insights
into his concerns involving art and society. Because they fall out
of the scope of this volume, however, their contents are not
detailed here, but they are useful in understanding Cogdell's
artistic progress and serve as an important supplement to his
travel narratives.

In 1808 Cogdell took at least a month-long trip from Charleston to Philadelphia and New York City. He left on August 29 on
board the *South Carolina* and reached Philadelphia on September
2. One of Cogdell's first stops was at the Peale Museum, where
he saw a number of portraits of American statesmen. He did not
think any of the portraits of George Washington were good and
remarked that he liked only one of two of Thomas Jefferson. The
likenesses of fellow South Carolinians Henry Laurens, David
Ramsey, and Thomas Sumter pleased him. Cogdell toured the
rest of Peale's museum and found it wanting. He wrote: "After
having examined the Academy of Physick at Florence, consisting
of all that can be imagined—from Reptiles up to Man in his
most deformed & perfect State—occupying forty Rooms—there
could not be very much at Peales museum to excite my wonder." Cogdell next visited the Pennsylvania Academy of the Fine
Arts, where he commented favorably on the paintings of Benjamin West, especially two that he called *Lear in the Storm* and

Orlando Rescuing Oliver from the Lion and the Serpent. The latter had been lent to the Pennsylvania Academy by Robert Fulton for its first exhibition. Reflecting his interest in social matters, Cogdell went to the Bettering House Hospital, later called the Pennsylvania Hospital, which served as an institution for the insane. He was impressed by the cleanliness of the place and wrote about what he could see of Philadelphia from the top floor: "From the top of the building we could have seen to advantage much of the surrounding country—but the Trees are so numerous about this Institution—as well as thro' all parts of the City (Market Street excepted) as to interrupt all perspective or view at any distance even of the fine edifices of the City." Cogdell also toured a prison and discovered that most of its inmates were sawing marble to fill construction orders caused by a local building boom. He commented that many of the inmates were black and noted further that some Philadelphians thought they committed crimes purposely in order to be incarcerated and to have a place to live and to gain credit for their labor. Judging from his dinner companions, Cogdell must have been well connected socially. On September 7, he ate with Benjamin Barton, a naturalist; Caspar Wister, a local physician; Benjamin Vaughan, a diplomat and economist; Charles Willson Peale, a painter; Stephen Elliott, a botanist from South Carolina; and Abraham Collins, who was identified in the Philadelphia city directory as a gentleman.

On September 8, Cogdell traveled through New Jersey to New York City. He visited the panorama of Edward Savage and termed it "the most surprising and Interesting piece of Machinery" he had ever seen. He called St. John's Church "beyond doubt the most superb Church in N.Y. & at this moment not yet finished."

In 1825 Cogdell traveled north again from Charleston. In Boston he met artists Gilbert Stuart, Washington Allston, Jonathan Mason, and Francis Alexander. Cogdell termed September 20 "one of the most grateful and interesting days I have spent at the North," for Allston escorted him to private homes in Boston where important paintings were located. Cogdell visited Stuart's rooms for the first time on September 22 and departed more impressed with him than ever. "His touch is so fine delicate & natural that I am more enraptured with his work than I ever was before," he wrote. On September 23, Cogdell met Mason, who "is very deaf but apparently a very pleasant young Man he has been 2 years in London pursuing his studies as an artist." Two days later they visited Mason's father and enjoyed looking at his collection of paintings. Francis Alexander, another Boston artist, led Cogdell to other residences to view private collections of paintings and also joined him for an evening at Stuart's home. In addition to spending time with Boston's community of artists, Cogdell was introduced to two prominent statesmen, presidents John Adams and John Quincy Adams.

In Philadelphia Cogdell characterized some of his contemporaries and their works. He visited the Pennsylvania Academy again. "The Large Room is still distinguished by Mr. Alstons splendid picture which I found more to be admired than 9 years ago." And, "Mr. West's painting Christ healing the sick is placed in a building suited for it. . . . The painting of Mr. West is lighted from above—but the Spectator does not see the light." Cogdell thought that Charles B. Lawrence would have a successful career as a painter; as he was a pupil of Stuart and Rembrandt Peale, he doubtlessly showed promise. Art historian William Dunlap wrote, however, that "Mr. Lawrence wisely relinquished painting, and has found employment in private life, where he is said to be very estimable." Cogdell confided to his diary that John Neagle was strong minded, had great talent, and was greatly improved as a painter. Neagle, who married a daughter of Thomas Sully, would eventually become a successful portrait painter and director of the Pennsylvania Academy. Of Thomas Doughty, Cogdell thought that he had taste of the first order, was clear and sparkling of thought, sensitive, and that life was seen in all of his work. Before he left Philadelphia, Cogdell purchased two of Doughty's paintings. As his life unfolded, however, Doughty enjoyed success in the 1830s as a landscapist but was impoverished thereafter.

Other papers relating to John Stevens Cogdell are located at the South Carolina Historical Society.

M20   Collingwood, Cuthbert, b. 1808.
[Autobiographical memoir]. 1880.
[1], 5 p.; 36 cm.
In 1880 an unidentified friend asked Cuthbert Collingwood to
write a letter in which he reminisced about his family and
childhood; this manuscript was the response. Collingwood
was born in Salem, New Hampshire. His grandfather was a
local blacksmith and his father a schoolteacher and post-
master. The family home was adjacent to the town green and
near the meetinghouse and graveyard. In 1814 Collingwood's
father decided to move the family to Boston. At first deeply
chagrined by this move, young Cuthbert grew to like his new
home and soon became fascinated by sights and experiences
in the city that he would never have encountered in rural Salem.
Collingwood "attended the Grammar, Latin & Eng. Classical
Schools; the latter was called the 'Boston College.' " He was
the president of the Scholars' Club and the Garrick Society.
Unfortunately, his father vetoed offers to pay for his college
education, so Collingwood was denied opportunities to attend
Harvard and Yale. From 1829, when his father met financial ruin, until 1845, when this short narrative ends, Collingwood alone was responsible for maintaining the well-being of
his family.

M21   Coney, Jabez.
[Diary]. 1867–68.
65, [7] p.: ill.; 20 cm.
Jabez Coney, a resident of Boston from 1863 to 1870, kept this
diary irregularly from January 26, 1867, until October 16, 1868, to
record ideas that he had for inventions. According to Boston city
directories, Coney was affiliated in some capacity with the Globe
Works Foundry in 1863 and was identified as a consulting engi-
neer between 1864 and 1870.

    Coney thought that he could make a better barrel. He noted
that barrels had been manufactured for centuries and that their
quality could not be improved. He believed, however, that they
could be made more cheaply and that their staves could be held
together using glue instead of hoops. In addition to the barrel,

Coney had ideas for a new, improved passenger elevator for hotels that would rely on two continuous steel bands for lifting and lowering, a new circular saw whose basic principle was explained in an article from *Scientific American*, a steam boiler described as "The Vertical Inverted Cone or Differential Shell with Vertical tubes of various lengths," and an all-metal wagon wheel. Finally, Coney was favorably impressed with a new kind of railroad tank car used to transport oil that was designed to allow for greater storage capacity than ever before.

M22 Cowles, Florence Ashmore, b. 1846.
[Diary]. 1866–68.
p. 21–234; 20 cm.
Sometime during the first half of 1866, Florence Cowles began writing in this diary. Unfortunately, the first twenty pages have been removed, so the beginning date is uncertain. Originally from New Orleans but residing in postbellum Petersburg, Virginia, Cowles was a newly married woman of nineteen in 1866. She revealed her feelings for her husband, Will: "To make Will unhappy for one minute is to me the most terrible thing in the world." And, "he thought I was reproving him. Oh Will! how could I reprove you?—you are so much better in all things than I." Will was a graduate of Randolph-Macon College, a Civil War veteran who had climbed the ranks to captain, and ten years older than his wife. As this diary was being kept, the couple was living with Will's parents, and Will probably was making a living as a farmer.

The most important element of Cowles's life was her family. She felt exceedingly close to her husband and looked forward to sending and receiving letters from her parents, her brother (a student at Washington College in Lexington, Kentucky), and her sisters. She became despondent in 1867 when she realized that she could not visit her family in New Orleans because she and her husband did not have enough money to pay for the trip. Cowles wrote movingly about a sister who had died young, remarking that when the death had occurred she believed that all purpose had been taken from her own life. Cowles looked forward to having children of her own, and on March 24, 1867, a son named

Will, Jr., was born. Throughout the pages of this diary, the growth and progress of the boy is recounted with delight. Perhaps the greatest disappointment in her family relationships was with her mother-in-law. Cowles noted that her husband's mother was usually in bad humor and highly critical, and she thought that Will did not realize how unkind his mother could be. For his part, Will said that his wife was the cause of estrangement between himself and his mother.

Despite living in Petersburg, the location of bloody Civil War fighting, on only one occasion does Cowles betray her feelings about Northerners. An acquaintance of the family, Katie Watkins, was being sent to school somewhere in the north because her father could not afford the cost of room and board at a southern school. He could afford a school in the north, however, where a family friend would house Katie. Cowles observed: "Its a shame for southern people to send their children to the North now. . . . I'm afraid Katie will lose her girlhood gentleness in that land of strong-minded females."

M23 Daily miniature diary for 1859.
[128] p.; 10 cm.
The keeper of this small diary resided in the vicinity of Richmond, Maine, and made his living as a trader, handyman, and farmer and from boarders who rented rooms in his house. His last name may have been Curtis, and his wife's maiden name could have been Brooks. It was common for him to work in his shop, repairing his wares, and then to load them on his wagon for the short ride into Richmond. The keeper routinely recorded the streets on which he traded and the names of the people in town with whom he ate and boarded. As the summer season approached, he spent more and more time with farm work, including planting, mowing, and barn repair. A representative diary entry was written on Saturday, July 2: "A storm threatens. loaded up took breakfast at Willises drove home arrived at 1/2 past 9 all well: brought 809 lbs. rags PM loaded up for another week—went to farm then house went to meeting." Beyond his work, the diarist was a devout Baptist; had relatives in Hingham, Massachusetts, whom he visited in September; enjoyed cel-

ebrating the Fourth of July; and was sympathetic to the
temperance movement. On August 1, he saved a woman from
committing suicide by hanging.

M24   Dexter, Henry, 1806–76.
          [Autobiographical sketch]. [Ca. 1850].
          [11] p.; 25 cm.
          Henry Dexter wrote this sketch of his life up to about 1850 in the
          form of a letter to someone named Miss Lee. His account begins
          with his birth and ends with notes about various busts that he
          had sculpted through the mid nineteenth century. Dexter was
          born on October 11, 1806, in Nelson, Madison County, New
          York. Sometime during his youth, a merchant from Utica, New
          York, moved into town and befriended the Dexter family. Por-
          traits that this merchant had hanging on his walls awakened
          young Henry's interest in art and were an early influence on his
          decision to become an artist. Shortly after the death of his father,
          or his father's disappearance as recorded in *Dictionary of Ameri-
          can Biography*, the remaining Dexters moved to Connecticut
          where Henry eventually became an apprentice to a blacksmith.
          He met Francis Alexander, an enterprising portrait painter, and
          later married his niece. Alexander dissuaded Dexter from earn-
          ing his living as an artist, suggesting instead that he continue
          with his work as a blacksmith. In 1836, after seven long years at
          that trade, Dexter opened his own art studio, working first in
          Providence, Rhode Island, and then in Boston. In Boston he
          again met Alexander, who now encouraged him to pursue a
          career as an artist. Finding little work in his chosen field of por-
          trait painting, Dexter turned to sculpture. By 1850 he had
          become a successful sculptor, working with both clay and mar-
          ble. His sitters included, among others, members of Boston soci-
          ety, political figures, and in 1842 Charles Dickens.
              Henry Dexter, Sculptor: A Memorial, written by John Albee
          and privately printed in 1898, offers a favorable biographical
          sketch and includes a portrait of the subject done late in his life
          and a catalogue of his works.

M25   [Diary of a New Castle County, Delaware, cabinetmaker].
1785–86.
[52] p.; 21 cm.
This diary was kept from May 19, 1785, to January 10, 1786, and
offers readers an indication of the different kinds of activities
that a rural cabinetmaker had to pursue to make his living in
postrevolutionary America. Despite having a primary interest in
furnituremaking, the unidentified diarist made coffins; helped
with barn raisings; constructed window sashes, frames, and shutters; fashioned architectural ornament; put up fences; shaved
shingles; and mended wheels. His talents for furnituremaking
and cabinetry are, however, most evident in his comments. The
diarist recorded when he worked on such things as tables,
desks, cradles, clothes presses, dressers, bureaus, chairs, and
cupboards. Often he would involve himself in the entire process
of manufacture, from gathering together the necessary wood and
metal ornaments to cutting the parts, joining and gluing them
together, affixing handles and hinges, smoothing the surfaces,
and either painting, staining, or otherwise finishing the piece.
    Regrettably, the name of the writer of this diary is
unknown. For a list of cabinetmakers working in Delaware from
the seventeenth to the nineteenth centuries, see Charles G. Dor-
man, "Delaware Cabinetmakers and Allied Artisans, 1655–1855,"
Delaware History 9, no. 2 (October 1960): [105]–217. The work
also was issued as a separate imprint in 1960.

M26   [Diary of a trip from Philadelphia to Boston]. 1791.
[14] p.; 12–17 cm.
The keeper of this diary was probably a member of the Richardson family. He left Philadelphia on July 14 with Jonathan Willis,
identified as a friend. Although the word *friend* was written in
lowercase, the writer may have used it to identify Willis as a
member of the Society of Friends, for the purpose of this trip
was to meet with Thomas Scattergood, a Quaker, in Boston.
    The two men traveled through New Jersey to New York
City by stage and then sailed from New York on a sloop bound
for Newport, Rhode Island. The writer described Newport as a

once-prosperous place that had gone into decline after the Revolution but noted that "the Inhabitants of this place appear to be a very Civil well behaved People & their appearance so much similar to those of Philad. that they seemed quite familiar." The writer took several walks in Newport and spent time looking at the windmills that were located on a hill just outside town. After two postponements because of unfavorable weather conditions, the short sail to Providence, Rhode Island, their next stop, began on July 22. From Providence the travelers went to Boston by coach.

Although the visit to Boston was for an unexplained, church-related reason, the writer had many opportunities to see the city. On getting about after dark, he wrote: "The streets of this City are not at present lighted at nights we were informed that it had been before the War but the Lamps being broke by the British Soldiers they have not since been replaced." On July 25, the writer and Willis left Boston and returned home, chiefly by land.

M27   [Diary of a young American in Europe]. 1852–53.
      [238] p.; 21 cm.
      This diary of a European visit begins on September 23, 1852, in New York City, and ends on March 5, 1853, in the hills of central Italy. Its unidentified keeper sailed on the *Southampton* for England, stayed in London for ten days, went to France—chiefly Paris—for a month, and finished his tour in Italy, staying there for three months.

The writer's comments about his ocean voyage include passages on the activities of his fellow travelers, other ships passed en route, weather conditions, latitudinal and longitudinal positions during the journey, and unexpected events, such as the sighting of leaping porpoises that he called "certainly the most ludicrous sight we have seen." Greeted on the coast of England by "a true English day"—sunshine, then clouds, then showers—the trip across the Atlantic ended in London, where everyone disembarked.

In London the writer and his companion, someone named Davenport, visited several attractions that also claim the attention of today's visitor: the Tower of London, Westminster Abbey, the British Museum, the National Gallery, Hyde Park, and Madame Tussaud's Gallery. At the last place, the wax figure of Napoleon I elicited a comment: "The Napoleon relick interested us much; his travelling carriage, so fitted that he could repose at full length, a desk on which he wrote his dispatches, dressing case and all accommodations for comfort, also his state carriage, and the one used by him at St. Helena." Unfortunately, the cultural places of London, the good food to be had there, and the homeyness of his rooms did not sufficiently counterbalance the weather: "We cant endure any longer the dull suicidal weather of London." So, the diarist and his companion hastily departed for the Continent.

From all indications, France was the highlight of this trip. The diarist's special appreciation of the wax figure of Napoleon is, thus, understandable. "Paris," he commented, "may in truth be called a gay city and the only wonder is that a Parisian can live contentedly elsewhere." With Davenport the diarist went to the Tuileries, the Louvre, the Pantheon, the Palaces of Luxembourg, Versailles, and the Hotel Cluny, and he promenaded on the boulevards and squares of the city. The detail used to describe the many churches of Paris suggests that he was either an expert in church architecture and history with a talent for vivid recall or that he copied descriptions from guidebooks to remind him of his experiences later. The author could speak enough French to be understood but had trouble understanding replies. On November 6, he recorded that the French "never laugh at mistakes, nor urge you to buy, and even refrain from showing their goods unless requested." On the character of the French, he stated that they were people of taste because even the humblest had access to great art treasures in palaces that were open free of charge to the general public. While in Paris, the diarist also saw the emperor, attended impressive religious services, and visited the Gobelin Tapestry Works.

In Italy, perhaps the final stop on his itinerary, the diarist spent most of his time in Naples and Rome. Although the classical sites in and around Naples were of great interest, the plethora of beggars seemed to impress him almost as much. On

November 15, the diarist went to the Grotto del Cane and was
forced to pay a local resident to guide him there. "Here, as
usual," he noted, "half the pleasure is lost by being followed by
a guide and getting into a quarrel with them or else submitting
to their demands [for money]." In Rome the diarist attended
Christmas mass in Saint Peters, visited the Coliseum, the Sistine
Chapel, the Baths of Diocletion, the Vatican Museum, and other
places of historical and religious interest. Judging from his comments, he must have had an aunt residing in Rome at the time
of his visit. In addition to Naples and Rome, the diarist went to
Genoa, Pompeii, and Pozznoli; traveled the Apian Way; and
wound up in the mountains near Florence.

M28   [Diary of an American on tour]. 1853.
      [111] p.; 16 cm.
      This travel narrative picks up the tour of an unnamed American,
      perhaps from New York City, on April 20 as he discussed the
      Cathedral St. Marco and other sites in Venice, Italy. He was less
      than impressed with the city, writing: "It is strange how quick a
      person uses up this town after a few rides in the Gondolas & vis-
      its to the Doges Palace & one or two churches in addition to the
      Cathedral St. Mark, one becomes wearied of the place and longs
      to get out of it." So he left after spending only three days there
      and headed for Vienna via the Alps and Trieste.
           Vienna was as impressive as Venice was disappointing.
      "This is really a fine city," he wrote, "the more I see of it, the
      better I like it." He lodged at the Archduke Charles Hotel and
      remarked that while the British were not held in very high
      regard by the Viennese, Americans were treated quite civilly.
      The traveler visited the Belvedere Palace, where he saw a collec-
      tion of armor and Egyptian antiquities; the Augustine Church,
      the location of the tomb of Emperor Leopold II; the Imperial
      Coach House, where a very impressive collection of centuries-
      old carriages was housed; the City Arsenal; the Volksgarten; and
      the Church of St. Stephen. He hoped to see the emperor on May
      Day but did not and was disappointed.
           The next stop on the itinerary was Dresden, and his impres-
      sion of it was not favorable. He spent five days there and visited

the Royal Palace; what he called the Historical Museum, where he saw a collection of weapons of war that supposedly rivaled the one in the Tower of London; the Japanese Palace, the location of an exhibition of porcelain and china that included items from Pompeii and Herculaneum; and the Orangery. On May 8, he noted that he would finally be leaving for Berlin the next day and commented, "I am glad to get out of this lonesome place."

In Berlin he settled at the Hotel du Nord and wrote that he was very pleased with the beauty of the city. He was favorably impressed with the wide, tree-lined streets, the fine public buildings, and the public grounds. He could not find an inferior building anywhere and reported that even "the poor people all live in nice houses." Visiting the Royal Palace, he commented that he witnessed some artwork being boxed up to be sent to New York for the world's fair scheduled for 1853 and 1854. Leaving Berlin on May 12, the diarist spent the next week and a half traveling through Germany to Frankfort and then Mainz, where he boarded the steamer *Joseph Miller* for a ride up the Rhine to Cologne. He compared the Rhine to the Hudson River by writing: "The scenery from many parts of it is truly magnificent & so is that of the Hudson." In Cologne he said that the cologne business was a mania there with twenty-five or thirty manufacturers and shop signs in many languages.

On June 1, the traveler left the continent for England. He arrived in London one day later and found a place to stay at the boarding house operated by a Mrs. Randall at 7 King Street, Cheapside. Remarking about London transportation, he wrote: "I find that I can get around as well as in N.Y. & no fear of getting lost." His chief objective in London was to see the crown jewels, which were not that impressive: "It was no great shakes after all." He saw Queen Victoria, Prince Albert, and three of their children leave Buckingham Palace in a coach and observed that "she is much older looking than I had expected & quite homely." At Madame Tussaud's Wax Museum he was favorably impressed with the carriage used by Napoleon on his unsuccessful foray into Russia. St. Paul's was not remarkable; in fact, "there is nothing very remarkable that I haven't seen the like of it on the continent." Further, "as to the story of England being a

Paradise, or the country one perfect garden, I must say that it is all humbug." He went to Liverpool to set sail for the United States and wrote: "I don't like Liverpool at all—nor the people—it is a *nasty smoky* place and I see more poor, squallid, rascally looking people, both male and female, & *more* drunkenness than in any place *yet*." On June 11, he left England and arrived in Boston on June 23.

M29 Doings on board the *Sloop Bec.* from Fire Island Bound to Three Mile Harbor. 1849.
[4] p.; 25 cm.
In this brief, matter-of-fact account, the writer chronicles a sea trip from the southern shore of Long Island west to New York City and then north on the East River to Three Mile Harbor. The writer traveled from December 3 to 14 and was probably a member of the Dominy family. He made note of the weather, his cod fishing on the way, a stopover at Raynortown near Hempstead, tying up at Pike Slip in New York, visiting with a Mr. Benson, attending a show at Burton's Theater, going to a museum, and sailing toward Throg's Neck and beyond.

M30 [Douglass, Anna Elizabeth Dexter].
[Diary]. [Ca. 1892–93].
98 p.; 12 x 20 cm.
In this travel narrative, Anna Douglass, a daughter of sculptor Henry Dexter, describes a trip from Boston to Daytona, Florida. Although there is some uncertainty concerning the years of this trip, comments about buildings in St. Augustine, Florida, and days and dates that have been related to a perpetual calendar suggest the years 1892 and 1893. There is no recorded beginning date of this account, but the last entry was made on February 17. Although Douglass's name does not appear anywhere in this manuscript, it came to Winterthur as part of the Dexter family papers, and the keeper's date of birth, recorded as February 14, is Douglass's.

    Most of Douglass's narrative concerns her weeks traveling along the east coast of Florida from Jacksonville in the north to St. Augustine and Daytona further south. At Jacksonville she took many train trips into the surrounding countryside, visited the Sub-Tropical Exhibition building, where products from the state of Florida were on display, and enjoyed the beach. Leaving Jacksonville, Douglass went to St. Augustine and toured many of the historic sites related to the settlement of that town. Although she did not lodge there, Douglass reviewed in detail what she saw at the newly opened Ponce de León Hotel, described the recently damaged Cathedral of Saint Augustine, and wrote at length about Fort Marion. At her final destination, Daytona, she met and spent many hours with friends and relaxed with activities appropriate to hot and rainy weather.

Douglass's travel narrative reveals little about her thoughts on society, people encountered, or traveling conditions. Rather, it concentrates on offering a good chronological account of her activities and fairly objective descriptions of what she observed as she took in the sights of a tourist.

M31   du Pont, Henry, 1812–89.
Diary for 1841; or, daily register for the use of private families and persons of business; containing a blank for every day in the year for the record of events that may be interesting, either past or future. 1841–42.
[140] p.; 15 cm.
This diary includes a few notes about events that transpired between January 19 and April 20, 1841, and records of crops in 1842. Without exception, the entries are only several words long and regretfully offer little that contributes to an understanding of du Pont's life. Most of the pages of the diary are blank.

M32   Fifield, Maria M., b. 1835.
[Diary]. 1857–62.
2 v.; 20 cm.
These volumes record the activities of a young woman who resided in Salisbury, New Hampshire. Married in 1854, Maria Fifield took care of the home that she and her husband, John, made for themselves. John was three years older than his wife. Although most of her days were taken up with the routine chores of a homemaker, including baking, ironing, spinning,

cleaning, churning butter, quilting, and making clothes, Maria
was able to find enough time to make hats to sell at a local store.
On May 5, 1860, she wrote: "Martha and I went to the village. I
carried down 14 hats (8¢) $1.12." A little later she put her sew-
ing talents to work for Civil War soldiers, offering to make clothing for them. On October 8, 1861, she noted that "[I] got me
some soldiers stockings to make." The following day she added
that "I like making the stockings first rate." Martha participated
in few social activities. She and her husband liked to sing, so
they belonged to a club whose members gathered regularly for
concerts. They also went to chuch, to meetings of a benevolent
society, to a lecture on spiritualism at the local schoolhouse, and
to the fair in nearby Concord. A daughter was born to Maria
and John on December 16, 1860.

    At the end of the second volume of Maria's diary, another
in a different hand begins. Much of what Maria wrote is dupli-
cated here, and judging from its contents, it would not be unreasonable to conclude that John kept it. It dates from 1860 to 1862
and is fifty-two pages long.

M33   Finley, Mrs. James A.
        Memoranda. 1881.
        [148] p.; 15 cm.
        Mrs. Finley was a resident of Odessa, Delaware. In autumn
1881, she traveled west to Iowa to visit relatives and friends and
to see the sights along the way. In Iowa she remarked, "The
country through here is rolley, good looking farmland—pretty
well improved—has more of the appearance of our Del. Farms—
good many cattle, some sheep." In Galena, Illinois, she stopped
at the home of former president Ulysses S. Grant and described
the place as "a rite nice comfortable looking place. Nothing very
extra." Near Chicago, Finley visited Pullman, the company town
of the train car manufacturing firm "where they build the Pullman P Cars have 5000 men employed this company own about a
thousand acres of land. This city is fine looking all new brick
buildings." In New Albany, Indiana, she stayed with family
friends, probably by the name of Gebhart. Mr. Gebhart had
moved from Pittsburgh to New Albany twenty years before with-

out much money to his name. He now supervised a woolen mill that employed six hundred men and women and was estimated to be worth $600,000. Finley toured the mill and saw every operation, from carding to dyeing. And in Oil City, Pennsylvania, again staying with friends, she witnessed the workings of the Oil Exchange, where, she claimed, 800,000 barrels of oil were sold every month.

M34   Fletcher, Martha.
Miss Martha Fletcher's journal. 1864–67.
[129] p.; 31 cm.
On January 1, 1864, Martha Fletcher began a diary of her daily activities. In a matter-of-fact manner, she noted such things as who she saw each day, weather conditions, family concerns, travel, and her troubles with men. Little mention is made of events of national significance, the exception being the assassination of Abraham Lincoln and the presence of his remains at Independence Hall in Philadelphia on April 23, 1865.

Fletcher was a resident of Delanco, a small rural town in southern New Jersey. She attended weekly church services and served as a Sunday school teacher and church librarian. She was a dressmaker and chair upholsterer, maintained a scrapbook, and enjoyed playing cards and backgammon. During the course of her diary, she recorded that her father, Thomas Fletcher, died on November 14, 1866, and that William, probably her brother, succumbed to alcohol and mental illness in the same year. George Yerkes and George Whitney occupied her romantic thoughts, but as matters developed, neither man proved worthy. Martha as well as other Fletcher family members made frequent trips to Philadelphia to go shopping, to carry out business transactions, and in 1865 to attend the Sanitary Fair.

In addition to Fletcher's diary, this volume contains a catalogue of 225 books in the Delanco library, including history, travel accounts, biographies, novels, children's books, and something called an "account of merchandise on hand." Since Maria's father and his partner in the silver and jewelry firm of Fletcher and Gardiner were forced into bankruptcy in 1842, this account undoubtedly relates to the auction held in that year to satisfy the creditors of the business.

Thomas Fletcher's career is outlined in Elizabeth Ingerman Wood, "Thomas Fletcher: A Philadelphia Entrepreneur of Presentation Silver," in *Winterthur Portfolio III*, ed. Milo M. Naeve (Winterthur, Del.: Henry Francis du Pont Winterthur Museum, 1967), pp. 136–71. He was the subject of Donald L. Fennimore, "Elegant Patterns of Uncommon Good Taste: Domestic Silver by Thomas Fletcher and Sidney Gardiner" (Master's thesis, University of Delaware, 1971).

Other papers relating to the family of Martha Fletcher are located at the Historical Society of Pennsylvania.

M35   Food at Astor, etc. 1857.
[12] p.; 20 cm.
This manuscript account was kept by an unidentified, well-to-do young woman, probably originally from Jersey City, New Jersey, who roomed on Twenty-third Street in New York City. The manuscript has two sections. The first includes concise records of menus and table settings at the Astor Hotel in New York and comments on the appearances and characters of the writer's fellow lodgers. The second section briefly describes the furnishings of hotels in Harvre, Rouen, Paris, Lyons, Dijon, Marseilles, and Nice, France, and in Genoa, Rome, and Florence, Italy, where the writer stayed beginning January 29, 1857.

M36   Foote, Lucinda.
A common place book containing variety: written in haste without premeditation, by Lucinda Foote while engaged as a matron in Auburn Prison. 1832–35, 1876.
[112] p.; 20 cm.
Auburn Prison was built in 1816 in Auburn, New York, and within ten years it had become a model for American prisons. It attracted visitors from England, Prussia, Canada, and France, most notably Alexis de Tocqueville and his traveling companion, Gustave Beaumont, who came searching for information for their study, *Du Système Penitentiaire aux Etas-Unis et de son Application en France*. By 1823 the so-called Auburn system of prison manage-

ment was firmly in place. It required accomodation in individual cells for the male inmates; work with fellow prisoners during the day; separation from the outside world, including contact with families; strictly enforced silence; and severe punishment, including flogging and solitary confinement. Every Sunday church services, Sunday school, and restriction to cells without work responsibilities were allowed. While twentieth-century standards would undoubtedly characterize this system as harsh, for the early nineteenth century it was quite revolutionary and was admired in some quarters.

Harriet Martineau visited Auburn and wrote her impressions in volume 1 of *Retrospect of Western Travel*, published in 1838: "The arrangements for the women were extremely bad at that time; but the governor [warden] needed no convincing of this, and hoped for a speedy rectification. The women were all in one large room, sewing. The attempt to enforce silence was soon given up as hopeless; and the gabble of tongues among the few who were there was enough to paralyze any matron."

Lucinda Foote expands on Martineau's observations. She remarked that she was shut up for ten hours per day with the female prisoners, "doing all in my power to reclaim them." When four new inmates arrived from Albany, New York, Foote wrote: "I will do the best I can to save them from ruin." Continuing, she noted that "they give pretty good attention to prayer reading the scriptures and instruction but if I touch upon vice they are manifestly displeased or entirely indifferent." Foote believed that she was treated with respect and kindness by the officials of the prison and responded enthusiastically when a select committee appointed by the New York state legislature visited her on three different occasions to solicit her opinions about the prison. Foote enjoyed meeting foreign visitors and recorded her activity when some Spanish people toured Auburn on July 25, 1834. She took them to her room, presumably the one where she watched over her charges, and showed them the chapel. She observed that the Spanish were well dressed, genteel, intelligent, and interesting. On May 6, 1835, Foote recorded that she had been working at Auburn Prison for three years and had "learnt much of human nature of depravity in all its degrees." Later that year she left her job: "With a struggle of mind that well nigh prostrated my body and soul I gave it up."

When Foote kept this diary, she was in her mid thirties and felt compelled to work. In another hand at the back of this volume someone recorded the date of Foote's marriage to Judge Henry Day of Indiana as October 16, 1846, when she was past her forty-seventh birthday. The diary entry for 1876 is in Foote's handwriting and is religious in nature.

The Development of American Prisons and Prison Customs, 1776–1845, by Orlando F. Lewis, published by the Prison Association of New York in 1922, discusses the Auburn system.

M37   Forney, Peter, d. 1881.
      [Diary]. 1858, 1861–62.
      3 v.; 13–15 cm.

Peter Forney was a cabinetmaker and furniture dealer who resided in Annville, Lebanon County, Pennsylvania. He claimed that he could provide furniture in the latest and most approved style and that he maintained a sizable stock to be seen in his warerooms. A broadside advertisement that Forney circulated began: "Being engaged in the manufacture of household furniture, I would respectfully invite you to call and examine my very extensive and elegant stock of new furniture and chairs, embracing every article in this line, required for comfort, utility and ornament in chambers, parlors, kitchens, &c." Forney implied that his prices would not be undercut, and he advised his prospective customers: "Do not be persuaded to purchase elsewhere, until you have seen my stock, and ascertained the prices."

The entries in Forney's diary for the most part reflect his business activities. For example, on April 22, 1858, he purchased furniture components, including bedposts and table legs, presumably to use in assembling finished pieces. This transaction, as well as others of a similar nature, reveal that he was familiar with a network of suppliers of furniture parts and that he did not necessarily customize his work as he claimed. On May 1, 1858, Forney sold a secretary for $28, and in 1862 he provided the North Annville Township school with a bench and a blackboard. Throughout Forney's diary he records when he made coffins and suggests that he acted as the local undertaker. On June 7, 1858, he wrote that he "made coffin for George Miller and took corps to Elizabeth furnace," Forney noted unrest by his workers: "Had been provoked very mush by the boyes in Shop."

Forney writes sparingly about personal matters. He states, however, that he attended a meeting regarding the establishment of a fire company, that he was elected assistant librarian of his church, appointed tax collector of the school board, and that "the young men of Annville met in my ware room in the evening to organize a Brass Band." On November 9, 1862, Forney writes without further elaboration: "William went to war."

M38 Gibbons, Mary P.
[Commonplace book]. 1819.
26 items: ill., ports.; 5–24 cm.
Mary Gibbons's work, consisting of twenty-five loose items and one small book, includes twenty-six silhouettes or cutouts of unidentified men and women; poetry on solitude, death, and disappointment; an illustration of the Philadelphia Patent Floor-Cloth Manufactory at Bush Hill; a view of the house of Joshua Waddington across the East River from Rikers Island, New York; and a portrait of the King of the Seminoles, Mico Chlucco, the Long Warrior. Mary Gibbons lived in and around Philadelphia and at one time operated a school on Orange Street. This commonplace book is part of the Gibbons family papers.

M39 Gilbert. W.
Journal of a voyage from Boston to Liverpool on board ship Hiram, capt. Samuel A. Whitney, commander. 1799–1800.
[31] p.; 19 cm.
Gilbert chronicles the events of routine crossings of the Atlantic Ocean during the last years of the eighteenth century. A typical entry, such as the one for July 31, 1799, reads: "Part of the day foggy. winds W. by N. & E. Course E. E. by S. Advanced 52 miles this day. I enjoy excellent health—eat, drink and sleep

hearty. I think I grow more fleshy." As the ship began to cross the banks of Newfoundland, those sailors who had never made the crossing before were given an initiation. They were assembled somewhere below, blindfolded, and taken up on deck. Next, they were tied down, and their faces were lathered up with a brush of tar. If any one of them shrieked, the tarred brush was shoved into his mouth. The sailors were then shaved and thrown in the tide to be washed. Finally, each sailor was required to take an oath: "He holds up his hand & swears that he never will eat brown bread when he can get white, that he never will lay with the maid when he can lay with the mistress, that he never will go to the Leward when he can get to Windward &c. &c." On September 1, the ship reached its destination at Liverpool, England, having been at sea for about five and a half weeks.

Gilbert's activities in England are for the most part unrecorded. He traveled through the country, stopping at various cities, including Nottingham, Sheffield, Wakefield, Leeds, Halifax, and Manchester. Unfortunately, he notes nothing about his stops, offering his readers only an itinerary of his trip.

On February 16, 1800, Gilbert was set to return to the United States on board the ship *John Adams*, which was headed for Boston under the able captaincy of Peleg Tollman. Gilbert and some of his mates left the ship off the coast of Scotland and went ashore to hunt birds for food during the journey home. Although they were unsuccessful on their hunt, they came across a cottage where they hoped they could get some food. Instead, they encountered a spot "where poverty and Happiness seemed united." The hunters entered the cottage through the cow stable that was attached to it. The woman who lived there was dirty and barefooted. Her daughter, a fat and healthy looking girl, was spinning flax. The daughter made no secret about her wish to leave Scotland for America as soon as possible. Gilbert observed that there was no chimney in the cottage but instead just a hole in the roof that let the smoke filter out. Gilbert returned to his ship and five days later set off for home, reaching Boston in mid April.

M40   [Gilman, Rufus King].
Diary. 1824.
19, [1] p.; 16 cm.
This short diary, attributed to Rufus King Gilman, covers a trip
from New London, Connecticut, to Dublin, Ireland, and Liverpool and Manchester, England, taken from February 14 to
June 7, 1824.

Gilman records his observations of Ireland and England
topically instead of chronologically. The country scenery surrounding Dublin was, to him, pleasant except that "the high
stone walls surrounding all the grounds tend to remind the traveller of the unsettled state of the country and the insecurity felt
by the proprietors." In 1824 Ireland was in the midst of one of
its crises between Protestant landowners and Catholics. Gilman
comments about Dublin's roads, greens, gas lighting, public
buildings, poverty, churches, and city statues. After spending a
week in Dublin, Gilman went to Liverpool, where he said there
was little of interest to the stranger, and then to Manchester,
which he characterized as a smoky, gloomy place.

Although he belittled Liverpool, Gilman's description of the
workings of the Herculaneum Pottery, which was located there,
is the highlight of his diary:

> I visited the Herculaneum Pottery while at Liverpool and
> saw the whole process of manufacturing the crockery and
> Porcelain—the Clay is brot to town by the Canals and by
> mixing with Water is made so thin as to pass through a fine
> muslin sieve—A quantity of flint burnt & made equally fine
> is then mixed with it & the Water is boiled away & the clay
> is then passed several times through a machine to work it,
> when it is cut in small pieces for the different articles &
> round ware, such as plates, bowls &c. are shaped on a
> stand in the manner stoneware is made in America, and
> when a little dried is turned in lathe, and it is while in the
> lathe that the brown lines that we see on enamelled ware
> are put on. Oval Tea Pots &c. are made in moulds of Plaster
> of Paris—the ordinary blue Painting is done by taking the
> impression from a Copper Plate on thin Paper which is

immediately placed on the Ware—this is done before glaz-
ing—another kind of Painting is done by taking the Copper
Plate impression in Oil on a sheet of glutinous substance
which is then laid on the article to be Printed—a brown or
red colour is then added which adheres to the Oil—the fine
landscapes, Gilding &c. is done with the pencil, as well as
the flowering of the enamelled Ware—Some of the Porcelain
is burnt three or four times once after each addition of Painting or Gilding—the Machinery is all operated & the boiling
done by Steam.

M41   Hewlett, Richard.
        Commonplace book. 1767.
        [99] p.; 16 cm.
        This commonplace book reveals that its keeper was a religious
man and that he was interested in having nearby examples of
texts of legal forms, including indentures, deeds of gift, bonds,
and promissory notes. Hewlett recorded prayers for many occasions and penned full texts of legal documents. In addition, he
wrote down riddles, very neatly printed the letters of the alpha-
bet, and copied an undated letter that he presumably sent to his
sister Hannah. Although Hewlett himself dated this manuscript
1767, dates as early as 1764 and as late as 1771 appear. Since the
handwriting style is consistent, Hewlett may have actually kept
his book for only a short while, perhaps anytime between 1764
and 1771.

It would not be unreasonable to conclude that this commonplace book belonged to the Richard Hewlett who, according to
an article in *The New York Genealogical and Biographical Record*, volume 54, 1923, page 209, is buried in Old Town Burial Ground,
Hempstead, New York. Born in 1846, this Hewlett would have
been twenty-one years old when he dated this manuscript. His
death occurred on September 18, 1794. A Hannah Hewlett, perhaps the sister to whom Richard wrote, is also buried in the cemetery. Having died in 1809 at age fifty-seven, she would have
been a fifteen-year-old girl when her brother wrote to her.

Other papers relating to the family of Richard Hewlett are
located at the Port Washington, New York, Public Library.

M42   Hoagland, Lavinia M.
          [Estate diary]. 1876–79.
          [28] p.; 20 cm.
          In September 1876, James M. Hoagland, husband of Lavinia,
          died intestate. This diary records Lavinia's activities during the
          settlement of his estate.

          At the time of Hoagland's death, the couple resided in New
York City at 153 West Forty-third Street. Hoagland's first appearance in a New York city directory was in 1861, but an occupation
was never recorded next to his name. Hoagland probably realized that death was imminent because he arranged to meet an
attorney, J. M. Guiteau, on either September 2 or 3 to draw up
his will. They drafted the document, but Hoagland died before
he could sign it. Lawyers questioned Lavinia about her husband's business affairs, account books, and the contents of his
safe. Apparently, the questioning became quite severe, for "Mr.
Clapp wanted the Auditor to enforce the law and put me in
prison." Hoagland's investments in insurance companies and
improvement bonds for the Southern Minnesota Railroad Company and the city of Jersey City, New Jersey, were sold. The
most serious problem that Lavinia had to face was the owner-
ship of a parcel of land in Monmouth County, New Jersey. Several members of the Hoagland family, including one of James's
nieces, and some tenants submitted claims for the property. On
November 8, 1877, the matter was to be settled in Chancery
Court. Unfortunately, the outcome is not revealed in Lavinia's
diary. Lavinia may have kept this diary to help her remember
how the events transpired and as a form of self-protection in
case she happened to be challenged on her testimony at some
future time.

M43   Hoxie, John M. S.
          [Journal of my life]. 1824–25.
          [15] p.; 33 cm.
          The journal kept by John M. S. Hoxie occupies only fifteen
pages of this volume. Approximately twenty-four pages contain
records of personal financial accounts while about 160 pages are
blank. The beginning date of Hoxie's journal is difficult to estab-

lish because he often shifted between listing his accounts and describing his activities. He probably began the journal sometime during the spring of 1824, and the journal ended abruptly on November 19, 1825. There are frequent gaps of unrecorded time. The title of Hoxie's work is taken from the heading on one of its pages.

Hoxie was a settler in the vicinity of current-day Daytona Beach, Florida. His activities included clearing land and operating a salt works, a business in which he claimed to be a half proprietor. Raising orange trees, however, seemed to be what he wanted most to do. Hoxie noted that he was unaware of any writings on the cultivation of orange trees, so he concluded that he would have to experiment until he achieved success. He started his venture in March 1825 and worked into the autumn to prepare the land for the eventual planting of his trees. Unfortunately, a hurricane struck in early October and ruined everything that he had done up to that time. Hoxie then wondered if he might be better off living and working in New River, a town to the south that would eventually become Fort Lauderdale. He summarized the advantages and disadvantages of moving there. Soon after, his journal ends.

Another of Hoxie's wishes was to be left alone by his neighbors: "[I wish] to have as little communications with my fellowmen as circumstances will permitt, for this reason that they are for the most part, a parcel of men unsuitable for society, ignorant, selfish to an uncommon degree, neither their friendship or enmity can be depended on. . . . My impression is that they are all a base contemptible race the very scum of the earth, at all events I shall consider them as such, and use them so."

M44   Jaques, George, 1816–72.
Diary and memoranda. 1840–46, 1852–56.
2 v.: ill., col. plan; 21–25 cm.
George Jaques was born in Brooklyn, Connecticut. He graduated from Brown University in 1836 and for several years thereafter taught at schools in Uxbridge, Massachusetts, and Nottaway County, Virginia. Jaques finally settled in Worcester, Massachusetts, where he again taught and also established a nursery spe-

cializing in fruit and ornamental trees. Jaques was active in the local horticultural society, preparing its *Transactions* in 1849 and serving as an officer. In 1869 he offered the city of Worcester seven acres for a park, but the city declined for financial reasons. Jaques was chosen a member of Worcester's local school committee and served as chairman of its high school committee. In 1871 he was elected treasurer of the newly established Worcester City Hospital. Upon Jaques's death the bulk of his estate was left to the city in a trust fund, its income earmarked for the maintenance of this hospital. Jaques was a Unitarian. He died on August 24, 1872, after a short illness.

Volume 1 of Jaques's diary covers his activities and thoughts from December 18, 1840, through January 29, 1846. He reviewed the progress of his education and wrote on topics that would claim his attention later in life. Jaques recorded in 1832 that he began to prepare for college at Northbridge. In subsequent years, he went to school at Leicester Academy and Drury's School in Pawtuxet, Rhode Island. Jaques wrote that he pursued studies of the classics, played the flute, and read a considerable amount of literature. Between 1840 and 1846, for example, he read, among other things, *Barnaby Rudge* and *Master Humphrey's Clock*, by Charles Dickens; *Proverbial Philosophy*, by Martin F. Tupper; *Tristram Shandy* and *The Sentimental Journey*, by Laurence Sterne; *Ten Thousand a Year*, by Samuel Warren; and two works by Andrew Jackson Downing: *Cottage Residences* and *Treatise on the Theory and Practice of Landscape Gardening*. Of *Cottage Residences*, Jaques commented that he thought only two of the places discussed therein were worthy.

In 1843 Jaques described himself using Orson S. Fowler's ideas about phrenology. He believed that he was inclined to underrate himself, had a nervous temperament, was sensitive, prone to sickness, refined, delicate, and eager. Several days later he wondered if he should not lead a life of celibacy and remarked that he wished his father had; Jaques never married. Also in 1843 he began to read law and two years later revealed his thoughts about the profession: "I propose spending a part of the winter in a law office if I can find nothing better to do." Jaques may have found something better, for on December 28, he started to teach twenty-nine young scholars at a local school. Jaques was a member of the Washington Temperance Society until early 1846, when he resigned after questioning the wisdom of a resolution concerning the patronization of people who sold liquor. Jaques thought that the society had no right even to vote on it. This resignation left him with membership in only one organization, the Worcester County Horticultural Society. Jaques's interest in horticulture was further manifested in the workings of his nursery at 270 Main Street, Worcester.

Volume 2 of Jaques's diary begins on January 20, 1852, and ends on September 24, 1856. Although he never became an attorney, many of the pages of this second volume are devoted to describing the legal details of property transfers in which he was involved. It is interesting to recall that twelve years earlier he had expressed disdain for the law. Jaques's reading habits changed slightly, reflecting his growing curiosity in architecture and travel. He read *Sir Uvedale Price on the Picturesque* and *Practical Hints upon Landscape Gardening*, by William S. Gilpin; *The Seven Lamps of Architecture*, by John Ruskin; *The American Cottage Builder*, by John Bullock; *Six Months in Italy*, by George S. Hillard; *Sunny Memories of Foreign Lands*, by Harriet Beecher Stowe; and *English Traits*, by Ralph Waldo Emerson. He kept up with Dickens by reading *Bleak House* and *Hard Times*. Jaques seemed to have lost interest in running his nursery by 1854, when he wrote: "I am aiming to get out of this tree-trading as I have better and more important business on my hands." In addition, he no longer wanted to cultivate varieties of trees for the sake of exhibiting them at shows; however, he remained a frequent contributor of articles to horticultural and gardening periodicals, including *Horticulturist*, *Gardener's Magazine*, and the *Journal of Agriculture*. In January 1856, he began preparing for a trip to Europe by reading the *North American Review* for hints on foreign travel. He arranged for a passport and attended a lecture on travel delivered by Bayard Taylor at the lyceum in Worcester. On September 1, after having been back home for a month, he wrote down his impressions of Europe, comparing it to his perceptions of the United States. Jaques observed that, unlike Europe, American buildings and bridges were flimsy and its streets poorly maintained; the people appeared haggard, feeble, and unhealthy; in matters of aesthetic taste, Americans were lagging far behind; concerning dress and manners, Europeans were much more graceful; and Americans were religious hypocrites, keeping laws on Sunday while breaking them all other days of the week.

In 1878 Albert A. Lovell, a personal friend of Jaques, published a short volume that contained selections from these diaries. Entitled *Memorial of George Jaques: Comprising Selections from His Journals and a Biographical Sketch*, it also included the record of Jaques's European trip.

M45   Johnson, Benjamin, 1766–1822.
[Travel diary in Europe]. 1796–97.
505 [i.e. 512] p.; 23 × 29 cm.
Benjamin Johnson enjoyed a successful career as a printer first in Reading, Pennsylvania, and then in Philadelphia. Among the items that he issued up to the time of his European trip were William Bartram's *Travels*; *The Life of Benjamin Franklin*; *Captain Cook's Third and Last Voyage*; three books by William Penn; *The Extraordinary Case of Elizabeth Hobson*, by John Wesley; an edition of Aesop's fables; sermons; children's books; a primer; a cookbook; the Bible; a bookkeeper's assistant; a surveyor's guide; and *Neue Unpartheyische Readinger Zeitung*, a newspaper. Johnson was an active member of the Society of Friends, which might explain his interest in printing materials of a religious nature. It certainly explains why he embarked for Europe and why he kept this travel journal. In 1796 and 1797, Johnson hoped to make contact with religious separatists in Germany and Quakers in France in order to hold Quaker meetings and to discuss the religious philosophy of the Friends.

Johnson and his party left America from New Castle, Delaware, on May 18, 1796, aboard the ship *Sussex*. The voyage to Liverpool, England, was not enjoyable: "We have had but little pleasant weather since we left the capes of Delaware." Johnson describes the North Atlantic storms that were encountered, fishing activities off Newfoundland, a meeting with a ship from England headed to the United States to exchange mail, and ship-

board occurrences. On June 16, the *Sussex* reached the Irish
coast, and two days later Johnson set foot on land at Liverpool.

From June 18 to August 4, Johnson was in England, spending most of his time in London. He found it advantageous to be
an American in Britain, for "it opens a source of conversation
very pleasing to most I meet with & in consequence [they] are
more willing to communicate such things as are interesting to
me." And, "the people here seem to respect the Americans
more than any other outlandish people (to use one of their own
expressions)." In London, Johnson met with a lifestyle quite dis-
similar to what he knew in Philadelphia. He wrote of the rag fair
on Rosemary Lane, Covent Garden; the manner in which a
household obtained its porter from tap houses; and how footwear was cared for by the abundant number of shoe blacks.
When his stay in London was at an end, he boarded the *Victoria*
for Bremen, Germany.

In Germany, Johnson was unfavorably impressed with living conditions: "So far the extreme filth, apparent poverty &
want of judgement in planning their houses are what most particularly strikes a stranger as extraordinary—our surprise was
still greater when G[eorge] D[ilwyn] who had been thro' Germany twice before, assured us that what we now saw was comfortable when compared with the wretchedness of some of the
interior parts of the country." He characterized the rural Germans that he met as impoverished, coarse, uncouth, ill man-
nered, and miserable.

In Bremen, Johnson found what he had been looking for:
"After considerable inquiry we found a small number of religious people . . . who were dissatisfied with the forms and cere-
monies in which they were educated and were seeking after
something more inward and spiritual and as such were the
objects which our little company were in search of." In town
after town in Germany, Johnson was told of persecutions that
resulted as a consequence of religious beliefs. In Celle, a
Lutheran clergyman even admitted that although he questioned
the rituals of religion, such as baptism and the Lord's Supper,
he went through the motions to support his family. In Magdeburg, the forty or so separatists who had banded together met in

seven different places so as not to attract too much attention or perhaps persecution. Johnson is both revealing and contradictory about his feelings on German separatists: "It is remarkable among these separatists of Germany that all are fluent upon religious subjects, have much to say and explain themselves with so much clearness as sometimes to have been a matter of astonishment to us. And tho' they talk a great deal they are generally willing to hear what Friends have had to say to them." Later he writes: "Like most others of the Germans, [they] talk religion to death and speak on the subject with as much fluency & familiarity as the people of Philadelphia do of the politics of Europe."

Johnson remained in Germany from early August until December 20 and then entered Holland so that his passport could be endorsed for a trip through France to Congenies, a village close to Montpelier where Quakerism had already been established. Unlike the living conditions in Germany, those in Holland were exceptional. Writing of Rotterdam, Johnson noted: "The public buildings and private houses in this place, as in almost all the other towns of Holland are remarkably neat, and everything as clean as water & scrubbing brushes can make it . . . It is as pleasant a place as I have ever seen." Finishing his business and meeting with the local population of Friends, Johnson left Holland in early February 1797 and headed for France.

On February 8, Johnson landed at Dunkirk, where he stayed for eight days and became acquainted with the Friends living there. He next traveled to Paris, not intending to stay for any length of time. "It is likely that we shall make but a short stay here as there is but little prospect of any religious service," he wrote. Johnson remained long enough, however, to form an opinion about the women of the city: "The women of Paris are supposed to be the most fashionable in Europe, but they are here confined to no fashion at all." Johnson left Paris after only four days and went south to Lyons, then Montélimar, Pont St. Esprit, Bagnoles, Nîmes, and finally to Congenies, his ultimate destination. At Congenies, he was welcomed warmly by approximately eighty Quakers—called Trembleurs by the residents—from the village and surrounding countryside. The colony there was established as a result of a visit by Friends Sarah

Grubb and George Dilwyn in 1788 and an even earlier contact by a Congenies resident with some Friends in London. Between March 13 and April 3, Johnson stayed in Congenies, working and meeting with the local Quakers. Before he left, he managed to reinstate the recently lapsed meeting on a regular basis. On April 13, Johnson was again in Dunkirk, but this time he headed north to England for a ship back to America. He had traveled 1,400 miles in France.

Before Johnson set out for Europe, he undoubtedly carefully orchestrated his trip, allowing for special situations at each stop. Frequently when he came to a town or city, he had a contact, suggesting a planned itinerary. In Germany at Bremen, for example, merchants named Moyer and Topkin were recommended, and in Hamburg, there was a bookbinder called Richter. A Herr Wunderling from Magdeburg wrote a letter of introduction for Johnson so that he might find a receptive audience in Berlin. Unfortunately, the letter was subsequently recanted, thereby creating serious problems for the traveler. In addition, Johnson took Quaker publications along to distribute where he thought they might do some good. Not coincidentally, at least one of these publications, William Penn's *No Cross, No Crown*, may have been drawn from Johnson's own press.

During the course of his trip, Johnson had no difficulty meeting dignitaries. Among those he saw were John Quincy Adams, James Monroe, the Duchess of Brunswick, Thomas Paine, and Benjamin West. Adams and Monroe helped get Johnson's passport in order for his journey through France while the Duchess conversed politely for thirty minutes, inquiring about the political situation in the United States following the violent overthrow of her brother's, George III's, rule. Thomas Paine, a resident of Paris, gave an "unsuccessful interview." Johnson reported that "we found him alone, sitting over a glass of grog—He appeared to have already taken enough of it." Paine said that the United States was becoming a confused nation and added "with much appearance of self importance, 'It will be necessary for me to go over among you soon and set matters right.' " Becoming vociferous, abusive, and turning to ridicule, according to Johnson, Paine criticized the Friends for not bearing arms and concluded by remarking: " 'Why! my books are more read and circulated thro' more countries than your Bible.' " Johnson's visit with the painter West was much more pleasant. Johnson delivered a letter from West's brother, William, who lived in Chester County, Pennsylvania. Johnson was given a warm reception from this "affable, agreeable man." Apparently familiar with West's family, Johnson wrote of the painter's wealth and contrasted it with his earlier circumstances: "His income, arising from his birth as painter to the king and paintings which he does for others is supposed to be ten thousand pounds sterling a year—This is the more extraordinary as but a few years ago he was a poor coopers son in Pennsylvania who gave Ben. many a sound whipping for drawing pictures on the casks instead of hooping them."

Johnson sailed back to America from Liverpool and landed at Wilmington, Delaware. He had been away for one year, four months, and eleven days. When he returned, he found his parents well and his two sisters, Rebecca and Ann, both newly married. Like most travel accounts, this one records conditions of travel, both pleasant and disagreeable. Unlike many others, however, Johnson comments infrequently about well-known tourist sights that might have been encountered along the way. Perhaps, however, it should not be surprising for a Quaker on a religious mission to ignore such things.

M46 [Journal of a printer's trip through Pennsylvania and West Virginia]. 1813.
[16] p.; 16 cm.
In 1813 an unidentified representative of the Philadelphia publishing firm of Kimber and Richardson traveled from Philadelphia through southern Pennsylvania to Pittsburgh and Wheeling, West Virginia, plying his employer's publications. Two works are specifically mentioned in this journal: *The Emporium of Arts and Sciences*, new series, and *Medical Inquiries and Observations upon the Diseases of the Mind*, by Benjamin Rush. The keeper of this journal recorded the names of people who bought or subscribed to his firm's publications. Every stop he made en route is noted as are conditions of overnight lodgings. Although

short, this journal nevertheless provides a glimpse into what early nineteenth-century printers and publishers were compelled to do to sell their books and journals.

M47 Journey from England through Sweden, Denmark, Russia, Prussia, Germany. 1817–18.
2 vols.: ill.; 15–19 cm.
Unlike many of the travel accounts in Winterthur's collection that cover journeys in western Europe, this volume includes a description of a trip through northern and eastern Europe. The unidentified diarist spent most of his time in Sweden and Russia. He left London, perhaps the city in which he resided full time, on July 12, 1817, for Goteborg, Sweden, a town that did not impress him favorably. He noted that the people there seemed to be dispirited and depressed, that the women resembled corpses, and that most of the residents were poor with little to call their own. The writer commented on their physical appearance, saying that they had high foreheads and cheekbones, flat noses, and light hair and eyes. At his next stop, Copenhagen, the traveler found a city better looking than he had expected. From there he went on to Kronshtadt, Russia, where he remained until his papers for entering St. Petersburg could be put in order. Kronshtadt was a military depot. "They who delight in things of this sort might find much to gratify their curiosity if not their envy or their malice," he observed. The traveler saw the Czar when he inspected his warships in the harbor at Kronshtadt. He was finally permitted to enter St. Petersburg, where the public buildings were beyond anything that he had ever seen; he thought that the city was splendid. He toured the Hermitage and the Winter Palace, "the largest Pile of Building I ever saw." On September 1, he left Russia and traveled through Germany, visiting Lubeck, Hamburg, Bremen, and Oldenburg. On September 16, he entered Amsterdam, Holland, and ten days later began his stay in Belgium at Brussels. Volume 1 of the diary ends while the traveler was in Ghent.

On March 9, 1818, the diarist left London for a brief journey to Paris via Dover and Calais. He was exceedingly impressed with the cathedral at Amiens, calling it the most perfect in

France and reminding himself that it had been built by the English during the regency of the Duke of Bedford. "Never have I seen the grand fortunes of the Gothick on such a scale," he wrote. On March 14, the diarist was in Paris. While there he visited the Louvre, the Tuileries, Notre Dame, and the Palace of Luxembourg.

The title of this manuscript diary was taken from a heading from the first volume. The illustration is of the battleground of Waterloo.

M48 Kinsey, John W.
Notes by J. W. Kinsey. 1850.
[40] p.; 21 cm.
"Having had a desire to visit the Western states for sometime past and knowing of a gentleman who was going, we made arrangements and packed up a few duds, bid farewell to those we left behind, and took cars for the Connecticut shore." Thus begins the diary kept by John W. Kinsey on a six-week trip with W. B. Bemans through the United States from Lowell, Massachusetts, as far west as Chicago.

The two men left Lowell on June 26 and headed south for Philadelphia, Kinsey's hometown. There he visited his Quaker parents, brothers, and sisters. They next traveled through Baltimore and then stopped in Washington, D.C. Kinsey sat in the gallery of the United States Senate on two occasions and wrote about both visits. He described the Senate chamber as "where the most wise and virtuous men which each state could produce should of been assembled, endeavouring to do that which would tend to the peace and prosperity of this great nation [and related that] just the opposite [was happening]: Henry Clay was in the chair presiding, only 1/3 of the Senate was present, & most seemed indifferent to Uppham of Vermont." There was a considerable commotion as Kinsey returned to the Senate a few days later: "We heard a great noise and soon found it to be Houstain of Texas roaring away on the boundary line of Texas and loudly denouncing Taylor and his Cabinet." Although the Senate was disappointing, Kinsey thought that the Patent Office was impressive but "not large enough to hold all American ingenuity."

From Washington, D.C., the travelers headed northwest through Harpers Ferry, Virginia, to Pittsburgh, where Kinsey met a friend, J. Richardson. He commented on the black smoke that frequently enveloped the town: "Many times you cannot see 3 Squares ahead it causes the bricks and paint to get black, and makes the buildings to look old and gloomy." Heading further west, Kinsey remarked that he approved of Cincinnati: "I like the appearance of Cincinnati very much it is regularly laid out and hansome." And even further west, he wrote about Chicago, saying that he "enjoyed the rich scene, the clear blue waves were lashing the shore." Midwesterners not only were kind to strangers but also seemed to be satisfied with their lives. Kinsey wrote that "they seemed to enjoy themselves as well or perhaps better than those who live in palaces. It is a true saying a contented mind is a continual feast."

Kinsey and Bemans then headed for home. Instead of retracing their steps, they journeyed along the Great Lakes to New York State and then New England. They stopped at Niagara Falls long enough for Kinsey to observe, "I can say nothing about the grandeur of this place, those only who visit it can appreciate such sublime and stupendious works of Nature."

M49   Konigmacher, A.
[Memorandum book]. 1817–20.
[80] p.; 32 cm.
On the pages of this manuscript A. Konigmacher mixes comments about his business as a hardware merchant and personal matters. Of the former, most of what concerned him related to the better organization of his business. He wrote a note to himself, for example, to make out a list of his customers organized by the towns in which they resided and another note to remind himself to buy some ledgers to record his financial activities. He also wished to get some bills of lading printed and bound. Konigmacher was interested in the activities of his employees, so he wanted to "draw a Sett of Rules & Regulations for the Government of my Boys & Store and have them framed and hung up in the Counting room." He needed to be able to forecast what he hoped to sell and to that end wanted to "make out a Statement

of the Sales of 6 mo. of the quantity of different kinds of articles on order to know how to regulate orders exactly." In addition, Konigmacher indicated that he would devise a list of the kinds of tools used by various craftsmen, including silversmiths, coopers, black- and whitesmiths, and enginemakers, to ensure that enough of them were on hand for sale.

Konigmacher wrote memos to himself regarding personal matters as well. He recorded that John Price borrowed his iron wedges, that he hoped to get a German style stove, and that he had just purchased a horse for $190. He hoped to write to his correspondents in Germany as soon as time would permit, was looking for Dutch herring, and needed to get his "bathing tub" painted. Konigmacher recalled that to destroy garlic it had to be pulled up while at seed and wrote about chimney care: "In order to obviate the necessity of Sweeping a chimney have the mortar with which you plaister the inside mixed with Salt and you will find that during the warm Season the Sut will all peal off and drop down and your chimney will be perfectly clean in the fall."

M50 Kunze, John Christopher, 1744–1807.
[Miscellaneous notebook]. 1785–93.
[154] p.; 19 cm.
John Christopher Kunze was born in Saxony at Artern on the Unstrut, Germany, and graduated from the University of Leipzig in 1763. He came to America in 1770 to assume a pastorate in Philadelphia under the tutelage of Henry Melchior Muhlenberg, the patriarch of the Lutheran Church in America. In 1784 Kunze moved to New York City and filled the pulpit of Christ Church, located at the corner of William and Frankfort streets. From 1784 until 1787 and again from 1797 until 1799, he taught oriental languages at Columbia College. Kunze was the author of many books on religion and was well versed in astronomy, astrology, numismatics, and languages. In addition to the languages of the Orient, his native German, and English, he knew Greek, Latin, Hebrew, Arabic, and Italian. Although he could never master the pronunciation of English himself, Kunze was responsible for recognizing the necessity of its use in America during the worship service of the Lutheran Church. John W. Francis character-

ized Kunze in his *Old New York* as someone who was out of touch with much that surrounded him: "He was so abstracted from worldly concerns and the living manners of the times, that like Jackey Barett, of Trinity College, Dublin, he practically scarcely knew a sheep from a goat, though he might have quoted to your satisfaction Virgil and Tibullus." Kunze married Margaretta Henrietta Muhlenberg, the daughter of his mentor, and was a favorite of New York society, counting Aaron Burr among his friends.

Much of what Kunze included in his book is in the form of lists. He listed the counties of Kentucky and New York, the townships of New York, the population of the United States state by state, memorable dates in American history, the recommendations made by George Washington in his farewell address, the salaries adopted by the United States Congress for governmental officials, a record of exports from the port of Goteborg, Sweden, and the names of the ships tied up in the harbor of New York City. Kunze also included a cure for cancer, a treatment for the bite of a mad dog, and a remedy for bugs.

Considering Kunze's knowledge of oriental languages and his vocation, it should not be surprising to find a description of Chinese worship. The Chinese deity, wrote Kunze, was a figure of a fat, laughing old man called a joss. The worshipper would come to him and bow his head three times. He would then throw two pieces of wood into the air, hoping they would land either with both round sides or both flat sides up; good fortune would then ensue. Devotion, called *chin chin*, followed. After *chin chin*, the worshipper bowed again, threw more wood, placed a lit taper in front of the joss, and departed.

The supplied title of this manuscript comes from a description of its contents that is written on page one. It is actually a commonplace book, and many of its early pages are in German.

M51   Mabie, Charles A.
       Diary for 1866.
       1 vol. (unpaged); 16 cm.
       In this short diary—it covers the keeper's activities from January
       1 through April 24 only—the reader encounters a twenty-year-

old Civil War veteran who was frequently depressed and despondent either because of his memories of the war or the death of his mother. Charles A. Mabie recalled his wartime experiences of a year before three times in this volume: on January 1, he remarked that a year earlier he had been with the army in South Carolina; on January 31, he remembered guarding rebel officers somewhere in Virginia; and on February 12, he wrote that he had been in New York City with a load of prisoners from South Carolina. As the diary opens, Mabie probably was working for his brother in Walton, New York, a small town south of Oneonta. By March 22, however, he had moved to Oneida, New York, for a better job with S. Chapin and Son, a jewelry firm. While there, he repaired glasses, rings, pins, clocks, and earrings. Many passages of Mabie's diary discuss his deeply held religious beliefs.

M52   [Manuscript diaries of a Boston artist: excursions, fishing, and bird hunting]. 1851–54, 1857–63.
2 v.: ill. (some col.); 25 × 30 cm.
The two volumes of this diary record journeys and contain eighty-one watercolors and pencil sketches by an unidentified Boston artist who traveled as far south as Havana and as far north as Montreal. The text has been transcribed and is available in typescript. The above title has been adapted from the supplied title of volume 1.
    Volume 1 contains an account of a trip that began in February 1851 and eventually took the diarist to Cuba. His first long stopover was in Charleston, South Carolina, where he had friends and relatives. In Charleston the traveler commented that he had "had a very pleasant ride with Mrs. Brewster about the city & noticed many improvements: if they do not secede this will be a large city." While he was there he heard a sermon by Dr. John Bachman, who in addition to his duties as a Lutheran clergyman was a noted naturalist and collaborator of John James Audubon. On March 1, he embarked on the steamer *Isabel*, for Key West, Florida, and on March 18, he landed in Havana. Two days later, he began to think that Havana was a stupid place and that he "shall be glad to get out of it." On March 23, he

attended a masquerade ball: "A grand bore it was—men smoking, atmosphere horrid, women ugly." After what must have been an interminable length of time, he left for home on May 9. On his way north, the traveler stopped again in Charleston, went through Annapolis and Philadelphia, then to New York City. There he attended an exhibition at the American Art Union, "where I saw a most execrable collection of trash, disgraceful to America, Art & Artists," a second exhibition that was far superior at what he called the National Gallery, and a third that turned out to be disappointing at the Dusseldorf Gallery. He admired the works of Asher B. Durand, John F. Kensett, and Jasper F. Cropsey that were on display in the second show. He met his friend Victor Audubon, a son of recently deceased John James, and accepted his invitation to spend a night at his country place. Victor's brother John was there, "the same old sixpence, without his wife."

The second volume includes a description of another visit to Charleston and a side trip to the nearby estate of Robert F. W. Allston. Allston, an important antebellum political figure, owned a large rice plantation and was known for his advanced techniques of scientific agricultural management. The diarist had a "long walk with Mr. Allston over his father's rice fields of which he has the care" and then commented: "His rice fields look queer enough." Heading further south, the diarist went to Jacksonville and St. Augustine, Florida, which he described as a miniature Havana.

During the latter half of the 1850s, the diarist traveled through New England and Canada and seemed to be taking part in incipient artists colonies in Vermont and Maine. Although such colonies would be fairly common and even formalized toward the turn of the century, at this time they had not found a place among this earlier generation of artists. The diarist records his activities as a member of these casual groups in volume 2.

Although the text that outlines the activities of the diarist is informative, his illustrations play an equal if not more important role in recording what he saw. The eighty-one pictures include seascapes done on Key West, a cathedral in Havana, the old Spanish gate and fort in St. Augustine, the Naval Academy and

State House in Annapolis, a depiction of the Brewster House in Charleston, the rice fields of the Allston plantation, city views in Montreal, local landmarks (such as the mill and railroad bridge in Brattleboro, Vermont), and the rocks at ocean's edge off Barnstable, Massachusetts.

M53   Marsh, E. S.
Memoir of the Centennial Exhibition of 1876. 1877.
4, [51] p., 8 leaves of plates: col. ill.; 25 cm.
E. S. Marsh composed these recollections of his three-week visit to Philadelphia's Centennial International Exhibition on August 13, 1877, from his residence in Brandon, Vermont. He wrote in a blank book that was prepared by the printing firm of J. H. Coates and Company and marketed at the fairgrounds of the exposition. In the preface to the book, called a publisher's note, Marsh read: "A personal narrative of one's own observations and impressions may be made a most interesting souvenir—for a present to a friend, or to lay aside for the next generation, or to preserve as a memento to oneself. . . . It would make an excellent paper to be read before literary societies and lyceums." Coates and Company added that "the finished writing must of course be done at leisure after the Exhibition has ended, but it will be advisable to take notes during the visit to furnish data for the full account." Coates and Company sold notebooks for just such a purpose.
Marsh toured the principal buildings of the fairgrounds and surveyed several of the smaller displays. He went through Machinery Hall, Memorial Hall, Agricultural Hall, and Horticultural Hall and wrote about such things as the Japanese dwelling, the Swedish schoolhouse, and the temporary encampment of the cadets of the United States Military Academy at West Point. Most of Marsh's comments resemble those of a guidebook and are very matter-of-fact. He did, however, reveal his thoughts in some observations; he believed that the exhibit buildings were fine specimens of architecture and regretted that all, except Memorial Hall, would be torn down when the exhibition ended. Marsh noted that the display of the Society for the Prevention of

Cruelty to Animals "was sadly interesting" and then described its rather gruesome contents.

At the end of Marsh's composition, he wrote: "At this point my enthusiasm, or my time, or something, failed me, and these 'memoirs' will never be carried out as far as I at first intended." He allowed, however, that his visit to the Centennial Exhibition was among his most pleasant memories and that because of the large size of the exhibition, nobody could comprehend it without great study. Marsh concluded: "I take pride in thinking that I was present at the Centennial Exhibition which commemorated the deeds of the old Revolutionary heroes, and the foundation of this Republic."

In addition to containing Marsh's handwritten text, this volume includes eight colored plates, published by Thomas Hunter of Philadelphia and credited to artist J. Aubrun, depicting buildings specially constructed for the exhibition. Their captions appear in English, German, and French.

M54 Mason, Hannah Rogers, b. 1806.
Diary; or, an account of the events of every day. 1825–27, 1830–34, 1836.
[92] p.; 21 cm.
Hannah Rogers Mason was the sixth and last child of Daniel and Elizabeth Bromfield Rogers. As she began to keep this diary, her father was on his deathbed, and one of her brothers, Henry, was so ill that he believed a trip to Europe was the only thing that could cure him. Many of the pages of this volume record descriptions of similar agonizing events: the death of Hannah's sister, Elizabeth, in 1826; the death of her mother in 1833; the impoverishment of the Rogers family; and the departure of her brother-in-law for Europe, leaving behind two young children in Hannah's care. Hannah's preoccupation with religion is revealed in her words. She noted after finishing a book by Madame de Stael on the French Revolution that the United States was fortunate to enjoy freedom of religion and not to have a Napoleon-like leader who encroached upon the rights of man. Hannah mentions a trip to the Catskill Mountains and another to Niagara Falls. She wrote in 1826 that she believed women should confine

themselves chiefly to performing good works for family and friends and that it was contrary to the female character to lead a public life. On October 24, 1831, Hannah married William P. Mason, an attorney from Boston. Her diary ends on July 2, 1837, with the birth of her second son.

Family information on Hannah can be found in *New-England Historical and Genealogical Register*, vol. 13 (1859), pp. 68–69, and vol. 26 (1872), p. 39.

M55 Mason, Jonathan, 1795–1884.
The recollections of a septuagenarian: written without any attempt at elegant phraseology or fine writing, but currente calamo as his thoughts and remembrances arose to his mind between sundown and dark: for the amusement of his grandchildren. 1881.
3 v.: ill., ports.; 20 cm.
Jonathan Mason, a native New Englander, recalls his childhood and early adult life in Boston in the first volume of his recollections. He describes what the city looked like, including its houses, stores, and street names; records the names of the residents of various dwellings; and details activities on the Common, such as the grazing of cattle. Mason was educated by tutors and also attended private schools run by Nathan Webb and William Welles. He entered Harvard in 1811. In 1813 he witnessed the battle between the frigates *Shannon* and *Chesapeake* thirty miles off Boston harbor. After college Mason traveled to Havana, Cuba, to recover from a tonsil operation and upon his return to Boston in 1817 entered the business world with Samuel Snelling as a commission merchant on India Wharf. In July 1822, Mason decided that he had no taste for commercial life and gave up his job.

From 1822 until 1824, Mason lived in England and France. In London he boarded at a number of houses before settling on a place on Great Marlborough Street. Although one of his duties in London was to procure medical instruments to be used in a new building being constructed for Massachusetts Hospital, most of his activities revolved around the city's artistic community. Mason befriended artists David Wilkie, Charles Robert Les-

lie, Gilbert Stuart Newton, and Chester Harding. He took a
drawing class at Sass Gallery and studied under Henry Fuseli.
"He was," wrote Mason of Fuseli, "often very cross when looking over the drawings but was excusable on account of his age
over seventy." Before leaving London for France in 1824, Mason
saw the future queen, Victoria, "then a little girl who we saw
one day playing hoop in the grounds fronting the [Kensington]
Palace."

In France Mason met Lafayette and was a fellow passenger
on the ship that took Lafayette to the United States for his trium-
phal tour in 1824. Mason regretted not having written down the
anecdotes that Lafayette told about George Washington, the capture of Maj. John Andre, and other incidents of the Revolution.
Mason described the reception for Lafayette in New York City's
harbor and recounted that afterward Lafayette had asked Mason
if he could travel with him in a private conveyance to Boston.
Mason replied that the United States government would
undoubtedly provide a carriage. Lafayette's "usual answer was
'you're very kind.' "

From 1824 until 1834, Mason lived again in Boston and in
his recollections wrote about the people he knew. As in London,
most of his friends were artists. Mason recalled, for instance, a
visit that he, Alvan Fisher, and Thomas Doughty made to the
White Mountains of New Hampshire to paint and sketch. Of
Thomas Cole he wrote: "He accompanied me back to Troy,
where taking my horse and waggon we crost the country to
Northampton and on the top of Mt. Holyoke Cole made the
drawing from which he painted his picture of the Connecticut
Valley." Later, Mason led Cole around Boston so he could find a
suitable scene for a painting that he had been commissioned to
do for Baring Brothers, a London banking firm. Mason enjoyed a
warm friendship with Cole and considered him to have great
moral worth. Whenever Cole was in Boston, he stopped at
Mason's house.

Mason studied art under Gilbert Stuart and even received
one of Stuart's portraits of George Washington as a gift. Mason
wrote: "He used to let me sit in his room where he was painting
which it was said he would not allow any other person, not

even his daughter, and although exceedingly eccentric which most great professional men are apt to be and often bearish to others I can conscientiously say I never recollect to have had an unkind expression of any kind from him." Recalling Stuart's advice, Mason wrote that "an artist is just half finished if he leaves out the character of the sitter," and "he must be a gentleman to understand how to paint a gentleman."

Mason compared the portraits of George Washington by Stuart and Rembrandt Peale: "Rembrandt Peale's portrait has very little of the dignity of Stuart's and gives a representation of a heavy unexcitable character of no great intellect and no commanding appearance, whereas Stuart's has all we have heard and read of Washington dignity, commanding appearance and graceful bearing." Mason concluded by remarking that although he greatly admired Stuart, Peale's work probably was historically accurate. Mason had spoken with Josiah Quincy, a Boston political figure and Harvard president, who had known Washington and claimed that he was neither of commanding appearance nor graceful but was a reticent country gentleman who did not seek notoriety.

Other artists also figure in Mason's recollections. He thought that Thomas Sully captured the likenesses of women better than he did of men: "Sully I have never estimated as a great artist, but he was the best female painter we had in those days Stuart being deceased." John Vanderlyn, a Stuart pupil, did portraits to make a living but had real talent for historical scenes. "Next to Allston I esteem him to have been the best colorist of those days in the United States."

Mason went to Europe again in 1834 and visited old friends and places. In London he met sculptor Horatio Greenough, whom he had known since 1825, and learned that Stuart Newton was in a mental hospital. Mason was married on November 25, 1834, in Florence, Italy. Greenough was his groomsman and accompanied the couple on their wedding trip through Italy, Switzerland, and France. Recalling this trip later, Mason mused that "it is not impossible (if we may judge from the discoveries since my boyhood) but that they [his grandchildren] may cross the Ocean on wings some day future."

From 1834 to 1851, Mason resided in Boston with his wife
and six children. In 1851 the family left Boston because of Mrs.
Mason's failing health to live in Pau, France, located at the base
of the Pyrenees. She died on April 6 of that year. Mason
remained in Europe for about twelve years, chiefly in Vevey,
Switzerland, where he rented part of a chateau that had been
built in 1839. While living in Switzerland, Mason had a close
brush with paralysis. He was confined to his room as a consequence of depression and "bodily complaints" and thought that
a course of hydropathy would cure him. After treatments with
cold water, he found that it was difficult to walk. Mason
stopped his therapy when he saw someone else who had under-
gone hydropathy and who was now unable to walk at all. "My
escape I consider providential," he reflected.

Mason's father was a prominent Boston political figure who
had served in the Massachusetts statehouse as well as in both
the United States House of Representatives and Senate. It
should not be surprising, therefore, to find references in these
recollections to American statesmen and current events. Mason's
father, for example, once gave Aaron Burr $100 to travel from
Boston to New York. In 1832 Mason visited vice president John
C. Calhoun, who received him in his bedroom while shaving
just before he delivered a speech in the Senate. Mason met
Andrew Jackson in Washington, D.C., in 1832 to ask for letters
of introduction and again in 1833 while the president was in Boston. Mason went to the Senate with Washington Irving to hear
Henry Clay speak on the Missouri Compromise. Finally, the politics that culminated in the Civil War led to the wounding of one
of Mason's sons, Herbert, and the death of another, Philip, in
1864.

These recollections are copies and except for a few notations
of corrections were written by someone other than Mason. The
final two pages, however, are in his handwriting. In 1881 Mason
complained about growing old and feeling alone, for three of his
six children were dead. Mason ended his recollections by writing
the twenty-third psalm. The illustrations and portraits show
Mason family members and are pasted on the inside of the
covers.

M56   Meigs, Henry, 1782–1861.
Meteorological notes &c &c commenced Jany 26, 1833. 1833–36.
[188] p.: ill.; 21 cm.

Henry Meigs was a native of New Haven, Connecticut, a graduate of Yale, class of 1799, a law student, and a practicing attorney for most of his life. Meigs was a member of the State
Assembly of New York, the 16th Congress of the United States,
and held several positions in the municipal government and
courts of New York City. He served as the recording secretary of
the American Institute from 1845 to 1861 and was the secretary
of the Farmers' Club. He was married in 1806, and his eldest
child, Julia, married the artist Walter Mason Oddie. Meigs died
on May 20, 1861, and was buried in Perth Amboy, New Jersey.

Meigs was a man of many intellectual interests. On October 18, 1835, for example, he passed an amusing evening with a
friend translating passages of the ancient Roman comic dramatist
Plautus. A few months later, he spent another evening reading a
second ancient Roman, the elegiac poet Sextus Propertius. In
addition, throughout the pages of his diary Meigs often wrote
comments in Latin and Greek. Interested in astronomy, Meigs
carefully noted his sightings of Halley's Comet in October 1835
and on October 15 sketched it as he saw it, magnified forty
times its actual size, through his own telescope. In order to further his astronomical interests and to enable others to enjoy the
wonders of the sky, Meigs hoped to persuade some city or state
to purchase a giant refracting telescope. Scientific experiments
also interested him. On March 6, 1836, he wrote: "Son Henry
has nearly completed an electrical machine with a cylinder of 14
inches—I've made a prime conductor of our Coffee Urn & drew
1/2 inch sparks from it." Meigs was also an observer of the
aurora borealis, generally thought to be of electrical origin. One
appearance fascinated him so much that he was prompted to
write a description of it for publication in the *Evening Star*, a
New York City newspaper. Finally, Meigs was a careful observer
of balloon ascensions, writing about one in detail on September 25, 1834.

Although Meigs was accomplished in many areas, most of
the pages of his diary were devoted to recording relatively sim-

ple pursuits, including gardening, family get-togethers, weather conditions, and the concerns of running an efficient household. He was proud of his family and delighted in his grandchildren. Writing of his son-in-law, artist Walter Mason Oddie, Meigs noted on July 22, 1833, that he had crossed into New Jersey to sketch from nature. On December 8, he added: "My Son in Law Walter has attained a distinguished rank as a Landscape Painter. His Bay of Naples is valuable." When a grandchild "of perfect form" was born to his daughter Julia on September 3, 1835, Meigs composed a poem and named it "Rosalie" in the baby's honor.

In addition to Henry Meigs's diary, Winterthur has two volumes entitled "Private Notes" kept by Walter Mason Oddie and described elsewhere in this volume. A privately printed genealogy, *Record of the Descendants of Vincent Meigs, Who Came from Doretshire, England to America about 1635*, by Henry B. Meigs, privately published in 1901, is instructive as well.

Other papers relating to Henry Meigs are located at the New-York Historical Society.

M57   Mendinhall, Estelle M.
          Places visited. 1905–6.
          3 v., bound; 18 cm.
          From July 18, 1905, through August 24, 1906, and beyond, Estelle M. Mendinhall and her traveling companions were on a tour of Europe and Egypt. Mendinhall's travel account offers a detailed record of her itinerary and a good account of the sights that she saw on the way.

The Mendinhalls—Estelle's husband, William, was among the group—arrived in Liverpool, England, and immediately headed for the Walker Art Gallery. A museum stop was not an uncommon feature of this trip. From Liverpool the group went to the Highlands of Scotland, then to Ireland and London. Leaving Great Britain on September 18, after having spent eight weeks there, they then traveled in Switzerland, Italy, and France. The Mendinhalls embarked for Alexandria, Egypt, from Marseilles on December 26 aboard the *Hohenzollern 3* of the North American Lloyd Line. Most of their time in Egypt was spent in Cairo, except for a two-week sail down the Nile to see ancient monuments and ruins. Leaving Egypt on February 15, 1906, they returned to Italy for about two months, headed into eastern Europe, cruised the Danube, and then visited Germany, the Netherlands, and France and England again. Although the travel account ends on August 9, 1906, notes that Mendinhall made on separate sheets of paper take the trip to August 26, when she visited Warwick Castle in England.

Although Mendinhall was relatively silent about her private thoughts while traveling, her writings reveal some of her background and interests. A resident of 1401 Pennsylvania Avenue, Wilmington, Delaware, she was a member of the city's upper class. Because she had a lively interest in literature, places associated with authors were important to her. In Scotland she went to Sir Walter Scott's house and grave and commented that she had planned to visit "Burns country" while around Glasgow. In Pisa, Italy, she saw Byron's house, and in Rome she quoted Dickens about the Coliseum; Browning about "The Crucifixion," by Guido Reni; and Shelley on the cemetery in which he was buried. A Greek statue in Rome that supposedly inspired Hawthorne to write *The Marble Faun*, the house in which Goethe was born in Frankfort, Germany, and the home of poet Hans Sachs in Nuremberg, Germany, all were important enough to mandate visits.

In addition to her literary inclinations, Mendinhall commented on the antiquities of Egypt and the art of Italy, suggesting that she must have been educated in those areas as well. The steamer *Ramses III* took her down the Nile to the ruins of ancient Memphis, Luxor, Aswan, and to the tomb of Amenophis, which had been opened only seven years earlier by Victor Loret and where excavations were still proceeding. She also visited the Sphinx and Giza pyramid. Mendinhall wrote on New Years day 1906 about her impression of Egypt: "We seemed to be living in some huge illustrated book of Bible stories."

In Italy, Mendinhall visited several palaces: the Vatican museums and library; galleries, including the Uffizi, Borghese, and Corsini; the Baths of Caracalla; and the ruins of the Pantheon, which she thought were disappointing. She made note of paintings by Tanzio, Albani, Titian, and Boticelli. A Protestant, she nevertheless had an audience with Pope Pius X. Writing of her two favorite Italian cities, she said: "To return to Florence seems like coming to an old & loved friend—such charm it ever possesses in its dignity and age." And of Rome: "How much to interest us at every turn in this wonderful Eternal City."

M58   Merritt, Benjamin H.
[Diary]. 1858, 1859, 1863, 1895, 1900–1902.
7 v.; 13–15 cm.
These volumes record the activities of a man in two phases of life: as a young adult getting started in his work and as a sickly old man who may have been close to death. In 1858 Benjamin H. Merritt's chief concern was building a house on a two-acre plot of land in Somers Center, New York, that he had purchased from J. Ruxer, the proprietor of a sawmill. Merritt finally made up his mind on March 3, 1858, to start construction, and he and some friends dug and "stoned" the cellar, did the carpentry, erected the chimney, made a mantel piece, laid the front steps, and painted. On July 28, he moved into his new home. As construction progressed, Merritt kept up with his work in a sawmill owned by Ruxer. In addition to cutting wood at the mill, Merritt turned banisters, made wagon hubs and spokes, and fixed the water wheel.

In 1863 Merritt was involved in a business venture at Sing Sing Prison near Ossining, New York. It is difficult to understand the exact nature of Merritt's work because his diary entries are not totally revealing. It would not be unreasonable to conclude, however, that he and a partner operated a training program for inmates who were interested in learning a trade that they could pursue upon their release. At any rate, Merritt's involvement at the prison was short lived, for on September 10, "[I] returned to Sing Sing this p.m. & sold my interest in business at Sing Sing to A. L. Finch."

In 1895 and from 1900 to 1902, Merritt recorded the activities of a man with a fair amount of leisure time. He did a lot of gardening, mowed his lawn, traveled to Long Island Sound to dig clams, fished, noted weather conditions, and spoke of his frequent trips to Purdys, New York. Merritt owned houses that he rented out and in 1900 described the roofing, siding, and construction of what he called a stoop—actually a large porch—on one of his properties. He knew or was related to Georgiana L. and Martha Vail, whose diaries are summarized elsewhere in this volume, and wrote about the times he spent with them. Merritt's diary ends abruptly on April 15, 1902, when he seemed to be quite ill.

Other papers relating to the family of Benjamin H. Merritt are located at the Minnesota Historical Society, St. Paul.

M59 Milhous, Sarah.
[Commonplace book]. 1786, 1806.
5–17, [31] p.; 16 cm.
In 1786 Sarah Milhous copied into this short book essays entitled, "The Cares of Greatness," "Thoughts on Happiness," "True Greatness (Instance of) in Henry 4 of France," "On Contentment," and "Reflections on Different Subjects of Morality." In a different hand and dated 1806 is poetry addressed to Elizabeth Coggeshell and Mary Morton, presumably friends of the writer. Milhous married into the Gibbons family, whose papers contain this commonplace book.

M60 Minutes of the western Virginia land excursion. 1839.
[46] p.; 17 cm.
On April 14, 1839, the unnamed keeper of this travel account left his residence in Sacketts Harbor, New York, bound for the southeastern section of present-day West Virginia. He journeyed principally by boat from his home to Buffalo, New York, then to Erie and Pittsburgh and finally to Wheeling and Charleston, Virginia. From Charleston he went by foot and horse along the Coal River to a place he referred to as the Promised Land. Although the writer does not state the reason for his trip, it probably involved either land speculation or an interest in examining the area before moving there from his upstate New York home.

The narrative is most valuable for its descriptions of a rural part of America, which is best known today for its production of coal, from a century and a half ago. The diarist wrote that the

newly populated "bottoms are all settled and have been some of
them more than 30 years which makes this an old settled country in the most proper sense of the question." The writer
described the many good springs in the vicinity but concluded,
"The streams are not right for mills owing to their general rapid
descent and climate that is habitually dry." He observed that
"Wolves, Panthers, and Bears have a place in society here as
well as the Rattlesnakes and Copperheads." Of the residents'
production of food and clothing, he said: "The people here have
a mill for grinding corn about every third Family, but their
wheat which they raise but little of they grind in their corn mills
and sift by hand. . . . They use the common sand stone for mill
Stones, every house has a loom and a woolen and linen wheel,
raise a good quantity of flax which they spin weave and wear
out."

    The diarist headed for home on May 1 and arrived on
May 11. One of his traveling companions summed up the excursion: "Mr. Platt thinks it is a very pretty country, verry pretty
timber, very pretty prospect, and he is pretty tired."

M61   Moore, Emeline.
           [Diary]. 1826–28.
           [28] p.; 22 cm.
           Emeline Moore, a young school-age girl, opened her diary by
           declaring her ambitious intentions: "I desire to be happy and use-
           ful in life and I consider that knowledge and virtue will promote
           my object. With the intention to improve my mind I have
           resolved to attend the Seminary a few months. At the commence-
           ment of the new year I enter school with a resolution to be more
           economical in the use of my time. . . . I will try to understand
           what I commit to memory and likewise to gain three distinct
           ideas on each day which will be selected by my Teacher. . . . O
           may I grow wiser and better every day." Although it is impossi-
           ble to discern whether Moore attained her goals, her comment
           on leaving the seminary suggests that she was serious in pursu-
           ing her endeavors. She wrote that she regretted parting from her
           fellow students and new-found friends but believed that she and

they had experienced "many pleasant hours in striving to gain useful instruction."

In addition to the diary entries that record her thoughts about school, Moore included "Extracts from different Authors on several useful subjects particularly on the various Sciences." In this section she wrote about the importance of education, astronomy, botany, mythology, and her understanding of the differences between the liberal and mechanical arts. Moore also wrote down definitions of words that she wanted to remember and included a recipe for lemon mince pie and instructions for stuffing a turkey.

An article by Elizabeth A. Ingerman in the *Winterthur Newsletter*, May 29, 1961, entitled "Introducing Emeline Moore, of Cornwall," also discusses this manuscript.

M62   Morris, James Pemberton.
Day book. 1823–25.
[55] p.; 32 cm.
Kept between January 1, 1823, and October 14, 1825, this short daybook records some of the activities on the farm owned by James Pemberton Morris, a resident of Bucks County, Pennsylvania, near Bristol. Much of Morris's writings concern the construction of a large barn, including preparing its cellar, digging its well, laying a stone foundation, raising girders, and putting on its siding and roof. Morris records his farm's planting schedules for such things as corn, oats, potatoes, and radishes. Morris had four daughters, was a vestryman of Saint James Church, Bristol, attended the General Convention of the Protestant Episcopal Church in Norristown, Pennsylvania, delivered the annual address of the Agricultural Society of Bucks County in 1823, was a subscriber to the Bristol Library, and was interested in expanding his landholdings.

An article by Edward R. Barnsley entitled "Agricultural Societies of Bucks County, Pa.," in *Papers Read before the [Bucks County Historical] Society and Other Historical Papers* (vol. 8, pp. 351–404), notes that James P. Morris delivered an address before the Bucks County Agricultural Society on April 28, 1823. The talk was printed and is listed in the Shaw/Shoemaker compi-

lation for 1823 as number 13402. The keeper of this diary
recorded that it was he who delivered this address. The 1830 census index includes a James P. Morris as a resident of Bristol,
Bucks County, Pennsylvania.

M63   Nichols, Francis.
A journal of a cruise on board the United States frigate *Chesapeake*. 1812–13.
[96] p.; 33 cm.
On June 1, 1813, the American frigate *Chesapeake* was challenged
thirty miles off Boston harbor by one of its British counterparts,
the *Shannon*. The American crew outnumbered the British but
was newly formed and lacked the necessary discipline required
for victory. The *Chesapeake* was pounded by the guns of the *Shannon* and finally succumbed to a fifty-man British boarding party.
The frigate was towed to Halifax, Nova Scotia, as a British prize.
The rallying cry of the United States Navy, "Don't give up the
ship!," is supposed to have been the dying command of James
Lawrence, captain of the *Chesapeake*, during this engagement. In
his *Pictorial Field-Book of the War of 1812*, published in 1868, Benson J. Lossing wrote that "history has recorded but few naval
battles more sanguinary than this. It lasted only fifteen minutes,
and yet, as Cooper remarks 'both ships were charnel-houses.'
They presented a most dismal spectacle."

Six months before its capture, the *Chesapeake*, then under the
command of Samuel Evans, set sail from Boston on a five-month
cruise of the Atlantic Ocean to try to harass and capture British
warships. Francis Nichols was on board in an unnamed capacity
and kept this sea journal of the activities of the *Chesapeake* from
December 17, 1812, to March 20, 1813. Most of his comments
concerned the details of sailing. The last half of his December 23
entry is typical: "At 1 fresh breezes from W.S.W. The wind coming on to blow heavy, furled the mizen top Sail the gale increas-
ing furled the fore and main top sail—at 3 hauled up the fore
sail And set the main Storm Stay Sail at 1/2 past 3 Sent down
fore and main topgallant yards and housed topgallant masts Set
the fore and mizen storm Stay Sails, At 4 Cloudy with light-
ning—Blowing a gale—At 8 difference between the Temperature

and water—4 Deg." Whenever the *Chesapeake* encountered other ships, however, Nichols was quick to take note. On January 1, the British merchant ship *Julia* was seized, and during the next five weeks the *Volunteer, Liverpool Hero,* and *Earl Percy* were similarly taken. Although the *Chesapeake* prevailed in these meetings, its successes were slight compared to its goal of destroying warships.

When the *Chesapeake* entered Boston harbor during a violent storm after this foray, it lost a top mast and several men who were aloft. This tragedy, the lack of activity on the voyage, and its reputation among sailors as an unlucky vessel foretold, perhaps, its capture a few weeks later.

For a list of ships captured at sea by the *Chesapeake* from December 13, 1812, through April 7, 1813, see pages 62 and 63 of *The Navy of the United States from the Commencement, 1775 to 1853,* published in 1853 by Gideon and Company, Washington, D.C.

M64 Nichols, Susan W.
[Diary and book of watercolor paintings]. 1816.
[7] p., 13 leaves of plates: col. ill.; 21 cm.
This small volume contains twelve watercolors of fruit trees, wildflower blossoms, and a butterfly and one preliminary pencil sketch of a flower. There are two diary entries, dated March 5 and 7, from Fairfield, Herkimer County, New York, that briefly discuss sermons and the keeper's lessons in Virgil, Cicero, and surveying.

M65 Norris, Albert Lane, 1839–1919.
A journal of Albert L. Norris, Epping, New Hamps. from April 1st 1858 to [March 11th 1860].
59 p.; 21 cm.
Albert Lane Norris, a native of Epping, New Hampshire, was educated at Phillips Exeter and Wilbraham academies and received a medical degree from Harvard College in 1865. During the Civil War, he served as an assistant surgeon and took part in the Peninsular Campaign of 1862. An obituary notice from the Boston *Transcript* noted that Norris met President Lincoln many

times and was a close personal friend of Gen. Lew Wallace. In 1869 Norris continued his medical education abroad at hospitals in Vienna, Berlin, Edinburgh, and London. When he returned from Europe, he settled in Cambridge, Massachusetts, and practiced medicine there until 1910. Norris married Cora E. Perley of Laconia, New Hampshire, in 1873 and had two daughters and one son, who also became a doctor. Upon retirement, he moved to Malden, Massachusetts. Norris was a member of the Grand Army of the Republic, the Military Order of the Loyal Legion, the New England Historic Genealogical Society, and the Massachusetts Medical Society. In 1890 he was a delegate to the Tenth International Medical Congress in Berlin and received an honorary degree from Wiley University.

Norris began this diary when he was nineteen years old. At that time, he was employed as a clerk at Tinkham and Company's dry goods store in Springfield, Massachusetts, and lived in a room above the store. Although Norris enjoyed his job, he left it after only four months, remarking, "I am convinced that it is a place of temptation and sore trial for a young man to live and do business in a city." Norris moved to rural Wilbraham, Massachusetts, and assumed another clerking position, this time at a store operated by S. F. Pickering. He remained with Pickering for more than a year and then moved to Boston to work in his third dry goods store, Palmer Waterman and Company's. Resigning this position after thirteen months, Norris continued his career as a merchant in partnership with Orien S. Currier. Commenting on his business life, Norris said: "I feel that I have been highly favored with good employers—good influences and good pay," and "I like store business very much indeed." Norris was a deeply religious man who rarely missed Sunday services at the local Methodist Church or camp meetings when they were close enough to attend. In his youth, he was an active member of the Union Philosophical Society of Wilbraham.

This volume predates Norris's years as a soldier and physician; however, loose sheets with notes and drafts of two letters to his sister reveal that he was eager to take part in the war and that he was concerned about his twin brother, Rufus, who was already in the army. Norris indicated his pro-Union sympathies on December 1, 1859, when he wrote from Wilbraham: "Tonight I helped with some 8 others to make and hang on the old Elm an image [of] Gov. Wise of Virginia in effigie." Wise is credited with quelling John Brown's raid on Harper's Ferry, Virginia, and thus helping to send Brown to the gallows. Norris would serve as a medical cadet in a hospital near Richmond during his summer vacation from Harvard in 1862.

A short obituary on Norris appeared in *New-England Ilislorical and Genealogical Register* (supplement to April 1920): lx[i]–lxii.

M66 Observations sur les Moeurs et des habitans de Distric a Maine, Nouvelle Angleterre, Ecrit a New Gloucester. 1797.
[46] p.; 16 cm.
In 1797 Maine experienced a rapid increase in population. Between the end of the Revolution and 1800, its residents grew in number from 96,000 to 152,000. This manuscript records observations by an unidentified visitor to Maine during this time of growth. Among the subjects he commented on were the farmers' lifestyle and peculiarities, the politics of the day, religious customs, the Shakers, and logging.

From what the writer observed during his stay in Maine, he concluded that the typical farmer was parsimonious, self-sufficient, not especially well educated, and uninclined to consider new ideas. Farmers were particularly proud of their houses and apparently spent a good deal of time improving them; yet the writer noted: "Being leisurely sometimes the house falls to decay before any of these improvements are adopted and sometimes the old part of the house is worn out before the new rooms are compleated. The individual, however, has the satisfaction of being called the owner of a large house."

The writer was not impressed by any political sophistication on the part of the residents of Maine. He commented that the people were generally apathetic, not wanting to abandon their tools or ploughs for political concerns. Stretching his observations on politics to cover the whole of New England, he wrote that this attitude fostered an aristocracy in government there, something that the Federalists advocated. The writer believed that political differences of opinion in Congress would force the

United States to split apart. He predicted that the North, being
aristocratic, would ally itself with Great Britain and that the
South, being democratic, would eventually enter into alliance
with France.

The writer was not kind in his remarks about what he called
religious reformations:

> Some fanatic preacher has generally liberally dealt out dam-
> nation, brimstone, hell, & the devil with great liberality has
> worked upon a number of weak minds who, frightened and
> terrified, have been led to put the care of their souls in the
> hands of the pious man who by virtue of this prerogative
> has governed the conduct of his flock with arbitrary sway
> constraining them to attend lectures 3 or 4 times a week
> besides performing double duty on the Sabbath. But, as
> their penance did not suit all constitutions it has happened
> that the majority have generally fallen off, leaving a few
> saints to brood over their superior sanctity in holy solitude.

The Shakers of Sabbathday Lake are considered on five
pages of this manuscript. Among the things discussed are the
Shakers' profession of celibacy, their public worship meetings,
their methods of education, and their hospitality toward strangers. Two misunderstandings concerning the Shakers are passed
on: first, the writer noted that early Shakers would "dance
naked and roll in the mire to show their humility." Second, he
stated that the most vigorous of the men "are permitted to
impregnate all the women who are fit for conception" in order
to increase the membership of the sect. The writer concluded
that the practices of the Shakers are "repugnant to common
sense."

Timber has always been an important Maine resource. As
the district grew and prospered during the last decades of the
eighteenth century, lumbering provided a living for many residents. In tandem and as a result of being located along the eastern seaboard, the shipbuilding industry of Maine also flourished.
The writer concluded his manuscript by discussing these aspects
of Maine's economic life. He lamented what he believed to be
the waste of good timber that originally was destined for the
masts of ships but was being destroyed for its perceived lack of

quality: "Several immense masts have been refused in consequence of a trifling flaw or very small knot of no real consequence. It is supposed that the District of Maine abt 30 years since contained masts enough to have supplied all Europe for centuries, but the impolicy before mentioned has caused such vast numbers to be destroyed."

In addition, the writer made remarks in shorter compositions about recipes, the local dialect, the influence of newspapers, relations with Indians, courtship, the militia, and the disregard for laws. One page of the text, as well as its title, is in French.

M67 Oddie, Walter Mason, 1808–65.
Private notes &c. 1828–29.
2 v.: ill.; 21 cm.
Walter Mason Oddie's notoriety as a painter came from his landscapes in the style of the early Hudson River school. He lacked extensive formal training and never traveled to England, where many of his contemporaries went for instruction. His early drawings revealed much natural ability and an eye for working from actual scenes. Oddie struggled continually with perspective, unable to show spatial depth effectively on a flat surface. Although he had been painting for years, Oddie waited until he was past forty before turning to art as a profession. At the time of his death, he had exhibited at the Boston Athenaeum, Pennsylvania Academy of the Fine Arts, Washington Art Association, and New Jersey Art Union.

The notes that Oddie made in these two volumes document his formative years as an artist and reveal concerns that remained with him throughout his life. Oddie married Julia Meigs in 1825, and from every indication he was a devoted husband. The couple had two children early in their marriage and saw both die. Baby Julia's death is chronicled in these pages. Oddie's entry on March 17, 1828, reveals the kind of life he hoped to lead: "Yesterday, Sunday, I enjoyed myself at home painting and sailing on our pond. I wish nothing better for the rest of my days." Unfortunately for Oddie, he was not a wealthy man and was forced to work for a living. His job during the course of this diary was with a merchant identified as W. Meyer, perhaps from the firm of Meyer and Hupeden of 28 Broad Street, New York City. Almost from the beginning of his entries, Oddie lamented that he was unable to achieve financial stability for his family. On July 28, 1828, he remarked that he needed a better paying job, perhaps with a bank; by August 13, he was $200 in debt; on October 2, he was forced to accept a suit of clothes paid for by his father-in-law, Henry Meigs; and on October 11, he wrote: "I shall know no peace of mind until I am once more free from the turmoils of debt—and stand independent of the world as far as relates to obligation."

Oddie was a voracious reader, and he used the pages of these volumes to record what he read and his thoughts about each book. Among the authors and works that he was attracted to were: *Belinda*, by Maria Edgeworth; *O'Donnel* and *Florence McCarthy*, by Lady Morgan; *The Life of Richard Savage*, by Samuel Johnson; *The Adventures of Roderick Random*, by Tobias G. Smollett; *The Clubs of London*, by Charles Marsh; *The Traveller's Oracle: or, Maxims for Locomotion*, by William Kitchener; *Posthumous Papers, Facetious and Fanciful, of a Person Lately about Town*, by Cornelius Webbe; *Travels through Spain in the Years 1775 and 1776*, by Henry Swinburne; *Sailors and Saints: or, Matrimonial Manoeuvers*, by William N. Glascock; *A Chronicle of the Conquest of Granada*, by Washington Irving; and *Devereaux*, by Lord Lytton. He read four of Sir Walter Scott's books: *The Monastery: A Romance, Redgauntlet: A Tale of the Eighteenth Century, Kenilworth: A Romance*, and *Life of Napoleon Bonaparte*. Rather than purchase these books, Oddie subscribed to the library of bookseller William B. Gilley at 94 Broadway, New York City, where he could borrow what he required and where he had access to periodicals from London.

Although Oddie claimed to disdain politics, he was a staunch foe of Andrew Jackson during the presidential campaign of 1828. On April 21, Oddie remarked about what he perceived as the violent tactics of Jackson's followers and called Duff Green's *Telegraph* (dubbed by some detractors as the *Tell-a-lie-a-graph*) as one of the most scandalous publications of the day. On July 16, he attended a political meeting held to elect delegates to a convention of young men at Utica, New York. Offended by what transpired, he wrote: "This is my first and last appearance in *public life*." One week later he noted that the election of Jackson would be "the greatest curse that could fall upon our country." Jackson was to Oddie "ignorant, ferocious & inexperienced." Just before the election, Oddie added: "I pray fervently he and his dastardly supporters may meet with the signal defeat their conduct merits from all civilized beings." Oddie made his final remark about politics on Jackson's first speech as president: "Jackson's inaugural address pleases none."

While Oddie kept this diary he was hoping to learn how to be a better artist. He enjoyed the many exhibitions in New York City. On April 8, 1828, for example, he saw the panorama painting of Mexico City by Robert Burford at the Rotunda. Oddie desccribed it in great detail and concluded that "I have just enjoyed one of the greatest treats in the fine arts that has come within my reach." Almost a year later he met the artist and looked forward to having some instruction in panorama painting. In 1828 and 1829, Oddie attended the third and fourth annual exhibitions of the National Academy of Design, where he saw works by Henry Inman, Samuel F. B. Morse, Charles C. Ingham, and Thomas Cole. He admired Cole's canvasses and later tried to copy *Hagar in the Wilderness*. Learning of a privately held collection of art, Oddie visited Samuel Maverick, an engraver who had ten paintings by William Hogarth. "I immediately went and examined what I now consider the most valuable specimens of the arts in America," Oddie exclaimed.

In addition to learning about painting from exhibitions, Oddie practiced his art by copying prints and taking lessons from portraitist Anthony Lewis DeRose. On November 3, 1828, he painted most of the day, copying a lithographic print lent to him by R. Ludlow. Oddie wrote: "I am much obliged to him at all events for lending me subjects for my pencil, not being able to afford to purchase them." Earlier he had spent time copying a lithograph of G. Engelmann, and Oddie deemed it one of his best pieces. In January 1829, Oddie began to sit for a miniature portrait painted by DeRose and soon was taking informal lessons from him. Oddie held his teacher in high regard: "For a young artist he is certainly far advanced in his art and some of his speci-

mens of painting do not lose in the comparison with our best artists." And "from calling frequently and observing closely the
fine effects produced by DeRose's pencil I am enabled to succeed
much better in my humble efforts."

Oddie was a man of refinement who was happiest when
with his family, reading, sketching, and painting. Oddie wrote
that he was fond of anything connected with intellect and
genius. He preferred life in the country to life in the city and
reflected this preference in his art.

See also in this volume the entry for Henry Meigs, Oddie's
father-in-law. In addition, see the spring 1980 issue of *American
Art Journal* for an article by Annette Blaugrund on Oddie entitled
"The 'Mysterious Mr. O.': Walter Mason Oddie (1808–1865)"
(pp. 60–77).

M68   Patton, Mary Shaw Bird, d. 1863.
Journal of Mary Patton. 1860–61.
[154] p.; 19 cm.
From June 3, 1860, until July 17, 1861, Mary Patton kept this journal of her wedding trip through western Europe. Mary's husband was a clergyman named William Patton who was noted for
his contributions to policies of the Presbyterian and Congregational churches in antebellum America. Reverend Patton's primary influences were in the areas of slavery, temperance reform,
education, and missionary work. Patton was born in Philadelphia in 1798, graduated from Middlebury College in 1818,
attended Princeton Theological Seminary for about two years,
and was ordained to the ministry by the Congregational Association of Vermont in 1820. Patton was one of four ministerial
founders of Union Theological Seminary, New York City, and
served as a director and instructor there between 1836 and 1849.
All of his pastorates were in New York City. Patton was a member of many professional groups and the author of several books
and articles. In fact, while he was in London on this trip, he
wrote articles for the English press explaining the antislavery
background of the Civil War and published a pamphlet entitled
The American Crisis; or, The True Issue, Slavery or Liberty. One of
his sons, William Weston Patton, followed him into the ministry

and served as the president of Howard University, Washington, D.C., from 1877 to 1889. Patton married three times. His second wife, Mrs. Mary Shaw Bird, also of Philadelphia, kept this journal. Patton died in New Haven, Connecticut, on September 9, 1879.

Although the Pattons were on their wedding trip, William attended meetings, renewed old acquaintances among the European clergy, and even conducted church services. On July 6, 1860, he went to a committee meeting of the Evangelical Alliance, an organization, which he was instrumental in establishing in 1846, that promoted Christian union and religious liberty throughout the world; three days later the Pattons spent the evening at the home of Rev. Dr. Davies, secretary of the London Tract Society; and one month later Reverend Patton filled the pulpit of Rev. B. Noel in London.

Many of the attractions that the Pattons enjoyed were religious in nature. In London they went to St. Paul's, which Mary described as elegant and beautiful; Westminster Abbey; and St. George's Chapel at Windsor Castle. In Edinburgh they stopped at John Knox's house, and in Italy the couple spent a considerable amount of time in churches everywhere. In Rome Mary commented that the floor of St. Peters was being redone "& I got two pieces of the old marble." They attended the 234th anniversary of the dedication of St. Peters on November 11, 1860, with many dignitaries, bishops, and cardinals. "The music & singing were very fine. . . . There were a large number of persons in the church but they were lost in the vastness of the building." On December 7, the Pattons were at the Church of the Holy Apostles in Rome, where they saw the Pope. Mary wrote that the Pope's guard lined the aisle and that the procession consisted of twelve priests carrying large candles, followed by the Pope in magnificent robes, then twenty-four cardinals, and finally the bishops. The Pope was carefully protected as he left the church in a gilt carriage pulled by six black horses.

In addition to their church activities, the Pattons took many opportunities to see the sights of the countries they visited: England, Scotland, France, Belgium, Germany, Italy, and Switzerland. Highlights included the Crystal Palace in London, which Mary described, saying that "the grounds [were] magnificent the palace wonderful—the ornaments of statuary, plants, lakes &c &c admirable wandered about for 45 minutes then took our seats for the concert." In England they also went to Covent Garden market, Hampton Court, Kew Gardens, and Sir John Soames museum, "the collection of a particular man of genius." After going to Madame Tussaud's Wax Museum, Mary wrote that "this exhibition strikes every beholder with its truly life like appearance." In Switzerland they rode horses to an elevation of 8,150 feet to see the glacier from which the Rhone River flowed. "This is the grandest glacier of Switzerland, " she wrote, "& to me it was a grand sight altogether different from any thing I had ever seen or even imagined." In Italy the Pattons visited many art galleries and spent two-and-a-half hours with American sculptor Hiram Powers, who had moved from the United States to Florence in 1837. Of Powers's studio, Mary observed: "I was delighted with him & his works particularly his America—fisher boy, etc." They also saw the leaning tower in Pisa, Vesuvius when it was smoking, and the ruins of Pompeii, where "there are strong indications of wealth, taste, & cultivation also of great debasement." While in France, the Pattons visited the Bois de Bologne, where they saw Emperor Napoleon III; the Louvre; the Gobelin Tapestry works; Versailles; and Napoleon I's tomb.

In addition to the people mentioned above, the Pattons met or saw several other well-known nineteenth-century figures. At the Crystal Palace in London, they witnessed a performance by Charles Blondin, a tightrope walker best known for crossing above Niagara Falls on a rope. In Rome they had an interesting interview with Harriet Hosmer, perhaps the most famous woman sculptor of her day. And again in Rome, on November 26, 1860, "Mr. Terry, the artist, called." Mary noted the election of Abraham Lincoln as President of the United States and wrote in Turin about the progress of Giuseppe Garibaldi, the Italian patriot and guerilla leader: "There was much excitement about the news of the victory. Many Garibaldi volunteers parading the streets, singing, &c."

M69   Randolph, R.
Sundry memos of R. Randolph, esq. 1835–37.
[17] p.; 16 cm.
From 1835 to 1837, R. Randolph traveled through Europe, Asia, and Africa with a Mr. and Mrs. R. H. Haight and their servants. He maintained this short diary to list the cities that he and his companions visited and the money they spent. At the beginning of this diary, Randolph and the Haights were in Leipzig, Germany. From there they journeyed to Hamburg and Stockholm, Germany; to St. Petersburg, Moscow, and Odessa, Russia; Alexandria, Egypt; Syria; Palestine; Paris; and London. Although much of their recorded expenses included money spent for accomodations and personal items, a number of entries enumerated works of art that were purchased along the way, including sixty-eight engravings, twelve color lithographs, clocks, and lamps in Paris, and more engravings in London.

M70   [A record of lessons in drawing]. 1855.
[13] p.; 21 cm.
From September 12 through November 15, the unnamed keeper of this diary recorded what he was taught during semi-weekly lessons in drawing from an instructor named Mr. Wood. He learned during his first class, for example, that when working with landscapes, it was advisable to draw the farthest object in sight first, to give the lightest color to the most distant clouds, and to make the edges of a drawing lighter than the center. He also studied the correct way to represent such things as trees, water, sky, shadows, mountains, and moonlight. He concluded that his lessons had been exceedingly valuable, for he wrote: "In this book is contained much important information."

M71   Remeniscenses of our trip to the Columbian Exposition from August 21/93 to August 31/93. 1893.
[87] p.; 17 cm.
Mary, Etta, and the unnamed keeper of this diary left by train from their home in Buffalo, New York, on August 21, 1893, for the World's Columbian Exposition in Chicago. Upon arrival,

they found a place to lodge opposite the fairgrounds at the Hotel
Garfield and enjoyed ten days of sightseeing in the fair and city.
Most of this diary is devoted to recording the various exhibitions
that the travelers visited and commenting on the highlights of
their experiences. They approved of Tiffany Company's display
and found much to admire in historical exhibitions. Writing
about the Convent de Larabita, the diarist observed: "This convent I consider the most interesting exhibit of all the exhibits in
this Columbian Exposition as it contains nothing but relics and
documents of Columbus." In addition, "the prettiest sight of all
is the Libby Glass works illuminated. It is only excelled by the
Ferris Wheel with its thousands of electric lights constantly moving around." The traveler's experiences at the fair were not
entirely pleasant, however. He thought the Irish Village was
merely a place to sell expensive goods and service, as its restau-
rant was poor. The beauty show, presented so that visitors
might see different native costumes, was "another of the many
fakes in the Midway Plaisance." While the group was there, an
explosion occurred in Machinery Hall, but nobody was hurt, and
there was little damage. Finally, the diary keeper could not
understand why the fair was open on Sundays while the restau-
rants on the grounds were closed. On August 30, the three travelers left the Hotel Garfield for the train station and took the 3:30
p.m. train for Buffalo. They arrived home at 8:00 the next morning, having spent $119.80 on their vacation.

M72   Richardson, Joseph G.
       Garden book. 1850.
       [32] p.: plan; 16 cm.
       In this manuscript, Joseph G. Richardson, a resident of Philadel-
       phia, described the schedule of planting in his vegetable and
       herb garden from March 15 to July 9, 1850. He offered instruc-
       tions on how to plant: "Corn in 2 rows plant about 3 in apart in
       the rows. rows thre feet apart & 9 in from the edge making 150
       rows." And, "peas in 3 rows 18 in apart & 9 from the edge
       plants 1 in apart in the rows making about 7300 peas." He also
       noted plans for subsequent years: "Lima beans in 26 hills have

got only 2 poles next year I must plant them deeper they were left uncovered by the rain."

At the front of his book, Richardson pasted a map of his garden that included the dimensions of the various plots and a numbered key that reminded him where his plants belonged. In all, there were eleven vegetables and herbs in the garden: cabbage, peas, beets, onions, eggplant, radishes, horse radish, tomatoes, potatoes, corn, and lima beans.

M73   Richardson, Ruth Hoskins, 1756–1829.
[Biographical sketch]. [Ca. 1829].
[24] p.; 19 cm.
Shortly after Ruth Richardson's death, one of her daughters wrote this sketch of her life. The subject was born in Burlington, New Jersey, and was one of twelve children of John and Mary Hoskins. "Her father's house was the resort of friends travelling in the work of the ministry." Apparently sickly as a child, Ruth suffered her first serious bout with disease at age seventeen, when she contracted a nervous fever. Later she would have yellow fever, bilious fever, cholera, and many less serious maladies that her daughter felt were not worthy to mention. On June 15, 1780, Ruth was married. Most of this narrative is tied to illness, suffering, and finding a lasting peace with God.

M74   Rumford, Charles G., b. 1841.
Pocket diary for 1864.
[400] p.; 11 cm.
Charles G. Rumford was a native of Byberry Township, Pennsylvania. He studied law with Judge E. W. Gilpin and Victor du Pont and was admitted to the Delaware bar in 1866. Rumford served as Deputy Attorney General of Delaware from 1867 to 1869, was a federal court clerk in 1873, and later Solicitor of the Court of Chancery of New Castle County, Delaware, and Clerk of the District Court under Judge Willard Hall. Rumford was elected a director of the Union Bank of Delaware in 1888. The diary that he kept in 1864 recorded his activities as a twenty-three-year-old soldier during the Civil War.

On January 19, Rumford and his unit were encamped near

Washington, D.C., ready to embark for Louisiana. They arrived near New Orleans by the end of February and started their trek through the state in March. At Chayneyville, Rumford remarked that "the country was fertile and but poorly cultivated. Negro & white men few, plenty of sugar & cotton along the road." On April 7, Rumford was around Pleasant Hill and witnessed the wounded being brought back to camp after a skirmish. Two days later he was at the front, where there was much commotion, confusion, and retreat. On May 19, two truce flags flew to allow for the exchange of prisoners. Rumford observed on October 4 that although it was a day of fasting, "did not fast at all. Soldiers do not appreciate the good intentions of the President in appointing days of fasting & prayer." Despite the disagreement between the soldiers and Lincoln on this matter, when the election of 1864 was held, Lincoln garnered sixty-two votes from Rumford's unit while his opponent, George B. McClellan, got only twenty-six. Rumford recalled an earlier battle after he returned to his old camp at Pleasant Hill in December: "Had our Gen. kept troops near each other . . . we would have had a victory at Mansfield than the total defeat which we recd. The panic was not much exceeding the 1st Bull Run."

M75   Rumford, Samuel Canby, 1876–1950.
      Life along the Brandywine between 1880–1895. 1938.
      48 p.; 28 cm.
      Samuel Canby Rumford was born into an old Wilmington, Delaware, family. His great-great-great-grandfather, Jonathan Rumford, had been an early resident of the city and had made his fortune in shipping. Samuel went to Friends' School in Wilmington and later to Penn Charter School in Philadelphia. He then attended medical school at the University of Pennsylvania and upon graduation practiced medicine, including surgery, in Wilmington. Looking for a position that promised regular working hours, Rumford then became the medical director of the Continental American Life Insurance Company. He married Beatrix Tyson in 1903, and they had two children, both sons.
         In this memoir of growing up in the city of Wilmington at the end of the nineteenth century, Rumford discusses a child-

hood probably dreamed of by many but experienced by only a few. He lived at the corner of Fourteenth and Market streets, and his recollections were drawn from an area bounded by Tenth Street, French Street, Delaware Avenue, and Augustine Mills.

Rumford's childhood revolved around his home. It was large, with a playroom and cellar in which to play. During the day peddlers brought goods to his door for sale, and unfortunately, the Rumfords feared that burglars wanted to break in to steal their household goods at night. So, every evening the shutters were closed, and the silverware was put away for safekeeping. A loaded revolver was always handy. The Rumfords used gas to light their house, operated one of the first telephones in Wilmington, and owned one of the first automobiles in town. Samuel's mother, the former Elizabeth "Lilly" Canby, enjoyed giving dinner parties and hired servants for these special occasions.

Like most children, Rumford was fascinated by firefighters and had a streak of adventurism. On fighting fires, he wrote: "Fire engines gave us the same thrill that children have felt in all times at the sight of running horses accompanied by the clanging of bells. In those days the number of the fire box from which an alarm was being sent was rung by all the engine houses and since we had memorized those numbers of interest to us we could easily tell from any part of town if the fire was near our home." In addition to chasing fires, young Samuel witnessed several illegal dog and chicken fights in which local talent was challenged by the finest representatives from Baltimore and Chester and Reading, Pennsylvania. The winners' owners made a lot of money off the efforts of their animals. Samuel looked forward to fireworks—especially the pinwheels—to celebrate the Fourth of July. He commented that "there were no public displays of fire works, each family having its own or a couple joining forces, with the ladies and children sitting safely in the background." Samuel also enjoyed shooting marbles, flying kites, trading cigarette cards, collecting stamps, keeping pets, and watching birds.

Rumford wrote about the sights of his city, including the old wooden and covered Market Street bridge, which was torn down in 1888 and replaced by an iron expanse, and the DuPont Company's building site at Tenth and Market streets, where the Hotel DuPont currently stands. He noted that open drain gutters carried household waste water to a creek, "so that a little stream of dirty water was constantly leaking thru their bottom into the drinking water below," leading to outbreaks of typhoid. Ninety years earlier similar unsanitary conditions in Wilmington led to an outbreak of yellow fever that John Vaughan discussed in his diary (entry M87). Rumford noted that because street lighting was inadequate and streets were unpaved, many families spent evenings at home.

Rumford concluded that he benefitted as a child from having to keep himself occupied. He wrote, "It has always seemed to me that children get much more out of life if they create their own amusements rather than having entertainment constantly provided for them and our minds were certainly fertile and productive."

"Life along the Brandywine," edited by Claudia L. Bushman, appeared in three issues of *Delaware History* (Fall/Winter 1988 through Fall/Winter 1989).

M76   Sea journal. 1804.
           [63, 13] p.; 43 cm.
           This manuscript contains an account of an Indian Ocean voyage from just west of the Azores to Mauritius (known in 1804 as the Isle de France) from April 13 to July 17, 1804. The ship may have been called the *Confederacy*, for the unnamed keeper of this journal worked on that ship at one time and referred in passing to his experiences as its supercargo, or person in charge of the ship's finances. Observations on the ship's passage include its latitude and longitude, distance traveled each day, sicknesses on board, religious worship, disciplinary actions, fishing activities, and sightings of other ships. As the vessel made for Mauritius, the writer summarized the weather conditions of the island of Mauritius during the different seasons of the year and offered instructions on how to dock a ship so that it would not be damaged by the ocean bottom.

The second part of the journal contains notes on the commerce of Calcutta, Canton, and Manila. The section on Calcutta includes remarks about the comparative worth of money from Great Britain, Denmark, France, Spain, Portugal, China, and the United States; import and export duties; and details about the purchase of sugar, opium, and indigo.

The writer's comments about the practice of trading in Canton summarize the conditions a westerner could expect to encounter as he attempted to establish his identity as a businessman acceptable to the Chinese. A trader would have to land at Macao and engage a river pilot, all the while being careful not to give the appearance of smuggling and taking care not to remove firearms from his ship. In addition, "should there be any female on board, they must be landed and left at Macao, for to carry a woman into China would produce your ruin." One of the first activities that had to be considered was the hiring of a *hong* (or united, licensed merchant) who was commissioned by the emperor and given the responsibility of carrying out trade with foreigners. A list of nine merchants, from Puanckeguay, described as the chief of all merchants, to Sonquoy, who was on the verge of financial failure, is provided. Unofficial contacts or outside merchants might also be considered; seven are listed by name and reputation. The writer cautioned that the longer a trader waited to find a merchant, the more the merchant would try to exact in fees.

Writing of Manila, the author noted: "There is not perhaps on Earth a Place that Requires greater Secrecy, precaution, and circumspection in the accomplishment of your views than at Manila." Within the context of securing sugar and indigo, two of the Philippine's most plentiful products, trading customs are described. In stark contrast to China, trade in Manila required dealing with women; men were considered idle and indolent and generally were prevented from carrying out serious business activities. All goods brought to Manila were inventoried and duties levied upon them. Western traders were housed separately in Binondo, then located across the river from Manila but now a part of Manila's old business district. Concluding his dis-

cussion of the Philippines, the writer noted that almost everyone
that a western trader would come into contact with would be dis-
honest; thieves who attacked foreigners were common, transportation was poor, the heat oppressive, and the water injurious to
one's health.

A good discussion of the trading situation in China can be
found in Yen-p'ing Hao, *The Comprador in Nineteenth Century
China: Bridge between East and West*, published by Harvard University Press, Cambridge, Massachusetts, 1970.

M77   [Sea journal of events from England to Jamaica]. 1765.
20 p.; 30 cm.

The unnamed keeper of this journal boarded his ship two miles
below Gravesend, England, on January 6 and landed at Port
Royal, Jamaica, on March 16. Nothing in the journal indicates
the purpose of the trip. The writer was aboard as a passenger
rather than as a hand and was supposed to establish residence
in Port Royal for "some time—but I hope not long." The writer
probably kept this record of shipboard activities for his wife and
young son, Dick, who had to remain at home in England.
Throughout the pages of his journal, the diarist lamented his separation from them. Writing on January 27, he confided, "I throw
myself to and fro upon my bed and in silent anguish bewail my
unhappy fate in being separated from you and my dr. child."
He also questioned whether he would ever return: "I now see
myself surrounded with nothing but this ocean, and if the wind
favors us, we shall see England no more,—farewell my native
land!—with tears in my eyes—I bid you farewell!"

The Atlantic crossing was anything but comfortable. The sea
was unusually high at times, the winds alternated between very
strong and nonexistent, and the weather was either bitterly cold
or oppressively hot. The captain remarked that he had never
experienced more disagreeable weather, and the diarist thought
that he must have been blessed with the constitution of a lion to
undergo such a rough voyage.

After arriving in Jamaica, the diarist wrote about several
unfamiliar matters. In order to protect himself from tropical dis-

eases, he commented that he drank three-quarters of a pint of salt water and as an extra measure made arrangements with the ship's doctor to be bled. At Kingston, he wrote about the natives' lack of clothing. And he described a fish that he had never seen, the shark: "This is a monstrous fish, as large as a ferry boat upon the Thames."

M78   Shank, Christian H.
       [Farm diary]. 1858–67.
       149, 69, [7] p.: ill.; 33 cm.
       Christian H. Shank lived in Annville, Lebanon County, Pennsylvania. The contents of his manuscript reflect the everyday activities of a seemingly prosperous farmer in mid nineteenth-century America. A typical entry, that of May 17, 1859, reads: "(Variable) Carpenters been here, Funcks went home this morning, cleaning Hay, Mow, Hauling Ground and Manure for tree planting, been to Hummelstown to Blacksmith &c." During the course of his diary writing, Shank would, among other things, tear down his barn and construct a new one, renovate his house, make fences, put in a pig sty, and lay out a new garden.
       Interested in lightening his workday burdens, Shank explored the possibility of acquiring a mowing machine and bought a smut machine, probably to combat crop disease. He also fancied himself an inventor, sending a model of a thrasher to Washington, D.C., to apply for a patent. Shank made no further remarks about his application, and it may have been turned down.
       Shank frequently commented about horse breeding as a source of income. In May 1860, he recorded that "Solomon Landis had a mare with my Horse this evening" and that Jacob Hoeker had paid him for two horses that his mare had had with Shank's horse. On May 10, he wrote with some chagrin: "The Sorrel mare with my Horse by accident. They were both hitched to the team."
       Although Shank's days were filled with farmwork, he was able to find time for recreational activities, including debates. One issue that he heard debated was whether Christopher

Columbus should be accorded more honor for discovering
America or George Washington for defending it. Columbus won
out. A second debate focused on whether the Union should be
dissolved; it should not was the debate's conclusion. And a third
question read: "Is the Distillation of Grain a benefit to the Community." The debater who argued in the affirmative was victori-
ous. Shank and his family often attended camp meetings, and
he noted that he once attended the "Collered camp-meeting" in
Middletown, Pennsylvania.

Shank's diary spans the Civil War, which affected him and
his family. On April 18, 1861, Shank observed, "Great war excitement prevails in the north against the South." In September of
the same year, his brother, Joseph, enlisted in the army. He
would later die in battle at Fredericksburg in 1863. On September 26, Shank noted that it was "a day appointed by the President of the United States as day [of] humiliation and prayer."
Shank joined a local outfit in 1862 and drilled with his company
in nearby Hummelstown, Pennsylvania. The men elected him a
second lieutenant. Following the defeat of Confederate forces at
Antietam, Shank and his company were discharged. In July
1863, Shank left home to visit the battlefield at Gettysburg. On
July 10, he observed: "Went on the Battle field again this morning until dinner. The destruction had been immense both in life
and Property. Men and horse were not buried yet from July 2nd
& 3rd." It would seem that Shank's early enthusiasm for the
war effort became tempered as time passed. The death of his
brother, Joseph, and what he saw at Gettysburg may have been
contributing factors. Shortly after traveling to Gettysburg, Shank
went to Harrisburg with a friend, J. Smith, to try to get him
exempted from the army; he was. And on January 28, Shank
attended a meeting in Hummelstown to raise money to buy
replacement recruits. He recorded that the effort was unsuccessful.

The title of Shank's diary comes from a page heading in the
early part of the manuscript. The illustration is a diagram showing plantings of fruit trees—identified by variety—around
Shank's farmhouse, the location of his bake oven, and fencing
and gates.

M79   Starr, John.
[Diary]. 1835–36.
[60] p.; 16 cm.

In this short diary—most of its sixty pages are blank—John
Starr records his observations of shipping activities in Wilmington, Delaware, from December 1, 1835, to April 20, 1836. Of the
ships that he mentions, the schooner *Pioneer* was the most important to him. The owner was a relative named Thomas Starr, who
used it to carry cargo that included flour and corn.

The shipping industry was important to the business life of
Wilmington. Henry C. Conrad wrote about it in his *History of the
State of Delaware*: "Before the advent of the steam railroad, all
shipping was necessarily done by water, and Wilmington, situated between the Christiana and Brandywine creeks only a short
distance from the broad Delaware, was admirably located for the
shipping trade." The steam railroad that Conrad mentions began
to have a great impact on American transportation during the
mid nineteenth century. Unaware that he was witnessing the
beginning of the country's great railroad era, Starr wrote on February 15 and 16 about the appearance of the *Elizabeth Frith*,
which had railroad iron on board. It ended up in Wilmington
after being towed by what Starr called the "TBoat" *Huckleberry*.
The iron may have been delivered to the Betts and Pusey Company of Wilmington, a firm that would be legally formed on
March 1, 1836, for the purpose of constructing railroad cars.

In addition to shipping activities, Starr faithfully recorded
the harsh weather conditions of the winter of 1835–36. The ice
on Brandywine Creek was at one time 16½ inches thick, and the
diarist remarked that someone told him that this winter was the
coldest in fifty years. Finally, there are detailed reports on wind
directions and speeds.

M80   Steen, Mary Service, b. 1837.
Journal. 1847–53, 1855–57, 1860–61.
6 v.; 20 cm.

Mary Service Steen began keeping her diary as a ten-year-old
girl and finished as she was just into her twenties. She was a resident of Philadelphia and interested in her studies at school, first

at Van Doren and David's Institute and later at Misses Gill's
School. In addition to the diary, the Downs Collection holds her
report card from September 25 to December 25, 1847, revealing
her interest in and aptitude for schoolwork.

Mary led what appears to be an ordinary life for a young
girl whose family was fairly well-to-do, taking part in the cultural activities of her hometown. On October 28, 1848, for example, Mary went to the Franklin Institute to see an exhibition
highlighting silver articles and then to another featuring drawings on rice paper. On May 16, 1849, she saw Walter McPherson
Bayne's panorama of a voyage to Europe, "which I thought was
very pretty." In New York City four years later, Mary visited the
Dusseldorf Gallery and the Crystal Palace. Throughout the years
that Mary kept her diary, she wrote of such activities as paper
flower–making, knitting, drawing, music lessons, singing, and
sewing. Mary was also an inveterate reader. Among the books
that she read were *The Maiden: A Story for My Young Coun-
trywomen*, by Timothy S. Arthur; *Hands not Hearts*, by Janet W.
Wilkinson; *The Mothers of England*, by Sarah Ellis; and *The City:
Its Sins and Its Sorrows*, by Thomas Guthrie of Edinburgh. Her
favorite magazines were *Miss Leslie's Magazine* and *Harper's*.
Mary was a religious girl. She attended church regularly, became
a member of the Dorcas Society, and often wrote in her diary
about sermons that she heard on Sundays.

Mary's father, Robert Steen, was a merchant who frequently
traveled to New York City on business. Mary noted on June 28,
1851, that he had been named a commissioner for the Great Exhibition of the Works of All Nations taking place in London. Her
father attended the fair during summer 1851.

During the course of these diaries, Mary traveled to England
and Ireland as well as to several places within the United States.
She landed at Liverpool, England, on June 18, 1852, and
remarked that the buildings appeared to have been constructed
to last for some time. She visited several stores and commented
that "our Philadelphia ones look like little things beside them."
On June 21, Mary headed for Dublin and points north to visit relatives. Her quarters in Carrickfergus brought to her mind a "pig-
sty hotel." Unfortunately, Mary's diary of her experiences in

Ireland and England ends before her trip conluded. Her last `adventure was a train derailment in which she and her family were thrown from their seats.

The Steen family spent part of their summers in Cape May, New Jersey. Mary led an active social life there, walking along the beach, swimming with friends, and attending hops. On July 17, 1850, she must have been in a quandary, for she had invitations to two hops, one at Congress Hall and the other at the Columbia. In 1852 Mary accompanied her father to Saratoga, New York, where he went for his health. In 1857 they revisited Saratoga and also stopped at Niagara Falls.

As time passed Mary's entries decreased. A passage in 1853 revealed her thoughts: "It seems almost impossible for me to find anything to write in my journal & as to giving my thoughts & opinions about things I cannot do it for I do not think I have any."

M81   Stover, Ralph.
Journal of a tour from Alexandria D of C to the western country: commenced May second one thousand eight hundred and thirty three, by A. F. Stover and Ralph Stover; and returned after an absence of thirty five days / by R. Stover.
[36] p.; 20 cm.
From May 2 to June 7, the Stovers traveled from Alexandria, Virginia to the Ohio–Indiana state line and back, averaging between thirty and forty miles per day. Unfortunately, there is nothing in the diary that would suggest a reason for this trip. Most of Ralph Stover's comments describe the scenery that he saw on the way. He wrote of Harpers Ferry: "The Situation of Harpers Ferry is extremely rugged and romantic with tremendous mountains guarding it on every side it bears the appearance of uncouthness and uncultivation." And of the Allegheny Mountains, he remarked: "The Alleghany at a distance you can trace as far as the eye can reach as it were the backbone of the Earth lifting its towering summit to the skies."

In Ohio, Stover became fascinated with the ancient burial mounds. On May 17, he wrote: "With numerable mounds of a very singular interesting and ancient appearance some of which are of a large size with circular and others square entrenchments around them it is universally believed to be the depository of the dead of some ancient nation of whom there is neither tradition nor history they are all covered with timber some of which is of a very large size." In Cincinnati, the travelers would visit what Stover called the Western Museum to see skeletons disinterred from the mounds.

Although Stover focused on scenery, he made a few political remarks. Without further elucidation, he commented on slavery as he entered Virginia (present-day West Virginia) from Pennsylvania: "There is an astonishing contrast between the two banks of the Ohio river between a free and a slave state." In addition, Stover referred to internal improvements that were important during President Andrew Jackson's administration. On May 12, he wrote, "We kept the U. States road which was in an unfinished state at some places we were obliged to take the old road through immense forests." And a bit later, "we crossed several streams which would have caused us considerable difficulty had it not been for the bridges recently built by the U. States." Finally, "we crossed the Miami Canal frequently which is a great improvement through that section of the country it is finished from Cincinnati as far as Dayton the contemplation is to extend it to Lake Erie."

At the end of Stover's narrative, he listed the names of the towns that he and his companion traveled through and the number of miles that separated one from the other.

M82   Studley, John M.
[Diary]. 1858–62, 1864–67.
9 v.: ill.; 13–18 cm.
As these volumes open, John M. Studley is working as a carpenter, building stairs in Worcester, Massachusetts. From 1858 to 1860, he made few entries and typically noted only where he was currently employed. On July 16, 1858, for example, he "worked on Cherry Rail for H. W. Eddy." In a more expansive mood, Studley wrote on February 1, 1858, that he "put up 3½ Mahogany rail two flights with 8 in Octagon Newel—1¾ in Bul-

ustrer—Birch. Price $50.00." In 1859 Studley was involved in
some kind of law enforcement but, as with his trade, did not record many details of his activities.

On July 1, 1861, the United States Army invited Studley to
attend Camp Scott, where he began his Civil War activities as a
Union soldier. On March 26, 1862, while stationed in Washington, D.C., as part of Gen. George McClellan's forces, he and his
company were ordered to march to Yorktown, Virginia. They
arrived on April 5, and all remained calm for a week and a half.
Writing on April 16, Studley observed that it was a "very pleasant Spring morning with the exception of an occasional dis-
charge of guns as quiet as a Sabbath in New England." At
7:00 A.M., however, the Union's artillery moved to the front line
and began shelling the Confederate's fortification at Yorktown.
On April 17, the rebels tried to advance but were turned back.
Matters then quieted, with alarms of supposed rebel movement
called only infrequently. On May 5, the Confederate forces
finally abandoned their position in Yorktown, and Studley and
his fellow soldiers advanced to assume control. McClellan's
troops then headed for Richmond, camping only twenty miles
away along the Pamunkey River on May 9.

On May 31 and June 1, Studley took part in the Battle of
Seven Pines at Fair Oaks, Virginia, and during the month of
June wrote about his activities as a soldier in the Peninsula Campaign. He remarked that there was a sharp engagement at Fair
Oaks Station on May 31 and that the Union forces remained
ready to defend their position all night. On June 1, Studley
wrote that he "moved forward at 4 a.m. some picket and Artillery firing on our side" and that "McClellan here today, enthusiastically received." By the end of June and after many
engagements with the enemy, Studley and his fellow troops
"were attacked again this P.M. after some hard fighting the
Rebels were driven back. commenced the march towards the
James river about midnight." On July 1, he recorded from near
the James River that there was "brisk commanding on both sides
for several hours."

Compared with June, the months of July and August were

calm for Studley. September, however, brought increased activity. On September 6, Studley found himself stationed near Rockville, Maryland. He wrote: "Rebels said to have crossed the river and within a few miles of us, preparations made to receive them." On September 14, his unit reinforced troops commanded by General Burnside at Boliver Gap, and on September 16, they were shelled by the Confederates for three hours. On September 17, Studley took part in the severe fighting at Antietam. His unit lost 363 men, counting those killed, wounded, and missing.

Studley was not involved in any other action until December 1863, when he was dispatched to North Carolina by boat. From New Bern, he traveled northwest to Goldsboro, meeting Confederate forces on the way. He helped burn a railroad bridge and then was ordered to "about face, the object of the expedition being accomplished."

Unfortunately, no diary survives for 1863, so Studley's Civil War activities for that year remain unrecorded. By 1864, he had been discharged from active duty, and he and his family were residing in Brooklyn, New York. His son, Eddie, was admitted to School 15, and his daughter, Fannie, began her first term at the Parker Institute. Studley worked in New York City at 100 Liberty Street for Theodore Studley, a relative who was identified in New York city directories as a merchant. In 1866 the Studley family moved to Providence, Rhode Island, where John found employment as a clerk.

M83   Thorn, William, b. 1739.
A journal of the proceedings of William Thorn in his occupation: together with the remarkable accidents happening within the limmits or hearing of him; liquise the draughts of the buildings which he hath been master of building; beginning in the year 1762. 1762–76, 1796–1813.
[148] p.: ill; 20 cm.
William Thorn was a carpenter during most of his working life and operated a sawmill beginning around 1800. He probably was a member of the Society of Friends. From April 13, 1762, to 1766, Thorn recorded information about houses, grist mills, and barns

that he helped construct in Dutchess County, New York. He sketched the framing of these buildings and identified their owners by name. When he wrote about grist mills, Thorn sometimes included drawings of the carving on their mill stones, sketches of water and cog wheels, and plans for mill dams and races.

Apparently Thorn lost interest in maintaining the journal, for he did not write in it again until 1796, when he decided to use it as a letter book. From 1796 to 1813, Thorn included copies of letters to family and friends about business concerns.

Thorn was a participant in many court cases involving his work. He denied to Jacob Brown in 1805, however, that he was "fond" of lawsuits, writing: "I can procure many instances where I have lost my debt rather than go to the law." He wrote of a particular distasteful experience in 1810: "The dispute was that I had charged him for sawing upwards of thirteen hundred feet more than I sawed." Thorn continued by suggesting that he cut the correct amount but that those who transported it from his mill failed to deliver the entire order. Whatever the case, Thorn, if only because he emphasized his legal problems in his writings, must have led an active life before the bench and bar.

M84 Vail, Georgiana L., b. 1851.
Excelsior diary. 1892–93.
2 v.; 11–13 cm.
Georgiana L. Vail's diary records the activities of a fairly ordinary resident of Somers Center, New York. Georgiana lived with her father, and they had at least one female servant. Her days were filled with making such things as pillow shams, bureau scarves, shawls, slumber robes, and silk quilts. Georgiana taught Sunday school regularly and vacationed in Ocean Grove, New Jersey, during the summer. There is nothing to suggest that Georgiana was married while she kept this diary, but she did have a ten-year-old daughter named Martha. Georgiana helped her daughter write letters, noted when she spilled ink on the carpet, taught her lessons, and recorded when she took her first music instruction. Martha's diary for 1899 is part of Winterthur Library's collection (entry M85).

Other papers related to the family of Georgiana L. Vail are located at the Minnesota Historical Society, St. Paul.

M85   Vail, Martha, b. 1883.
           Diary. 1899.
           [408] p.; 10 cm.
           On Christmas day 1898, Martha B. Vail's mother, Georgiana, gave her this diary, and in it Martha wrote about her concerns and the events of her young life in Somers Center, New York. Martha's mother, Georgiana, kept diaries as well, two of which are in Winterthur's collection (entry M84).
                   Martha went to school in Katonah, New York, and was a good student. She received a report card on April 7 that recorded a mark of 100 in deportment and an 85 average in her scholastic studies. She noted that she once failed geography and physiology tests but that she did well on a reading test with a score of 100 and a writing test with a 90. Martha noted that she had circulated her autograph album in school and made some remarks about boys. "Elbert," she said, was "very nice to me to night. He will hardly treat Jennie civil." On April 20, she sat next to Harry Robertson in the library, "& he was very loving." The same afternoon, she was next to Will Boner, and "Will stunk like everything." Although many of the girls at school belonged to a baseball club, Martha did not. In July Martha's mother thought about sending her to Drew Seminary in Carmel, New York, but in the autumn Martha found herself back in class at Katonah.
                   Martha had definite likes and dislikes. She enjoyed ice skating, making candy, shopping, riding her bicycle, and attending the local strawberry ice cream festival. She did not, however, like her summer vacation at the shore in Ocean Grove, New Jersey. It was simply too hot there. Martha tried to make the best of things, however, spending time at the merry-go-round and the beach. She attended a lecture delivered by Theodore Roosevelt, at that time the governor of New York, and noted his dress: "He had on a little white sailor hat, a light pair of pants & black coat & vest."

Other papers relating to the family of Martha E. Vail are located at the Minnesota Historical Society, St. Paul.

M86 Vandegrift, Harrison, 1840–1931.
[Diary]. 1863–64.
[180] p.; 15 cm.
On Sunday, June 28, 1863, Harrison Vandegrift was encamped with other troops of Company C, 1st Regiment, Delaware Volunteer Cavalry, near Westminster, Maryland. The next day a small scouting party that included Vandegrift and his brother Willie was dispatched to check on reports of southern troops in the area. They quickly encountered what turned out to be the large advance guard of J. E. B. Stuart's cavalry, then traveling to Gettysburg, Pennsylvania, only twenty-five miles further north. Knowing nothing of the force they had met, Vandegrift's party impetuously attacked Stuart's guard. They quickly were driven back, and Willie was killed. Vandegrift fled through a wheat field into nearby woods but was forced to throw off his haversack along the way. In it were his rations and the original copy of his Civil War diary. Stuart's men gave up the chase, thinking that their foe had successfully escaped. W. G. Rinehart, the owner of the property through which Vandegrift had run, found the haversack some time later and kept the diary. In 1908 a chance meeting between Vandegrift and Rinehart descendants prompted the return of the diary to its author, then sixty-eight years old. The diary in Winterthur's collection is a faithful copy of the original.

Vandegrift's diary records his Civil War experiences from January 1 to June 29, 1863, and for all of 1864. He enrolled in the army in Wilmington, Delaware, on August 29, 1862, and spent his first months as a soldier in a nearby camp. During this time, he wrote about routine drills and inspections, living conditions of soldiers, dress parades, saber exercises, and leisure time at Wilmington concerts. On February 18, 1863, he was ordered to Camp Wallace, near Salisbury, Maryland, where his main responsibility seemed to involve policing the general area for deserters and smugglers and then arresting them. All things considered, Vandegrift's life was not too unpleasant. He was away from the

violence of the battlefield and could control the situations in
which he found himself. In addition, "our fare now is very
good. The old Negro does his duty and prepares our meals at
the proper time." Moving in Maryland from Vienna to Westminster to Baltimore and then to Port Tobacco, Vandegrift learned
on May 22, 1864, that his unit had just been ordered from the
cavalry into the infantry, something that pleased neither him nor
his fellow Delaware volunteers.

On June 5, Vandegrift was assigned to the 6th Army Corps,
Army of the Potomac. Shortly thereafter, he was only 1,200
yards from the front, near Petersburg, Virginia, where there was
heavy fighting. "It is," he observed, "very amusing to see the
boys trying to dodge the bullets. It makes a man feel queer." In
order to clear the dead, a truce was called one morning. "Our
men and the Rebels during the truce were friendly and socia-
ble." Then the guns started firing again. Vandegrift got to within
one mile of Petersburg and commented erroneously that the
Union troops had taken it. Six weeks after becoming a member
of the Army of the Potomac, he was reassigned to the cavalry,
headed back north, and on July 22, he went to the theater in
Baltimore.

From the time he was again a cavalryman until the end of
1864, Vandegrift returned to his former duties of general police
work. Apart from his chance encounter with Stuart's advance
guard and participation in the Petersburg campaign, this diary
provides a good firsthand account of routine life as a Civil War
soldier. The diary might be used profitably with William P.
Seville, *History of the First Regiment, Delaware Volunteers*, published by the Historical Society of Delaware, Wilmington, 1884.

M87   Vaughan, John, 1775–1807.
Medical diary no. 3: commenced January 1st AD 797; containing a
meteorological table for every month with a nosological description of the diseases which occur in their respective months & a
pathological narration of such as are unusual or otherwise important. 1797–1802.
[270] p.; 20 cm.
John Vaughan was educated in Chester, Pennsylvania, and in

1793 and 1794, while studying to be a doctor, attended lectures on medicine at the University of Pennsylvania in Philadelphia. Vaughan practiced medicine in Delaware, first in Christiana Bridge and later in Wilmington. He was a member of several professional organizations, including the Philadelphia Academy of Medicine, the Medical Society of Philadelphia, the American Medical Association, and the Delaware Medical and Philosophical societies. Vaughan was a prolific author, lending his pen to topics of medical and scientific importance. He kept his "Medical Diary No. 3" before and during the serious yellow fever epidemic of 1802. Vaughan died in 1807 of typhoid fever.

Vaughan was an assiduous observer of Wilmington's climate conditions, often listing the daily temperature, wind direction, and weather. He believed that these conditions influenced the occurrence of diseases at certain times of the year. Thus, on one group of pages Vaughan recorded weather information for a given month, and on another group he noted what his patients suffered from during the same period.

Occasionally, Vaughan broke this pattern to copy an article that he had read, something he had heard, or a letter that he had either written or received about a medical matter. One of his correspondents was Dr. Benjamin Rush. A man of science and medicine, Vaughan wrote perhaps in amusement to substantiate his theory on the influence of weather on disease: "Mr. Alrichs, an ingenious watch maker, informed me that sickly seasons were always characterized by the breaking of watch springs— that the fact was so well established as to be proverbial & that it was peculiarly so this season." On August 26, 1800, Vaughan said: "Bad accounts from Baltimore & Norfolk—yellow fever spreading with great mortality."

In 1802 a severe yellow fever epidemic broke out in Wilmington. Vaughan is reputed to have been the only doctor to have remained in town to administer to those who had contracted the dreaded disease. One year later, the American Philosophical Society requested that he write a pamphlet about the incident. *A Concise History of the Autumnal Fever which Prevailed in the Borough of Wilmington in the Year 1802* resulted. Vaughan's manuscript diary features the author's immediate and private observances of the spread of the disease. In the pamphlet Vaughan detailed why he thought the yellow fever epidemic started, how he thought it spread, and what he thought had to be done to eradicate it. In his diary Vaughan recorded his early visit with Ann Davidson, whom he later identified as the initial carrier of the disease, and noted the conditions in the house neighboring the Davidson's: "Hadley's cellar, adjoining Davi[d]sons has been for a long time full of water—& the common receptacle of every filth . . . oft condemned as a nuisance by the corporation, but neglected. Wm. Cloud complained of its being very offensive to them." Vaughan wrote of the activities of Wilmington residents on September 13: "3/4 of the people left the lower parts of the town—below second street—great alarm. Board of Health disorganized in effect—some resigned—President fled—are not mankind reverting to Barbarism."

Vaughan probably used his diary, serving as it did as a chronological record and source of valuable details, to construct the narrative of his pamphlet. On September 23, for example, Vaughan wrote a letter on the status of the disease to the president of the Board of Health, Isaac Dixon; he copied this letter into his diary, and it appeared subsequently in the circular. At the end of his pamphlet, Vaughan listed the people who died from the epidemic; in his diary he recorded the names and addresses of those stricken and noted whether they recovered or died.

Vaughan never totally abandoned the original intent of his diary—to demonstrate a cause-and-effect relationship between weather conditions and the incidence of disease—to write about the outbreak of yellow fever in Wilmington. There are, in fact, numerous references to weather conditions during the epidemic, and the concept plays an important role in his *Concise History*.

M88   Wales, Salem Howe, 1825–1902.
[Diary]. 1867–68.
5 v.; 22 cm.
Salem Howe Wales was born in Wales, Massachusetts. He attended its local schools and then the Academy of Attica in upstate New York. In 1846 Wales went to New York City, where

he joined an importing business. Two years later he began his affiliation with the *Scientific American* and served as its managing editor from 1848 until 1871. In 1855 Gov. Horatio Seymour of New York appointed him a commissioner to the Paris exposition, which he subsequently visited and reported on in a series of letters published in the *Scientific American*.

During the Civil War, Wales was an active member of the Christian Commission, an organization devoted to caring for the sick and wounded. In politics, Wales was a delegate to the Republican national conventions of 1872 and 1876 and a presidential elector in 1872; in 1873 he was called to be a New York City park commissioner by reform mayor William F. Havemeyer; and in 1874 he ran unsuccessfully as the Republican party's candidate for mayor of New York City. Wales was an officer of the Union League Club of New York, served as a trustee of the Middletown, New York, insane asylum, assisted in establishing Hahnemann Hospital and the Metropolitan Museum of Art, and was a director of the Bank of North America and the Hanover Trust Company. Wales traveled widely and from May 4, 1867, to March 6, 1868, kept a diary of his trip to Europe.

The Great Exhibition of Industry of All Nations held in Paris occasioned this trip, Wales's second, to Europe. In addition to France, Wales visited nearly every western European country. Of travel accounts in general Wales commented: "The whole business of telling what one sees abroad has been so thoroughly overdone in books, pamphlets, and newspapers that I shall forbear many such details. . . . I propose to jot down a few items of information which may be useful to a few inexperienced travelers." His remarks about the countries that he stayed in and comparisons with experiences in the United States reveal his keen intellect and gift for observation.

Wales's feelings about France were mixed. Early in his trip he advised that foreigners needed to know the language and that women should arrive with adequate clothing because apparel prices were unrealistically high. "Genteel begging," he revealed, "is done here to perfection." On the other hand, he marveled at the French demeanor and fairness and the good quality of life in Paris. Cab drivers, for example, were uninclined to violate the fare structure or take riders out of their ways in order to inflate charges. He observed that "architecturally the city is rapidly changing its character by the opening of broad boulevards and the necessary destruction of those streets and houses where revolutions have kindled their fiercest fires." And he commented on the French character: "I desire to make my acknowledgements to the French people for the politeness and kind consideration a foreigner every where experiences among them. Undoubtedly they are the pleasantest people in the world for a stranger to deal with . . . [and] the most tasteful people in the world."

As much as Wales liked France, even with its few shortcomings, he despised Spain. Wales noted that American travelers usually bypassed Spain because it was out of the way and later observed that Spanish food was bad (he encouraged fasting and prayer as good substitutes) and that Spaniards were naturally suspicious, dull, and taciturn. He continued by recording that "the rural hotels in Spain are not intended to accommodate any body" and that "the [railroad] cars are usually dirty, a national habit, scrupulously observed." Wales's introduction to the country was abrupt. At the border between France and Spain, his train came to a sudden stop because it could pass no further on Spain's wider gauge track, constructed, according to Wales, to inhibit hostile invasion from France during wartime. Wales wrote: "Toledo is the most singular, dried up specimen of an old city that we have ever seen," and he thought that the bullfights there were cruel and inhuman. "There was nothing whatever in this spectacle which deserves to be called a fight. It is simply a cruel method of torturing to death a few bulls—and old worn out horses." Wales seemed, however, to be able to extract something good from every situation, even his days in Spain. He noted that "the chief attraction of all Spanish cities seems first to center in the old Cathedrals," and the Royal Gallery in Madrid possessed "the finest collection of pictures in Europe."

Art was never far from Wales's attention. "Germany," he contended, "is the only country on the continent where the art of painting flourishes with any considerable boldness and singularity; and the seat of this department of fine arts has been transferred from Rome and Florence to Munich." In Florence, Italy, Wales visited American sculptors Hiram Powers, Joel Tanner Hart, Thomas Ball, and Larkin Goldsmith Mead. Hart was working on a bust of Andrew Jackson that had been modeled in 1839 at Jackson's Tennessee home, the Hermitage; Mead was laboring over an order of capitols for ornamental pilasters of the Treasury Building in Washington, D.C.

Wales visited other countries on his tour, including Austria, the Netherlands, Belgium, and England. As was his custom, he picked out things to admire in each place and isolated things to criticize. Even in Switzerland, a country that most travelers raved about, Wales found something to denigrate, commenting negatively on the curious living conditions of the rural Swiss: "The chalets are constructed to shelter under the same roof, men, women, children, cows, goats, and pigs."

Wales commented freely on gambling, drinking, and smoking and judging from what he said, disapproved of all of them. He noted with disdain that the chief income of Monte Carlo was derived from gambling and added that "lottery offices are about as numerous in Rome as the churches." In France he wrote about tobacco: "Villainous tobacco, at villainous prices, is the staple. If you know of any who wished to return a kindness to a Frenchman, recommend sending him a box of good cigars." In Spain everyone smoked. He observed in Italy that "barroom tippling, the curse of our own country, is a thing almost unknown in Italy," and "drunkenness, as we so well understand it, is also a thing unknown." According to Wales, the rowdiness that stemmed from what he called rum shops, so commonplace in New York, did not occur in Paris: "Monstrous public nuisances cannot propagate as freely here as they do in the cities where less vigor is exercised by the municipal authorities. This fact is being learned in New York by the forcible application of the law, under the guidance of its present energetic chief magistrate."

Although five volumes of Wales's trip to Europe are cited, only two are in diary form. The other three volumes contain lengthy chronological summaries of his observations and are in another person's handwriting.

M89   Ward, William E., b. 1821.
Notes of European travel taken by William E. Ward. 1867.
[248] p.; 21 cm.
On April 20, 1867, William E. Ward embarked for Europe on the
steamer *St. Laurent* from pier 50, New York City. He arrived in
Brest, France, on April 30 and recorded his activities as a traveler
and observer of the European scene through August 19. Ward, a
Quaker who probably resided in New York City, celebrated his
forty-sixth birthday on this trip and was, from all indications,
involved with the iron industry.

Ward began his sightseeing in Paris and then journeyed to
Italy, passing through Lyons, Marseilles, Nimes, and Nice. Of
Genoa he wrote: "I never approached a place with less, or left it
with *more* satisfaction than Genoa." Similarly impressed with
Naples, Ward commented that "I prepared for leaving Naples
having spent more time there than I expected, but feeling better
satisfied and repaid for my labor than any other place yet visited." In Rome Ward found so much to occupy his time that he
noted: "I despair of doing even moderate justice to any of the
'land marks' around me, and shall only mention the most con-
spicuous points of interest I shall visit, leaving to *Murray* the
task of a fuller narrative than I have time to give." Upon leaving
Florence, he remarked, "I can truly say it is the only place I have
left on this side of the Atlantic with regret that I could not conve-
niently stay longer."

Ward next headed for Switzerland and on June 5 was in
Geneva. From there he went to Chamonix, France, to see the
Mer de Glace, a glacier and famous tourist attraction. He pro-
nounced the sight "thrilling" and added: "At one glance I saw
the Modus Operandi or whole operation of these stupendius
engines of nature, in tearing up and pulverizing rocks in their
slow and steady, but irresistible march down the side of mountains." Ward traveled in the Alps of Switzerland and France for
about ten days and summed up his experiences by writing: "The
whole tour through the mountains, on and by the lakes, cities,
villages, rural districts and all, have imported a refreshing tone
to my feelings and thoughts." Then, from June 17 until July 5,

Ward was back in Paris to continue his sightseeing and to attend the Exposition Universelle of 1867. At the exposition Ward was most interested in the displays of manufacturers of metal products. Of the London Bolt and Nut Company's exhibit, he said, "I was glad to find that I had been over the same ground." Further, he observed that the French system of making bolts was as crude as the English. Ward concluded that the Whitworth Company from Manchester, England, made superior engines and tools and that W. Sellers and Company of Philadelphia had a "creditable display of tools." He believed that European safes, especially those manufactured in France, were of excellent quality. "In cast iron ornamental work, although the French do well the Prussians still maintain their supremacy." In summing up the exposition, Ward wrote, "The progress made in the working of metals in Europe is truly astonishing," and "I find so much more of interest to me there than anywhere else I have been in Paris."

Ward left Paris early in July and traveled in Germany, Austria, and the Netherlands. He cruised the Rhine from Cologne and observed that "though delighted with the day's trip, I was somewhat disappointed not at finding the Hudson river more successfully rivalled by the over strained reputation of the Rhine." Ward noted that "my experience thus far in Germany is that a day in one small town gives one an idea of most of them." He announced that Munich was his favorite city east of Italy, that the Danube reminded him of the Schuylkill River of Pennsylvania, that Berlin was impressive for its architecture, and that the Hague was pleasantly neat.

Ward returned to Paris on August 4 and instead of spending a great deal of time back at the exposition, took in some Parisian sights. On August 7, for instance, he visited the Gobelin tapestry works and said: "I was very much disappointed, I expected to see an elaborate institution, instead of a cluster of old superannuated apartments, where the famous fabrics are patiently woven up, the work is pretty but does not compare in beauty or interest with the Roman Mosaic." Ward also visited the catacombs, where bones of the disinterred from cemeteries in Paris were stacked in "artistic order" in lines measuring some 1,000 feet in length, and the Garden of Acclamation, where he saw a magnificent collection of live birds.

During his trip Ward met some important figures of American history and sculpture. In Paris he made arrangements to talk with Abram S. Hewitt "in an investigation of the iron interest." Hewitt, the noted iron manufacturer and philanthropist, had just been appointed commissioner to the Paris exposition by President Johnson. In 1870 he would manufacture the first steel of commercial value in the United States, and at this exposition he spent time with Ward reviewing the way it was currently being produced in Europe. Ward recorded in his diary that Hewitt was favorably impressed with the quality of the steel and that "Hewitt seems determined that the same results shall be accomplished in our country." In Rome on May 25, Ward visited John Rogers, who achieved both critical and popular acclaim for his bronze statues at the Paris exposition, and Harriet G. Hosmer, called by some the most famous woman sculptor of her day. In Florence on May 27, Ward visited Hiram Powers, who "seems to delight in entertaining his countrymen."

M90   Watson, John Fanning, 1779–1860.
[Travel diaries]. 1804–6, 1822–23, 1825–27, 1829, 1831–35, 1839, 1842–45, 1852, 1855–56, 1858.
12 v.: ill.; 20 cm.
John Fanning Watson was born in Batsto, New Jersey, the son of William and Lucy Fanning Watson. After the Revolution the Watsons settled in Philadelphia, where William was engaged as a sea captain in the coastal trade. Both William and John's brother, Wesley, died in a shipwreck off Cape Hatteras in 1804. The details of John's education are unknown, although he did obtain some business training from James Vanuxem, the operator of a countinghouse in Philadelphia. From 1798 to 1804, John worked for the United States War Department and was headquartered in Washington, D.C. He subsequently returned to Philadelphia and opened a mercantile house. Later business endeavors included the operation of a book store, publishing, banking, and railroads.

Watson is well known as a historian of Philadelphia and New York City. His mother, Lucy, a Methodist mystic, probably influenced her son to appreciate history through her interest in genealogy and through stories of her youth in New England. Whatever the case, Watson published, among other works, *Annals of Philadelphia, Historic Tales of Olden Time Concerning the Early Settlement and Advancement of New York City and State*, and *Historic Tales of Olden Time Concerning the Early Settlement and Progress of Philadelphia and Pennsylvania*. He also wrote newspaper and magazine articles that focused on history. Watson was a founder of the Historical Society of Pennsylvania and the Society for the Commemoration of the Landing of William Penn. He used oral history as early as 1821 in assembling reminiscences of elderly inhabitants of Philadelphia, studied archaeological evidence in an effort to support written documentation, and frequented Philadelphia's various archives. Watson's travel diaries are a natural extension of his interest in history and indicate a knack for keen observation.

Watson's early travels took him west to New Orleans and then south to Cuba. In 1804 he was engaged by Gen. James O'Hara of Pittsburgh, former quartermaster-general of Anthony Wayne's Indian army, in a shipping venture. O'Hara's business was centralized in New Orleans. On March 10, Watson left Philadelphia for Pittsburgh, where he was scheduled to board a boat to sail south on the Ohio and Mississippi rivers for New Orleans. He observed that the widespread burning of so much coal in Pittsburgh made the houses look more like forges than dwellings. He was generally pleased with the towns that he stopped in on the way. In Cincinnati, for instance, the houses were neat and beautiful, and New Madrid, Missouri, was beautifully situated.

Watson landed in New Orleans in late May and learned about the deaths of his father and brother. He wrote: "This afternoon as I lay contemplating the clouds was impressed with observing a strong likeness of Maj. Swain & immediately after a striking one of my father. I search them for the appearance of my brother but the clouds went off without it showing any." New Orleans was larger than Watson had expected, and he found that the residents there were more engaged in business than in Philadelphia. In addition, he witnessed few high houses, rampant disregard for observing the sabbath, many lizards, expensive tailors, a lot of shrimp and gumbo to eat, and people of different ancestry—French, Spaniards, and Americans—keeping separate societies.

Watson left New Orleans on November 11, 1805, and arrived in Cuba on November 26. He did not like the city of Havana very much but did enjoy the Cuban countryside. The Havana of Watson's day, as he observed it, was walled with narrow, dirty, and crowded streets. The large gothic buildings were constructed, Watson said, with oblong stones, and they featured little ornamentation and no exterior window shutters. Watson wrote that "every other man you meet is either a Priest, Friar, or soldier" and that "the streets abound with beggars." He felt that "living here is extremely unpleasant." On the other hand, the country "in comparison with any other that I have seen is a perfect Paradise." Nobody, Watson believed, should starve because there was plentiful game and abundant wild fruit and vegetables. Many of the houses in the Cuban countryside had thatched roofs.

Philadelphians have always traveled to the New Jersey shore for summer vacations; Watson and his family were not exceptions. Because so many of John Fanning Watson's diaries have survived, readers are given the opportunity to compare the observations of one man on the same places over a span of nearly thirty-five years. For example, in 1822 Watson said that the ocean was 165 feet from Aaron Bennett's boardinghouse in Cape May. He added that, in 1804, it had been 334 feet away and that during the mid eighteenth century more than 600 feet off. During Watson's visit of 1834, he recorded that Bennett's house had been reached by the ocean. On another occasion, he commented: "The Inlets & the beach have much altered in 50 years. It was once covered with cedar trees—now all are gone—The Inlets in the War of the Revolution admitted two frigates to come in & now there is only water for small vessels." Over the course of time, Watson found himself acquainted with fewer and fewer of his fellow vacationers. In 1822 he wrote about Roger B.

Taney, an attorney and future chief justice of the United States Supreme Court, who had a room in his boardinghouse. By 1839 Watson was regretting that he knew so few faces and that everyone looked so young. Watson was never impressed with ostentation. During the 1820s, he wrote about his activities and friendships with glee, but by 1856 he was noting that "the Society [at Cape May] seems to be generally the class of lucky traders—such as started low—& have had success and now think renown is won by expensive display!"

Reflecting the travel patterns of many of his contemporaries of early nineteenth-century America, Watson took in the sights of Niagara Falls and Mauch Chunk, Pennsylvania. He went to Niagara Falls in July of 1827 by stagecoach and boat. Watson's observations were religious in orientation and mirrored those of other visitors: "Oh, how the *first* sense of this mighty Cataract overwhelms the Soul & makes it stand *in speechless awe*! It gives the blood a *moral flow* & for the moment it makes the worst devout." Despite being a location for coal mining, Mauch Chunk was a place frequented by travelers because of the way railroad cars were used to move coal, then a novelty. Watson sketched the scene as he saw it from his hotel window.

Watson made frequent trips to New York City. He visited in December 1835 and reviewed the remains of a recent devastating fire. The area that had burned had recently been rebuilt "in costly grandeur," said Watson, having been the site that the Dutch had originally occupied. According to Watson, the only building that remained standing was owned by John Benson, a copper merchant, and was located at 83 Water Street. Many out-of-towners were touring the area, while the wonder of native New Yorkers had subsided. Watson thought that much of the destruction was due to inferior construction methods that featured walls that were too thin and cheap lime from New England. In 1855 Watson came back to New York after a five-year absence and extended his travel to Long Island. He mentioned that Long Island had always seemed little visited until the railroad made transportation easier. Watson remembered the New York of his youth and recalled seeing Dutch houses that were painted red. He remembered when expenses were moderate "and hospitality and friendly greetings were everywhere abounding." Watson noted that the New York of his old age was a busy, pushy, noisy, vainglorious show where there were abundant riches and palatial expenditures. "I felt," Watson confided, "that New York was a place to visit & to see wonder, but not to abide."

Watson also made quick trips to places in the vicinity of his home in Philadelphia. In addition to Cape May, he went to other New Jersey shore towns, including Long Branch and Manahawkin, where he stayed at "The Mansion of Health." Watson traveled on the Delaware Canal; went to Harrisburg, Pennsylvania; and journeyed through Chester County, Pennsylvania, where he owned property, and through several New Jersey towns where he had friends and in which he had spent time as a youngster. What Watson saw in Mount Holly, New Jersey, occasioned a pensive remark: "The young and beautiful, especially among the females, had become faded & motherly, & some of their daughters were fast growing up into their former place—But the houses & streets seemed to have renewed their age by improvements, & the glare of paint & ornament." In 1826 Watson visited King Joseph and Prince Charles of Spain at their home at Point Breeze, New Jersey. He wrote of them: "The opinion that I then formed, was, that neither the King, nor the Prince would have been noticed as *uncommon* men in any mixt company."

Watson summarized his thoughts on the keeping of travel journals in 1856 as he paid a visit to his birthplace of Batsto: "I feel & know, that I am a queer man—that is, a man by myself, in this preserving the record of my movements in the brief life—I just know, that when I shall have made my exit, & shall be no more seen of men, I shall have some descendants who shall like to travel over these pages—possibly to see the same land."

In addition, see "Philadelphia's Boswell: John Fanning Watson," by Deborah Waters, in the *Pennsylvania Magazine of History and Biography* (January 1974): 3–52. Under her maiden name, Deborah Dependahl, Waters wrote her thesis, *John Fanning Watson, Historian, 1779–1860*, in 1971 for the University of Delaware.

Other papers relating to the family of John Fanning Watson are located at the Historical Society of Pennsylvania, Philadelphia, and the Henry E. Huntington Library, San Marino, California.

M91   Watson, Lucy Fanning, d. 1834.
[Reminiscences]. 1803, [1834?], 1860.
3 v.; 20–25 cm.
These three volumes were written by either Lucy Fanning Watson herself or dictated by her to her son, John Fanning Watson, who then made final written copies. Because the nature of one is so different from the others, each is discussed separately.

1. Wesley M. Watson family history. 1803.
Despite the title of this manuscript, it is not a history of Wesley M. Watson's family but rather a genealogical account by Wesley's mother, Lucy, of much of the Fanning family. Wesley, the brother of John Fanning Watson, died in a shipwreck that also claimed the life of his father—Lucy's husband—in 1804. The account focuses primarily on New England, and the few dates that are mentioned are from the late eighteenth century. Most of the account details familial relationships without the benefit of any record of time periods. At the bottom of page fourteen is an explanation of the Watson coat of arms.

2. Experience & incidents in the life of Mrs. Lucy Watson, who died at Germantown, Pa. 5th June 1834, aged 79 years. [1834?]
This manuscript contains three sections. The first is a narrative of the life of Lucy Watson; the second, a diary kept by her spo radically between 1805 and 1828; and the third, a copy book containing some of her letters. The volume is homemade, assembled from these three elements sometime after 1834, the year of Lucy's death. The narrative was penned by Lucy's son, John Fanning Watson, while the diary entries and letters seem to be in another hand, presumably Lucy's.

These writings are chiefly religious. Lucy was born in Groton, Connecticut, and was the youngest of ten children. Her parents were New Light Baptists. Lucy felt that God had spoken directly to her for the first time when she was five or six, after she nearly died from a fall off a stone wall. Lucy claimed that she lost sight of God after moving from New England to Little Egg Harbor, New Jersey (a town that she considered ungodly) and then marrying. Eventually Reverend James, a country minister, persuaded her to rejoin a church. When she moved to Philadelphia later in life, she joined the Methodist church.

From an early age Lucy was preoccupied with death. As a child, she believed that she was close to death at least four times, and as an adult, she suffered the loss of her husband, William, and a son, Wesley, in a shipwreck. She dreamed regularly of her dead relatives and wrote in her diary about conversations she had with them. On May 9, 1805, she remarked about a message from Wesley: "Dreamed of being in the mud, awakened and thought it denoted trouble, slept again and dreamed one said, The comforts of religion is the only thing that can support us through." In 1807 she dreamed that her late husband was bringing her a coffin that had been used by the apostle Paul, whose bones were still inside. Lucy believed that someone in the family was to make use of it. In 1810 she summed up her feelings: "I think much of death since I have been debilitated in body; Is it because it is near; Or is it my natural gloomy turn of mind?" Sixteen years later she said she thought funeral sermons were tedious and useless if too long. She hoped that the biblical text of her own funeral would be: "And they that were ready went in with him to the marriage, and the door was shut."

3. Mrs. Lucy Watson's memory & account of new settlers in the American woods—1762, chiefly at Walpole, N.H. 1860.
Sometime during the mid 1820s, Lucy Watson told her son, John Fanning Watson, about her childhood experiences in New Hampshire and asked him to write them down. In 1860, shortly before he died, John copied his original manuscript into this small volume. At the end of his mother's reminiscences, John remarked that he, as a chronicler of New York City and Philadelphia, probably inherited his sense of history from his mother and that he regretted that none of his children shared it.

In 1762 Lucy Fanning left Stonington, Connecticut, with her family and headed north to settle at Walpole, New Hampshire.

Her father owned a sloop called the *Sea Gull* in which they began their journey up the Connecticut River. At Enfield, Connecticut, they bought a barge to continue their trip, and further north they switched to a wagon and oxen. Because the oxen were unable to pull the weight of the wagon, the Fannings were forced to lighten the load by leaving a chest of drawers by the roadside. When they arrived at Walpole, the Fannings bought 150 acres and constructed a house. "Walpole looked new—had probably but 12 or 15 houses—All wooden ones—Most of them of logs and none of them fine to look at. The Meetinghouse was of frame and not quite finished—No Indians were seen at the Church or about the Town—It lay near the River." The Fannings raised corn and soon were able to produce ten acres of wheat. They fished, hunted, tapped maple trees for sugar, picked berries, and made their own clothes. Finding that the weather was not to their liking, at the end of four years, they moved south to Batsto, New Jersey, where it was much warmer. Here John Fanning Watson was born in 1779.

Other papers relating to the family of Lucy Fanning Watson are located at the Historical Society of Pennsylvania, Philadelphia, and the Henry E. Huntington Library, San Marino, California.

M92 Watson, Selina.
Journal, October from the 8 to 21–1837.
20 p.: ill.; 17 cm.
This account, written when Selina Watson was young, covers the first long journey of her life, from Germantown, Pennsylvania, where she lived, to New York City. Much of her narrative focuses on walks that she took on Broadway and other streets in New York, visits that she made to relatives and family friends, and church attendance. She was impressed by Castle Garden, remarking that "it was surprising that man could invent any thing so magnificent" but generally withheld substantive comment on her other activities. Returning home, she wrote of New Jersey: "The scene from Brunswick to Bordentown was nothing worth mentioning; it was all woods except now and then we

would come to a house." The illustrations are pencil sketches of views of New York City and Philadelphia.

When grown, Watson, who was the daughter of historian John Fanning Watson, married Charles Willing, a member of a socially prominent Philadelphia family.

Other papers relating to the family of Selina Watson are located at the Historical Society of Pennsylvania, Philadelphia, and the Henry E. Huntington Library, San Marino, California.

M93   White, Enos, 1803–[ca. 1852].
          [Diary]. 1821–51.
          [150] p.; 19 cm.
          Enos White's diary covers his adult years from the time he moved out of his father's house at eighteen until shortly before his death. He did not record his daily activities but rather recapped events of his life in annual or occasional entries. For most of his life White lived in Weymouth, Massachusetts.

On November 26, 1821, White decided to strike out on his own; he left his boyhood home and boarded with the widow Jane Humphrey. He soon left, however, and on May 13, 1822, recorded that he was working with his father "at the cabinet business." In 1826 he bought his father's shop and one year later purchased half of his father's house. In 1828 White married Jane Humphrey, probably the daughter of his former landlady, and in 1829 they had a daughter, Jane Augustus.

White was concerned with finances throughout his life. On August 10, 1829, he wrote: "The deplorable state that I have considered my father's circumstances to be in together with the view of the misfortunes of my brothers and the dread of poverty myself with all its inconveniences has induced me to make a slave of myself since I was of age to work for my own support." In an effort to find a more lucrative vocation—his furniture business had been off by $\frac{1}{3}$ in 1829—White changed his occupation to shoemaker and entered into a partnership with Abner Nash. The two men moved to Cincinnati, Ohio, in autumn 1830 to start their new work and soon realized that there was not enough trade there to sustain them. They returned to Weymouth in February 1831. White had no regrets, claiming that he had learned more about the world than if he had remained at home, and resumed furnituremaking.

In 1835 White's brother, probably living in New York City and somehow connected to the medical profession, asked him to make wooden cases for surgical instruments. This proved quite profitable, and because White himself was ill, it proved doubly welcome, since it required less strenuous physical exertion. In 1837 White, still sick, again left furnituremaking. He wrote: "As I never expected to do any more work in the shop I sold all the Furniture and stock that I had on hand at auction." He began making frames for looking glasses and in 1838 returned to shoemaking. All the while White farmed his property.

The 1840s was a decade of personal change. On January 7, 1843, White's wife died after having delivered a baby; three days later the infant, named Stephen, died. In November White's seventy-year-old mother died, and on March 5, 1844, his father, age seventy-eight, died. On September 16, 1846, White married Mary Ann Fowler, age thirty-three. By 1849 White's children were in school: Jane attended Miss Blanchard's School; Lucy Ann was at the Charlestown Academy; and Charles, who would eventually become a shoemaker like his father, went to New Hampshire Academy. Shortly before the end of his life, White wrote that his health was still bad, that his farm was not doing well, and that he had entered into land speculation that proved unsuccessful.

M94   Whitefield, Edwin.
[Travel diary]. [Ca. 1855]–63.
8 v.: ill; 17–25 cm.
Edwin Whitefield, a native of England, emigrated to the United States around 1840 and soon embarked on a career of landscape and flower painting. He began his work in America by sketching and painting numerous scenes of the Hudson River valley. In 1845 Whitefield contributed the illustrations to *American Wild Flowers in Their Native Haunts*, by Emma C. Embury, and two years later published a series of views entitled *North American Scenery*. During the 1880s, Whitefield lived in Boston and Reading, Massachusetts, and began to issue volumes of *The Homes of Our*

Forefathers, featuring depictions of early New England
architecture. Whitefield's artistic endeavors were financially
rewarding, for during the 1850s and 1860s, he made several trips
to the Midwest to explore and promote real estate ventures. In
1888 he even remarked about returning to Great Britain so that
he could encourage English settlement in Minnesota.

The Downs collection includes diaries kept by Whitefield on
some of his trips through the Midwest. While they lack, for the
most part, personal observations, they include many entries that
vividly describe a developing and prosperous region of the
nation. Of Jonesboro, Illinois, Whitefield wrote: "The land rises
quite high and is rather broken quite enough to be picturesque.
Woods all around." And commenting about Cairo, Illinois,
Whitefield focused on architecture: "Several large three story
brick stores and one 4 story. Then the new hotel nearly finished
is a large and handsome brick edifice 4 stories high." In addition
to describing Cairo, Whitefield sketched a picture of the hotel.
Many of Whitefield's text descriptions were supplemented with
pictorial representations. Whitefield's interest in the picturesque
and in architecture, revealed in the diaries, culminated in his
publication of the aforementioned series, *Homes of Our Forefathers*.

The extent of Whitefield's diaries—eight volumes—suggest
a sizable amount of literature. Many of the volumes number
only a few pages, and most are succinct. These diaries are valuable, however, when used with the larger body of Whitefield
papers, prints, and books in Winterthur's collection.

Whitefield's travels are discussed by Bettina A. Norton,
Edwin Whitefield: Nineteenth-Century North American Scenery (Barre,
Mass.: Imprint Society, 1977), pp. 15–31. Other Edwin White-
field papers are located at the Society for the Preservation of
New England Antiquities, Boston, and the Minnesota Historical
Society, St. Paul.

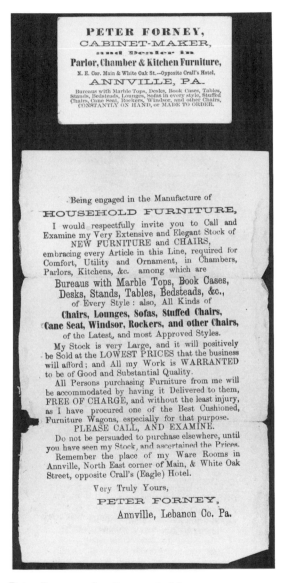

Peter Forney advertisement. M37

John Fanning Watson. From *Annals of Philadelphia, and Pennsylvania, in the Olden Time . . .* (Philadelphia: J. M. Stoddart, 1879), pl. facing p. [11]. M90

From manuscript diaries of a Boston artist, 1850s, vol. 2, pl. 2. M52

Jonathan Mason. From Jonathan Mason, "The Recollections of a Septuagenarian . . . ," 1881, vol. 1, inside front cover. M55

Carving design. From Charles E. Adams diary, vol. 4, p. 136. M1

Nov 11th 95-

Portrait of a woman. From Horace Robbins Burdick diary, 1895. M14

David Clapp. From *New England Genealogical and Biographical Register* (Boston: New England Historic Genealogical Society, 1894), pl. facing p. 145. M17

From Albert A. Lovell, *Memorial of George Jaques, Comprising Selections from His Journals and a Biographical Sketch* (Worcester, Mass.: Privately printed, 1878). M44

Pencil sketch. From Walter Mason Oddie, "Private Notes &c," 1828–29.
M67

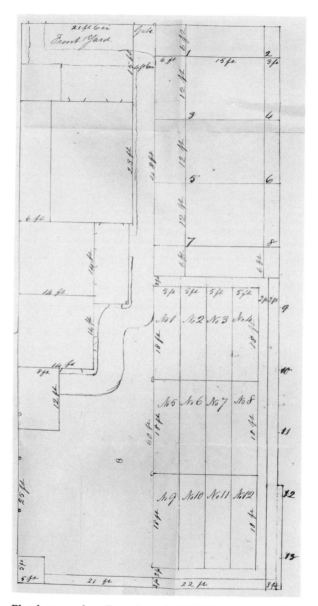

Plot for a garden. From Joseph G. Richardson, garden book, 1850. M72

Yellow fever list. From John Vaughan, medical diary no. 3, 1707–1802. M87

Salem Howe Wales. From *The National Cyclopaedia of American Biography*, vol. 3 (New York: James T. White, 1893), p. 310. M88

Published Travel Accounts

P1 Abbott, Jacob, 1803–79.
New England and her institutions / by one of her sons. Hartford, Conn.: S. Andrus and Son, 1847.
271 p.; 20 cm.

P2 Adams, Paul, 1862–1920.
Vues d'Amérique. Paris: Société d'éditions litteraires et artistiques, 1906.
[6], 568 p.; 19 cm.

P3 Adgar, the father.
Recollections of rambles at the South / by Father William [pseud.]. New York: Carlton and Phillips, 1854.
196 p., 5 leaves of plates: ill.; 15 cm.
Howes no. W443.
Clark, *Old South*, vol. 3, no. 506.

P4 Aikman, Louisa Susannah Wells, 1755?–1831.
The journal of a voyage from Charlestown, S.C., to London: undertaken during the American Revolution by a daughter of an eminent American loyalist [Louisa Susannah Wells] in the year 1778 and written from memory only in 1779. New York: Printed for the New York Historical Society, 1906.
121 p., 2 leaves of plates: ill.; 26 cm.

P5 Alcala Galiano, Dionisio.
Atlas para el viage de las goletas Sutil y Mexicana al reconocimiento del estrecho de Juan de Fuca en 1792, publicado en 1802. Madrid: Imprenta Real, 1802.
8 p.ℓ., cixviii, 185 p.; 21–30 cm.
Howes no. G18.
Sabin no. 69221.

P6 Ampère, Jean-Jacques Antoine, 1800–1864.
Promenade en Amérique / par J. J. Ampère; précédée d'une étude sur J.-J. Ampère par C.-A. Sainte-Beuve . . . Paris: Michel Lévy Frères, 1874.

xliii, 299 p., 11 leaves of plates: ill.; 27 cm.
Howes no. A222.
Sabin no. 1347.

P7   Anburey, Thomas.
      Travels through the interior parts of America in a series of let-
      ters / by an officer. London: Printed for William Lane, 1789.
      2 v.: ill.; 21 cm.
      Howes no. A226.
      Sabin no. 1366.

P8   Anburey, Thomas.
      Travels through the interior parts of America / by Thomas
      Anburey, lieutenant in the army of General Burgoyne, with a
      foreword by Major-General William Harding Carter . . . Boston
      and New York: Houghton Mifflin Co., 1923.
      2 v.: ill.; 23 cm.
      Howes no. A226.

P9   Arese, Francesco, conte, 1805–81.
      A trip to the prairies and in the interior of North America (1837–
      38): travel notes by Count Francesco Arese, now first translated
      from the original French / by Andrew Evans [pseud.]. New
      York: Harbor Press, 1934.
      xxiv, 217 p., 1 plate (fold.): ill.; 20 cm.

P10   Arfwedson, Carl David, 1806–81.
      The United States and Canada in 1832, 1833, and 1834 / by C. D.
      Arfwedson . . . London: R. Bentley, 1834.
      2 v.: ill.; 22 cm.
      Howes no. A304.
      Sabin no. 1943.

P11   Baily, Francis, 1774–1844.
      Journal of a tour in unsettled parts of North America in 1796
      & 1797 / edited by Jack D. L. Holmes. Carbondale and
      Edwardsville, Ill.; London; Amsterdam: Southern Illinois

University, [1969].
xxvi, 336 p., 8 leaves of plates: ill.; 22 cm.

P12   Ballard, Joseph, 1789–1877.
England in 1815 as seen by a young Boston merchant: being the
reflections and comments of Joseph Ballard on a trip through
Great Britain in the year of Waterloo. Boston; New York:
Houghton Mifflin Co., 1913.
viii, 181 p., 1 plate: ill.; 21 cm.

P13   Barrow, John, Sir, 1764–1848.
Travels in China: containing descriptions, observations, and comparisons, made and collected in the course of a short residence
at the Imperial Palace of Yuen-min-yuen, and on a subsequent
journey through the country from Pekin to Canton . . . / by John
Barrow. London: T. Cadell and W. Davies, 1806.
x, 632 p., 10 leaves of plates: ill. (some col.); 28 cm.

P14   Bartlett, John Russell, 1805–86.
Personal narrative of explorations and incidents in Texas, New
Mexico, California, Sonora, and Chihuahua: connected with the
United States and Mexican boundary commission during the
years 1850, 1851, 1852, and 1853 / by John Russell Bartlett. New
York; London: Appleton, 1854.
2 v.: ill.; 25 cm.
Howes no. B201.
Sabin no. 3746.

P15   Bartlett, William Henry, 1809–54.
Walks about the city and environs of Jerusalem / by W. H. Bartlett. London: George Virtue, [1846?]
viii, 255 p., 31 leaves of plates: ill.; 25 cm.

P16   Bartram, John, 1699–1777.
A journey from Pennsylvania to Onondaga in 1743 by John Bartram, Lewis Evans, [and] Conrad Weiser / introduction by Whit-
field J. Bell, Jr.; illustrations by Nathan Goldstein. Barre, Mass.:

Imprint Society, [1973].
132 p.: ill.; 22 cm.

P17   Bartram, John, 1699–1777.
       Travels in Pensilvania and Canada / by John Bartram. Ann
       Arbor, Mich.: University Microfilms, [1966].
       94 p., 1 plate (fold.): ill.; 19 cm.

P18   Bartram, William, 1739–1823.
       Travels through North and South Carolina, Georgia, East and
       West Florida, the Cherokee country, the extensive territories of
       the Muscogulges, or Creek confederacy, and the country of the
       Chactaws: containing an account of the soil and natural produc-
       tions of those regions . . . / by William Bartram. Philadelphia:
       Printed by James and Johnson, 1791; London: Reprinted for
       J. Johnson, 1792.
       xxiv, 520, [12] p., 8 leaves of plates (some fold.): ill.; 22 cm.
       Howes no. B223.
       Sabin no. 3870.

P19   Bartram, William, 1739–1823.
       Travels through North & South Carolina, Georgia, East and
       West Florida: a facsimile of the 1792 London edition embellished
       with its nine original plates, also seventeen additional illustra-
       tions and an introduction by Gordon DeWolf. Savannah, Ga.:
       Beehive Press, [1973].
       xx, 534 p.: ill.; 24 cm.

P20   Baudry des Lozières, Louis Narcisse, 1761–1841.
       Voyage à la Louisiane et sur le continent de l'Amérique Septentri-
       onale fait dans les années 1794 à 1798: contenant un tableau his-
       torique de la Louisiane . . . / par B*** D***; Orné d'une belle
       carte . . . Paris: Dentu, an xi, 1802.
       viii, 382 p., 1 plate (fold.): ill.; 20 cm.
       Clark, *Old South*, vol. 2, no. 76.
       Howes no. B243.
       Sabin no. 3979.

P21   Bayard, Ferdinand Marie, b. 1768?
Travels of a Frenchman in Maryland and Virginia with a description of Philadelphia and Baltimore in 1791; or, travels in the interior of the United States, to Bath, Winchester, in the valley of
the Shenandoah, etc., etc., during the summer of 1791 / by Ferdinand-M. Bayard. [Ann Arbor, Mich.]: Edwards Brothers, [1950].
xxvii, 182 p.; 23 cm.

P22   Bayard, Ferdinand Marie, b. 1768?
Voyage dans l'intérieur des Etats-Unis à Bath, Winchester, dans
la vallée de Shenandoha etc. etc. etc. pendant l'été de 1791 / par
Ferdinand-M. Bayard . . . Paris: Chez Cocheris, Imprimeur-
Libraire, An cinquième de la République, (1797, vieux style).
xvi, 336 p.; 20 cm.
Howes no. B255.
Sabin no. 4022.

P23   Beaumont, [Jean François] Albanis, 1753?–1811.
Travels through the Maritime Alps from Italy to Lyons across the
Col de Tende by the way of Nice, Provence, Languedoc, &c.:
with topographical and historical descriptions; to which are
added some philosophical observations on the various appearances in mineralogy &c. found in those countries / by Albanis
Beaumont . . . London: Printed by T. Bensley, 1795.
[6], 127, [2] p., 18 leaves of plates (1 double): ill., maps; 44 cm.

P24   [Beckford, William], 1760–1844.
Recollections of an excursion to the monasteries of Alcobaça and
Batalha / by the author of "Vathek." London: R. Bentley, 1835.
xi, 228 p., 1 plate: ill.; 23 cm.

P25   [Bell, Andrew], of Southampton, w. 1838–66.
Men and things in America: being the experience of a year's resi-
dence in the United States in a series of letters to a friend / by
A. Thomson [pseud.]. London: W. Smith, 1838.
viii, 296 p.; 18 cm.
Sabin no. 4447.

P26   Bell, Margaret Van Horn (Dwight), 1790–1834.
            A journey to Ohio in 1810 as recorded in the journal of Margaret
            Van Horn Dwight / edited with an introduction by Max Farrand.
            New Haven: Yale University Press, 1913.
            vi, 64 p.; 22 cm.

P27   Bell, William Abraham.
            New tracks in North America: a journal of travel and adventure
            whilst engaged in the survey for a southern railroad to the
            Pacific Ocean during 1867–8 / by William A. Bell . . . London:
            Chapman and Hall; New York: Scribner, Welford, 1870.
            lxix, 564 p., 24 leaves of plates: ill.; 22 cm.
            Howes no. B330.

P28   Beltrami, Giacomo Constantino, 1779–1855.
            A pilgrimage in Europe and America leading to the discovery of
            the sources of the Mississippi and Bloody River: with a descrip-
            tion of the whole course of the former and of the Ohio / by J.C.
            Beltrami. London: Hunt and Clarke, 1828.
            2 v.: ill.; 22 cm.
            Howes no. B338.
            Sabin no. 4605.

P29   Benjamin, Israel Joseph, 1818–64.
            Three years in America, 1859–1862 / by I. J. Benjamin; translated
            from the German by Charles Reznikoff with an introduction by
            Oscar Handlin. Philadelphia: Jewish Publication Society of
            America, 1956.
            2 v.: ill.; 24 cm.

P30   Bernhard, Karl, duke of Saxe-Weimar-Eisenach, 1792–1862.
            Reise Sr. Hoheit des Herzogs Bernard zu Sachsen-Weimar-
            Eisenach durch Nord-Amerika in den Jahren 1825 und 1826. Wei-
            mar, Ger.: Wilhelm Hoffman, 1828.
            2 v. in 1: ill.; 23 cm.
            Howes no. B385.
            Sabin no. 4953.

P31   Bernhard, Karl, duke of Saxe-Weimar-Eisenach, 1792–1862.
Travels through North America during the years 1825 and 1826 /
by His Highness, Bernhard, duke of Saxe-Weimar-Eisenach. Phil-
adelphia: Carey, Lea, and Carey, 1828.
2 v. in 1; 23 cm.
Howes no. B385.
Sabin no. 4954.
Shaw/Shoemaker no. 32277.

P32   [Berquin-Duvallon].
Travels in Louisiana and the Floridas in the year 1802: giving a
correct picture of those countries / translated from the French
with notes &c. by John Davis . . . New York: Printed by and for
J. Riley, 1806.
viii, 181 p., 18 cm.
Clark, *Old South*, vol. 2, no. 79.
Howes no. B389.
Sabin no. 4965.

P33   [Berquin-Duvallon].
Vue de la colonie espagnole du Mississippi, ou des provinces de
Louisiane et Floride Occidentale, en l'année 1802 / par un obser-
vateur résident sur les lieux . . . Paris: A l'Imprimerie Expédi-
tive, l'an XI, 1803.
xx, 318, 5, [4] p., 2 leaves of plates (fold.): ill.; 21 cm.
Clark, *Old South*, vol. 2, no. 79.
Howes no. B389.
Sabin no. 4962.

P34   [Biddle, Richard], 1796–1847.
Captain Hall in America / by an American. Philadelphia: Carey
and Lea, 1830.
120 p.; 23 cm.
Sabin no. 5247.
Shaw/Shoemaker no. 538.

P35   Bierce, Lucius Verus, 1801–76.
Travels in the Southland, 1822–1823: the journal of Lucius Verus
Bierce; edited with a biographical essay by George W. Knepper.
Columbus: Ohio State University Press, [1966].
x, 139 p.; 23 cm.

P36   Bigelow, Timothy, 1767–1821.
Diary of a visit to Newport, New York, and Philadelphia during
the summer of 1815 / by Timothy Bigelow; edited by a grandson
. . . Boston: Printed for private distribution; [Cambridge, Eng.:
Cambridge University Press], 1880.
[5], 29 p.; 23 cm.

P37   Bigelow, Timothy, 1767–1821.
Journal of a tour to Niagara Falls in the year 1805 / by Timothy
Bigelow; with an introduction by a grandson [Abbott Lawrence].
Boston: Press of John Wilson and Son, 1876.
xx, 121 p.; 23 cm.
Howes no. B437.

P38   Bingley, William, 1744–1823.
Travels in North America from modern writers: with remarks
and observations; exhibiting a connected view of the geography
and present state of that quarter of the globe / by the Rev. William Bingley. London: Printed for Harvey and Darton, 1821.
346 p., 3 leaves of plates: ill.; 18 cm.
Sabin no. 5463.

P39   Birkbeck, Morris, 1764–1825.
Letters from Illinois / by Morris Birkbeck . . . Philadelphia:
Printed for the author; Dublin: Re-printed for Thomas Larkin,
1818.
[xv], 112 p.; 23 cm.
Howes no. B467.

P40   Birkbeck, Morris, 1764–1825.
Notes on a journey in America from the coast of Virginia to the
territory of Illinois . . . / by Morris Birkbeck. London: James

Ridgway, 1818.
iv, 156, 2, [2], 4 p., 1 plate (fold., col.): ill; 18 cm.
Clark, *Old South*, vol. 2, no. 4.
Howes no. B468.
Sabin no. 5569.

P41   Birket, James.
Some cursory remarks made by James Birket in his voyage to
North America, 1750–1751. New Haven: Yale University Press
[etc., etc.], 1916.
vi, 74 p.; 22 cm.

P42   Blanc, Marie Thérèse (de Solms), 1840–1907.
Les Américaines chez elle / Th. Bentzon [pseud.]. Paris:
Hachette, 1904.
358 p.; 19 cm.

P43   [Blane, William Newnham], 1800–1825.
An excursion through the United States and Canada during the
years 1822–23 / by an English gentleman. London: Baldwin, Cradock, and Joy, 1824.
[3], 515 p., 2 leaves of fold. plates: ill.; 24 cm.
Howes no. B521.

P44   Bloodgood, Simeon de Witt, 1799–1866.
An Englishman's sketch-book; or, Letters from New-York. New
York: G. and C. Carvill, 1828.
[2], iv, [7]–195 p.; 20 cm.
Sabin no. 22625.
Shaw/Shoemaker no. 32401.

P45   Blouët, Paul, 1848–1903.
A Frenchman in America: recollections of men and things / by
Max O'Rell [pseud.]. . . . with over one hundred and thirty illustrations by E. W. Kemble. New York: Cassell Publishing Co.,
[1891].
x, 365, [3] p., 1 plate: ill.; 21 cm.

P46   Bodichon, Barbara Leigh Smith, 1827–91.
An American diary, 1857–8 / edited from the manuscript by
Joseph W. Reed, Jr. London: Routledge and Keagan Paul, [1972].
[8], 198 p., 2 leaves of plates: ill.; 23 cm.

P47   Bontekoe, William Ysbrantsz, 1587–1647.
Memorable description of the East Indian voyage, 1618–25 /
translated from the Dutch by Mrs. C. B. Bodde-Hodgkinson and
Pieter Geyl . . . with an introduction and notes by Professor
Geyl. New York: Robert M. McBride, 1929.
168 p., 10 leaves of plates: ill.; 23 cm.

P48   Bossu, [Mons. Jean Bernard], 1720–92.
Nouveaux voyages dans l'Amérique Septentrionale, contenant
une collection de lettres écrites sur les lieux par l'Auteur à son
ami, M. Douin . . . ci-devant son camarade dans les nouveau
monde / par M. Bossu . . . Amsterdam: Changuion, 1777.
xvi, 392, 4 leaves of plates (1 fold.): ill.; 20 cm.
Howes no. B627.
Sabin no. 6470.

P49   Boudinot, Elias, 1740–1821.
Elias Boudinot's journey to Boston in 1809 / edited by Milton Hal-
sey Thomas. Princeton: Princeton University Press, 1955.
xiii, 97 p., 4 leaves of plates: ill.; 24 cm.

P50   Bourke, John Gregory, 1843–96.
The snake dance of the Moquis of Arizona: being a narrative of a
journey from Santa Fé, New Mexico to the villages of the Moqui
Indians of Arizona; with a description of the manners and customs of this peculiar people and especially of the revolting religious rite, the snake dance . . . / by John G. Bourke. New York:
Charles Scribner's Sons, 1884.
xvi, 371 p., 31 leaves of plates (some col.): ill.; 23 cm.
Howes no. B655.

P51 Bowles Samuel, 1826–78.
Across the continent / by Samuel Bowles. Ann Arbor, Mich.: University Microfilms, [1966].
xx, 452, p., 1 plate (fold.): ill.; 20 cm.

P52 Braam Houckgeest, Andreas Everard van, 1739–1801.
Voyage de l'ambassade de la Compagnie des Indes Orientales Hollandaises vers l'empereur de la Chine dans les années 1794 & 1795 . . .: le tout tiré du journal d'André Everard Van Braam Houckgeest . . . Philadelphie: Chez l'éditeur [etc.], 1797–98.
2 v.: ill.; 27 cm.
Evans no. 31860.

P53 Brackenridge, Henry Marie, 1786–1871.
Views of Louisiana: together with a journal of a voyage up the Missouri River in 1811 . . . / by H. M. Brackenridge. Pittsburgh: Cramer, Spear, and Eichbaum, 1814.
304 p.; 22 cm.
Clark, *Old South*, vol. 2, no. 136.
Howes no. B688.
Sabin no. 7176.

P54 Bradbury, John, b. 1768.
Travels in the interior of America in the years 1809, 1810, and 1811: including a description of upper Louisiana, together with the states of Ohio, Kentucky, Indiana, and Tennessee, with the Illinois and western territories; and containing remarks and observations useful to persons emigrating to those countries / by John Bradbury. Liverpool: Printed for the author by Smith and Galway and published by Sherwood, Neely, and Jones, London, 1817.
364 p.; 23 cm.
Clark, *Old South*, vol. 2, no. 137.
Howes no. B695.
Sabin no. 7207.

P55 Bradbury, John, b. 1768.
Travels in the interior of America in the years 1809, 1810, and

1811 / by John Bradbury; foreword by Donald Jackson. Lincoln:
University of Nebraska Press, 1986.
320 p.: map; 20 cm.

P56   Bremer, Fredrika, 1801–65.
        The homes of the New World: impressions of America / by Fre-
        drika Bremer. London: Arthur Hall, Virtue, 1853.
        3 v.: ill.; 20 cm.
        Howes no. B745.
        Sabin no. 7713.

P57   Brissot de Warville, Jacques Pierre, 1754–93.
        The commerce of America with Europe, particularly with France
        and Great Britain . . .: shewing the importance of the American
        Revolution to the interests of France and pointing out the actual
        situation of the United States of North-America in regard to
        trade, manufacturers, and population / by J. P. Warville and
        Etienne Clavière; translated from the last French ed., rev. by Bris-
        sot, and called the second volume of his View of America . . .
        New York: T. and J. Swords, 1795.
        xxxv, 228 p.; 17 cm.
        Evans no. 28343.
        Howes no. C464.
        Sabin no. 8016.

P58   Brissot de Warville, Jacques-Pierre, 1754–93.
        New travels in the United States of America performed in 1788 /
        by J. P. Brissot de Warville; translated from the French . . . Dub-
        lin: W. Corbet, 1792.
        xliii, viii, 46–482 p., 1 fold. plate: ill.; 20 cm.
        Sabin no. 8025.

P59   Brissot de Warville, Jacques-Pierre, 1754–93.
        New travels in the United States of America performed in
        MDCCLXXXVII . . . / by J. P. Brissot de Warville. London:
        Printed for J. S. Jordan, 1794.
        3 v.: ill.; 22 cm.
        Sabin no. 8027.

P60 Brissot de Warville, Jacques-Pierre, 1754–93.
Nouveau voyage dans les États-Unis de l'Amérique Septentrio-
nale fait en 1788 / par J. P. Brissot (Warville) . . . Paris: Chez
Buisson, 1791.
3 v.; 21 cm.
Sabin no. 8035.

P61 Broughton, William Robert, 1762–1821.
A voyage of discovery to the north Pacific Ocean: in which the
coast of Asia, from the lat. of 35° north to the lat. of 52° north,
the island of Insu (commonly known under the name of the land
of Jesso), the north, south, and east coasts of Japan, the Lieu-
chieux and the adjacent isles, as well as the coast of Corea, have
been examined and surveyed; performed in His Majesty's sloop
Providence and her tender in the years 1795, 1796, 1797, 1798 /
by William Robert Broughton. London: Printed for T. Cadell and
W. Davies, 1804.
xx, 393 p., 6 leaves of plates (some fold.): ill., maps; 28 x 22 cm.
Howes no. B821.
Sabin no. 8423.

P62 Bryant, Edwin, 1805–69.
What I saw in California / by Edwin Bryant. Palo Alto, Calif.:
Lewis Osborne, 1967.
xiv, 480, [10] p., 15 leaves of plates: ill., maps; 23 cm.

P63 Buckingham, James Silk, 1786–1855.
America, historical, statistic, and descriptive / by J. S. Bucking-
ham. London: Fisher, Son, 1841.
3 v.: ill., map.; 23 cm.
Howes no. B921.
Sabin no. 8892.

P64 Buckley, Michael Bernhard, 1831–72.
Diary of a tour in America by M. B. Buckley of Cork, Ireland, a
special missionary in North America and Canada in 1870 and
1871 / edited by his sister, Kate Buckley. Dublin: Sealy Bryers

and Walker, 1886.
384 p., 1 plate: ill.; 19 cm.

P65   [Burlend, Rebecca], 1793–1872.
A true picture of emigration; or, Fourteen years in the interior of
North America; being a full and impartial account of the various
difficulties and ultimate success of an English family who emigrated from Barwick-in-Elmet, near Leeds, in the year 1831. London: G. Berger, [1848].
62 p.; 18 cm.
Howes no. B992.
Sabin no. 97133.

P66   Burnaby, Andrew, 1734?–1812.
Burnaby's travels through North America: reprinted from the
third edition of 1798 / with introduction and notes by Rufus
Rockwell Wilson. New York: A. Wessels Co., 1904.
265 p.; 22 cm.

P67   Burritt, Elihu, 1810–79.
Walks in the black country and its green border-land / by Elihu
Burritt. London: S. Low, Son, and Marston, 1868.
vi, 448 p., 1 plate: ill.; 21 cm.

P68   Busch, Moritz, 1821–99.
Travels between the Hudson and Mississippi, 1851–1852. [Lexing-
ton]: University Press of Kentucky, [1971].
xix, 295, p.; 24 cm.

P69   [Butel-Dumont, Georges Marie], 1725–88.
Histoire et commerce des colonies angloises, dans l'Amérique
Septentrionale. A Londres et se vend á Paris: Chez Breton,
[etc.], 1755.
xxiv, 336 p.; 18 cm.
Howes no. B1049.
Sabin no. 9602.

P70 [Caldwell, John Edwards], 1769–1819.
A tour through part of Virginia in the summer of 1808: in a
series of letters, including an account of Harper's Ferry, the Natural Bridge, the new discovery called Weir's cave, Monticello,
and the different medicinal springs, hot and cold baths, visited
by the author. New York: Printed for the author [by] H.C. South-
wick, 1809.
31 p.; 23 cm.
Clark, *Old South*, vol. 2, no. 139.
Howes no. C23.

P71 [Candler, Isaac].
A summary view of America: comprising a description of the
face of the country, and of several of the principal cities, and
remarks on the social, moral, and political character of the people; being the result of observations and enquiries during a journey in the United States / by an Englishman. London: T. Cadell
and W. Blackwood, 1824.
viii, 503 p.; 22 cm.
Howes no. C110.
Sabin no. 10672.

P72 Carr, George Kirwan.
A short tour through the United States and Canada, October
10th to December 31st, 1832: the journal of Lieut. George Kirwan
Carr / edited with notes by Deoch Fulton. New York: New York
Public Library, 1937.
34 p., 3 leaves of plates: ill.; 26 cm.

P73 Carroll, Charles, 1737–1832.
Journal of Charles Carroll of Carrollton during his visit to Canada in 1776 as one of the commissioners from Congress / with a
memoir and notes by Bantz Mayer. Baltimore: John Murphy,
1845.
84 p., 1 plate: ill.; 23 cm.
Howes no. C179.
Sabin no. 11068.

P74   Carver, Jonathan, 1710–80.
Three years travels through the interior parts of North-America
for more than five thousand miles . . . / by Captain Jonathan
Carver. Philadelphia: Key and Simpson, 1796.
xx, 360, 20 p.; 21 cm.
Evans no. 30169
Howes no. C215.
Sabin no. 11185.

P75   Carver, Jonathan, 1710–80.
Three years travels throughout the interior parts of North-
America for more then five thousand miles . . . / by Captain Jon-
athan Carver. Boston: John Russell for David West, 1797.
xvi, [5]–312 p., 18 cm.
Evans no. 31920
Howes no. C215.
Sabin no. 11185.

P76   Carver, Jonathan, 1710–80.
Travels through the interior parts of North America in the years
1766, 1767, and 1768 / by J. Carver. London: C. Dilly [etc.], 1781.
[4], 22, [22], xvi, [17]–543, [21] p., 7 leaves of plates (some fold.
& col.): ill.; 23 cm.
Howes no. C215.
Sabin no. 11184.

P77   Casey, Charles.
Two years on the farm of Uncle Sam: with sketches of his location, nephews, and prospects / by Charles Casey. London: Richard Bentley, 1852.
ix, 311 p.; 20 cm.
Howes no. C219.
Sabin no. 11326.

P78   Cather, Thomas.
Journal of a voyage to America in 1836. London: Rodale Press;
Emmaus, Pa.: Rodale Books, 1955.
48 p., 6 leaves of plates: ill.; 21 cm.

P79   Chambers, William, 1800–1883.
Things as they are in America / by W. Chambers. Philadelphia:
Lippincott, Grambo, 1854.
vi, 364 p.; 20 cm.
Howes no. C275.
Sabin no. 11807.

P80   Chandler, Richard, 1738–1810.
Travels in Asia Minor; or, An account of a tour made at the
expense of the Society of Dilettanti . . . Dublin: Printed and sold
by R. Marchbank, 1775.
xxviii, 283 p.; 21 cm.

P81   Chandler, Richard, 1738–1810.
Travels in Greece; or, An account of a tour made at the expense
of the Society of Dilettanti / by Richard Chandler. Oxford:
Printed at the Clarendon Press, 1776.
4, xiv, [2], 304 p., 7 leaves of plates (some fold.): ill.; 28 cm.

P82   Charlevoix, Pierre-François-Xavier de, 1682–1761.
Journal of a voyage to North America / by Pierre de Charlevoix.
Ann Arbor, Mich.: University Microfilms, [1966].
2 v.: ill., map; 19 cm.

P83   Chastellux, François Jean, marquis de, 1734–88.
Travels in North-America in the years 1780, 1781, and 1782 / by
the Marquis de Chastellux . . . London: Printed for G. G. and J.
and J. Robinson, 1787.
2 v.: ill.; 22 cm.
Howes no. C324.
Sabin no. 12229.

P84   Chastellux, François Jean, marquis de, 1734–88.
Voyages de M. le marquis de Chastellux dans l'Amérique Septentrionale dans les années 1780, 1781, & 1782. Paris: Chez Prault,
1786.
2 v.: ill.; 21 cm.

Howes no. C324.
Sabin no. 12227.

P85   Chastellux, François Jean, marquis de, 1734–88.
Voyages de M. le marquis de Chastellux dans l'Amérique Septentrionale dans les années 1780, 1781 & 1782. Paris: Prault,
1788–91.
2 v.: ill.; 22 cm.
Howes no. C324.
Sabin no. 12227.

P86   Cipriani, Leonetto, conte, 1812–88.
California and overland diaries of Count Leonetto Cipriani from
1853–1871: translated and edited by Ernest Falbo. [Portland,
Ore.]: Champoeg Press, 1962.
[6], 148, [5] p., 1 plate: ill.; 27 cm.

P87   Clarke, Edward Daniel, 1768–1822.
Travels in various countries of Europe, Asia, and Africa / by
Edward Daniel Clarke. Hartford, Conn.: John W. Robbins, 1817.
2 v.; 18 cm.
Shaw/Shoemaker no. 40486.

P88   Cobbett, William, 1763–1835.
Rural rides in the southern, western, and eastern counties of
England: together with tours in Scotland and in the northern
and midland counties of England and letters from Ireland / by
William Cobbett. London: Peter Davies, 1930.
3 v., ill.; 26 cm.

P89   Cobbett, William, 1763–1835.
A year's residence in the United States of America . . .: in three
parts / by William Cobbett. New York: Clayton and Kingsland,
1818.
134 p.; 19 cm.
Howes no. C525.
Sabin no. 14021.
Shaw/Shoemaker no. 43654.

P90   Coke, Edward Thomas, 1807–88.
            A subaltern's furlough / by E. T. Coke. New York: J. and J.
            Harper, 1833.
            2 v.; 20 cm.
            Howes no. C546.
            Sabin no. 14239.
            Shaw/Shoemaker no. 18320.

P91   Coleridge, Henry Nelson, 1789–1843.
            Six months in the West Indies in 1825 / by Henry Nelson Cole-
            ridge. London: John Murray, 1832.
            8, 311 p.; 16 cm.
            Sabin no. 14319.

P92   [Colles, James], 1828–98.
            Journal of a hunting excursion to Louis Lake, 1851. Blue Moun-
            tain Lake, N.Y.: Adirondack Museum, 1961.
            [79] p.: ill., facsims.; 29 cm.

P93   Collins, John Sloan, b. 1839.
            My experience in the West / edited by Colton Storm. Chicago:
            R. R. Donnelley and Sons Co., 1970.
            xxxv, 252 p.: ill.; 17 cm.

P94   Colman, Henry, 1785–1849.
            European life and manners in familiar letters to friends . . . Bos-
            ton: Charles C. Little and James Brown; London: John Pether-
            ham, 1849.
            2 v.; 21 cm.

P95   Comettant, Jean Pierre Oscar, 1819–98.
            Voyage pittoresque et anecdotique dans le Nord et le Sud des
            Etats-Unis d'Amérique / par Oscar Comettant. Paris: A. Laplace,
            Libraire-Editeur, 1866.
            vii, 469 p., 22 leaves of plates: ill. (some col.); 27 cm.

P96   Cooley, James Ewing, 1802–82.
            The American in Egypt: with rambles through Arabia, Petraea,

and the Holy Land during the years 1839 and 1840 / by James
Ewing Cooley. New York: D. Appleton, 1842.
8, [xx], 610, [4], 12 p., 17 leaves of plates: ill.; 22 cm.

P97   Cooper, James Fenimore, 1789–1851.
        Notions of the Americans: picked up by a travelling bachelor.
        Philadelphia: Carey, Lea and Carey, 1828.
        2 v.; 18 cm.
        Howes no. C750.
        Sabin no. 16486.
        Shaw/Shoemaker no. 32827.

P98   Cooper, Thomas, 1759–1839.
        A ride to Niagara in 1809 / by T. C. Rochester, N.Y.: George P.
        Humphrey, 1915.
        49 p., 1 fold. plate: ill.; 24 cm.

P99   Cox, Ross, 1793–1853.
        Adventures on the Columbia River: including the narrative of a
        residence of six years on the western side of the Rocky Moun-
        tains, among various tribes of Indians hitherto unknown;
        together with a journey across the American continent / by Ross
        Cox. London: Henry Colburn and Richard Bentley, 1831.
        2 v.; 22 cm.
        Howes no. C822.
        Sabin no. 17267.

P100   [Crèvecoeur, Michel Guillaume St. Jean de], 1735–1813.
        Voyage dans la haute Pensylvanie et dan l'état de New-York /
        par un membre adoptif de la nation Onéida; traduit et publié par
        l'auteur des Lettres d'un cultivateur Américain. Paris: Maradan,
        An IX, 1801.
        3 v.: ill.; 21 cm.
        Howes no. C884.
        Sabin no. 17501.

P101   Crockett, Davy, 1786–1836.
        An account of Col. Crockett's tour to the North and Down

East . . . / written by himself. Philadelphia: E. L. Carey and
A. Hart, 1835.
234, 34 p., 1 plate: ill.; 19 cm.
Howes no. C896.
Sabin no. 17565.
Shaw/Shoemaker no. 31203.

P102   Cuming, Fortescue, 1762–1828.
Sketches of a tour to the western country through the states of
Ohio and Kentucky: a voyage down the Ohio and Mississippi
Rivers, and a trip through the Mississippi territory and part of
West Florida . . . / by F. Cuming. Pittsburgh: Cramer, Spear and
Eichman, 1810.
504 p.; 18 cm.
Clark, *Old South*, vol. 2, no. 13.
Howes no. C947.
Sabin no. 17890.

P103   Danckaerts, Jasper, b. 1639.
Journal, Jasper Danckaerts 1679–1689 / edited by Bartlett Bur-
leigh James . . . and J. Franklin Jameson . . . with a facsimile
and two maps. New York: Barnes and Noble, 1952.
313 p., 3 leaves of fold. plates: ill.; 22 cm.

P104   Danckaerts, Jasper, b. 1639.
Journal of a voyage to New York and a tour in several of the
American colonies in 1679–80 / by Jasper Dankers and Peter
Sluyter. Brooklyn: [The Society], 1867.
xlvii, 440, viii p., 12 (i.e. 13) leaves of plates (some col. & fold.):
ill.; 25 cm.

P105   D'Arusment, Frances (Wright), 1795–1852.
Views of society and manners in America: in a series of letters
from that country to a friend in England during the years 1818,
1819, and 1820 / by Frances Wright. London: Longman, Hurst,
Rees, Orme, and Brown, 1822.
x, 483 p.; 22 cm.
Sabin no. 105597.

P106   Davis, John, 1774–1854.
Travels of four years and a half in the United States of America
during 1798, 1799, 1800, 1801, and 1802 / with an introduction
and notes by A.J. Morrison. New York: Henry Holt, 1909.
xi, [5], 429 p.; 23 cm.

P107   Defoe, Daniel, 1661?–1731.
A tour thro' the whole island of Great Britain, divided into cir-
cuits or journeys: giving a particular and diverting account of
whatever is curious and worth observation / by Daniel Defoe,
gent.; with which is included a set of maps of England and
Wales divided into counties and a map of Scotland, composed
by Herman Moll, geographer; with an introduction by G. D. H.
Cole. London: P. Davies, 1927.
2 v.: ill., maps; 25 cm.

P108   Denon, Dominique Vivant, 1747–1825.
Viaggio nel Basso ed Alto Egitto: illustrato dietro alle tracc e ai
disegni del Sig. Denon. Firenze: Presso G. Tofani, 1808.
2 v.: ill.; 55 cm.

P109   Denon, Dominique Vivant, 1747–1825.
Voyage dans la basse et la haute Egypte pendant les campagnes
du Général Bonaparte. Paris: P. Didot l'aîné, An X, 1802.
2 v.: maps; 67 cm.

P110   De Roos, Frederick Fitzgerald, 1804–61.
Personal narrative of travels in the United States and Canada in
1826: with remarks on the present state of the American navy /
by Lieut. the Hon. F. Fitzgerald De Roos. London: William Harrison Ainsworth, 1827.
xii, 207, [14] leaves of plates (1 fold.),: ill.; 22 cm.
Howes no. D268.
Sabin no. 19677.

P111   Description de l'Egypte; ou, Recueil des observations et des
recherches qui ont été faîtes en Egypte pendant l'expédition de
l'armée française; publié par les ordres de Sa Majesté l'Empereur

Napoléon le Grand. Paris, 1809–22.
23 v.: ill.; 41–110 cm.

P112   Dickens, Charles, 1812–70.
American notes for general circulation / by Charles Dickens. London: Chapman and Hall, 1842.
2 v.; 21 cm.
Howes no. D316.
Sabin no. 19996.

P113   Dickinson, Jonathan, 1663–1722.
Jonathan Dickinson's journal; or, God's protecting providence; being a narrative of a journey from Port Royal in Jamaica to Philadelphia between August 23, 1696 and April 1, 1697 / edited by Evangeline Walker Andrews and Charles McLean Andrews.
New Haven: Yale University Press, 1945.
x, 252 p., [4] leaves of plates: ill.; 21 cm.

P114   Dilke, Sir Charles Wentworth, bart, 1843–1911.
Greater Britain: a record of travel in English-speaking countries during 1866 and 1867 / by Charles Wentworth Dilke. New York: Harper and Brothers, 1869.
xiii, 561, [2] p.: ill.; 20 cm.
Sabin no. 20155.

P115   Dix, John, 1800?–1865?
Local loiterings and visits in the vicinity of Boston / by a looker-on. Boston: Redding, 1845.
147 p.; 19 cm.
Sabin no. 20344.

P116   Dixon, James, 1788–1871.
Personal narrative of a tour through a part of the United States and Canada: with notices of the history and institutions of Methodism in America / by James Dixon. New York: Lane and Scott, 1849.
431 p., 1 plate: ill.; 19 cm.
Sabin no. 20370.

P117   Duden, Gottfried, 1785–1855.
Report on a journey to the western states of North America and
a stay of several years along the Missouri (during the years 1824,
'25, '26, and 1827) / Gottfried Duden; an English translation;
James W. Goodrich, general ed. . . . Columbia: State Historical
Society of Missouri, 1980.
xxiv, 372 p.; 24 cm.

P118   Duflot de Mofras, Eugène, 1810–84.
Exploration du territoire de l'Orégon, des Californies, et de la
mer Vermeille: exécutée pendant les années 1840, 1841, et 1842 /
par M. Duflot de Mofras . . . Paris: Arthur Bertrand, 1844.
3 v.: ill.; 24–54 cm.
Howes no. D542.
Sabin no. 21144.

P119   du Pont de Nemours, Victor Marie, 1767–1827.
Journey to France and Spain, 1801 / by Victor Marie du Pont. Ithaca, N.Y.: Cornell University Press, 1961.
xxvi, 144 p.: ill.; 23 cm.

P120   Duvergier de Hauranne, Ernest, 1834–77.
A Frenchman in Lincoln's America = Huit mois en Amérique:
lettres et notes de voyage, 1864–1865 / by Ernest Duvergier de
Hauranne; translated and edited by Ralph H. Bowen; with introduction and notes by Ralph H. Bowen and Albert Krebs. Chicago: Lakeside Press; R. R. Donnelly and Sons Co., 1974–75.
2 v.: ill.; 18 cm.

P121   Dwight, Theodore, 1796–1866.
Things as they are; or, Notes of a traveller through some of the
middle and northern states. New York: Harper and Brothers,
1834.
252 p., 1 plate: ill.; 21 cm.
Howes no. D609.
Shaw/Shoemaker no. 24249.

P122   Dwight, Timothy, 1752–1817.
        Travels in New-England and New-York / by Timothy Dwight.
        London: W. Barnes and Son; Edinburgh: H. S. Baynes, 1823.
        4 v.: ill; 22 cm.
        Howes no. D612.
        Sabin no. 21559.

P123   Edwards, Amelia Ann Blandford, 1831–1892.
        A thousand miles up the Nile / by Amelia B. Edwards; with
        upwards of seventy illustrations engraved on wood by G. Pear-
        son . . . London [etc.]: G. Routledge and Sons, 1890.
        499 p., 1 plate: ill.; 23 cm.

P124   Ellis, William, 1794–1872.
        A journal of a tour around Hawaii, the largest of the Sandwich
        Islands. Boston: Crocker and Brewster; New York: J. P. Haven,
        1825.
        xii, 264 p., 6 leaves of plates, 1 fold. map: ill.; 19 cm.
        Shaw/Shoemaker no. 20399.

P125   Ellison, Frank.
        A facsimile of A journal of a trip Down East, Aug. 1858 / by
        Frank Ellison; foreword by Isaac Oelgart. Dallas: Somesuch
        Press, 1981.
        viii, [10], 33, [10] p.; 7 x 8 cm.

P126   [Engelbach, Lewis].
        Naples and the campagna felice: in a series of letters addressed
        to a friend in England in 1802. London: R. Ackermann, 1815.
        4, 400, [ii] p., 18 leaves of plates: col. ill.; 26 cm.

P127   European delineation of American character as contained in a let-
        ter from a foreign traveller in New York to his friend in London.
        New York: Printed for the booksellers [by] J. Gary, 1820.
        16 p.; 22 cm.
        Sabin no. 23111.
        Shaw/Shoemaker no. 1126.

P128   Eustace, John Chetwode, 1762?–1815.
A classical tour through Italy . . . / by the Rev. John Chetwode
Eustace. Philadelphia: M. Carey, 1816.
2 v.: ill., plans; 22 cm.
Shaw/Shoemaker no. 37528.

P129   Faithfull, Emily, 1835–95.
Three visits to America / by Emily Faithfull . . . New York:
Fowler and Wells Co., 1884.
xvi, 400 p.; 20 cm.

P130   Faux, William.
Memorable days in America: being a journal of a tour to the
United States principally undertaken to ascertain by positive evi-
dence the condition and probable prospects of British emigrants
. . . / by W. Faux. London: W. Simpkin and R. Marshall, 1823.
xvi, 488 p., 1 plate: ill.; 22 cm.
Howes no. F60.
Sabin no. 23933.

P131   Fea, Allan, b. 1860.
Picturesque old houses: being the impressions of a wanderer off
the beaten track / by Allan Fea . . . with numerous illustrations
by the author. London: S. H. Bousfield, [1902].
xii, 224 p.: ill.; 23 cm.

P132   Fearon, Henry Bradshaw, b. ca. 1770.
Sketches of America: a narrative of a journey of five thousand
miles through the eastern and western states of America; . . .
with remarks on Mr. Birkbeck's "Notes" and "Letters" / by
Henry Bradshaw Fearon. London: Printed for Longman, Hurst,
Rees, Orme, And Brown, 1818.
xi, 454 p.; 22 cm.
Howes no. F65.
Sabin no. 23956.

P133   Felton, Mrs.
American life: a narrative of two years' city and country resi-

dence in the United States / by Mrs. Felton. Bolton Percy, Eng.: By the author, 1843.
136 p., 1 plate: ill.; 18 cm.
Sabin no. 24044.

P134   Ferguson, William.
America by river and rail; or, Notes by the way on the New World and its people / by William Ferguson. London: James Nisbet, 1856.
viii, 511 p., 1 plate: ill.; 24 cm.
Sabin no. 24100.

P135   Ferri-Pisani, Camille.
Prince Napoleon in America, 1861: letters from his aide-de-camp / by Lieutenant-Colonel Camille Ferri Pisani; translated with a preface by Georges J. Joyaux; foreword by Bruce Catton; illustrations by Gil Walker. Bloomington: Indiana University Press, 1959.
317 p., ill.; 21 cm.

P136   Fidler, Isaac.
Observations on professions, literature, manners, and emigration in the United States and Canada made during a residence there in 1832. New York: J. and J. Harper, 1833.
viii, 247, 6 p.; 20 cm.
Howes no. F110.
Sabin no. 24261.
Shaw/Shoemaker no. 18807.

P137   Fiennes, Celia, 1662–1741.
Through England on a side saddle in the time of William and Mary; being the diary of Celia Fiennes / with an introduction by the Hon. Mrs. Griffiths. London: Field and Tuer [etc.]; New York: Scribner and Wilford, 1888.
xi, 336 p.; 23 cm.

P138   Finch, Marianne.
An Englishwoman's experience in America / by Marianne Finch.

London: Richard Bentley, 1853.
viii, 386 p.; 21 cm.
Howes no. F132.
Sabin no. 24354.

P139   Finch, Marianne.
An Englishwoman's experience in America / by Marianne Finch.
New York: Negro Universities Press, 1969.
viii, 386 p.; 23 cm.

P140   Flint, Timothy, 1780–1840.
Recollections of the last ten years passed in occasional residences
and journeyings in the valley of the Mississippi: from Pittsburgh
and the Missouri to the Gulf of Mexico and from Florida to the
Spanish frontier; in a series of letters to the Rev. James Flint of
Salem, Massachusetts / by Timothy Flint. Boston: Cummings, Hil-
lard, 1826.
[2], 395 p.; 23 cm.
Howes no. F204.
Sabin no. 24794.
Shaw/Shoemaker no. 24553.

P141   Fontaine, John, 1693–1767.
The journal of John Fontaine, an Irish Huguenot son in Spain
and Virginia, 1710–1719 / edited with an introduction by Edward
Porter Alexander. Williamsburg, Va.: Colonial Williamsburg
Foundation, [1972]; distributed by the University Press of Virginia.
xii, 190 p.: ill.; 24 cm.

P142   Fordham, Elias Pym.
Personal narratives of travels in Virginia, Maryland, Pennsylvania, Ohio, Indiana, Kentucky: and of residence in the Illinois Territory, 1817–1818 / by Elias Pym Fordham. Cleveland: Arthur H.
Clark Co., 1906.
248, [10] p., 5 leaves of plates: ill.; 24 cm.
Howes no. F257.

P143 Forman, Samuel S., 1765–1862.
Narrative of a journey down the Ohio and Mississippi in 1789–90 / by Samuel Forman. New York: Arno Press, 1971.
67, [5] p.; 23 cm.

P144 Fortune, Robert, 1813–80.
Two visits to the tea countries of China and the British tea plantations in the Himalaya: with a narrative of adventures and a full description of the culture of the tea plant, the agriculture, horticulture, and botany of China / by Robert Fortune. London: John Murray, 1853.
2 v.: ill.; 21 cm.

P145 Fowler, John.
Journal of a tour in the state of New York in the year 1830: with remarks on agriculture in those parts most eligible for settlers; and return to England by the Western islands in consequence of shipwreck in the Robert Fulton / by John Fowler. London: Whittaker, Treacher, and Arnot, 1831.
333 p.; 20 cm.
Howes no. F299.
Sabin no. 25310.

P146 Frazier, William, 1812–85.
Copy of a journal by William Frazier, Esq., of Virginia: of his journey in the year 1843 by horseback, stage coach, and river steamer into the middle west thence to Niagara Falls and beyond. Richmond: Dietz Printing Co., 1930.
88 p.: ill.; 24 cm.

P147 Frémont, John Charles, 1813–90.
Report of the exploring expedition to the Rocky Mountains in the year 1842: and to Oregon and North California in the years 1843–44 / by Brevet Captain J. C. Frémont. Washington, D.C.: Gales and Seaton, 1845.
693 p., 18 leaves of plates (some fold.): ill.; 23 cm.
Howes no. F370.
Sabin no. 25845.

P148   Gass, Patrick, 1771–1870.
A journal of the voyages and travels of a corps of discovery
under the command of Capt. Lewis and Capt. Clarke of the
Army of the United States: from the mouth of the river Missouri
through the interior parts of North America to the Pacific Ocean
during the years 1804, 1805 and 1806 . . . / by Patrick Gass. Philadelphia: Printed for Mathew Carey, 1810.
262 p., 6 leaves of plates: ill.; 18 cm.
Howes no. G77.
Sabin no. 26741.
Shaw/Shoemaker no. 20185.

P149   Gass, Patrick, 1771–1870.
A Journal of the voyages and travels of a corps of discovery
under the command of Capt. Lewis and Capt. Clarke of the
Army of the United States: from the mouth of the river Missouri
through the interior parts of North America to the Pacific Ocean,
during the years 1804, 1805, & 1806 . . . / by Patrick Gass. Philadelphia: Mathew Carey, 1812.
262 p., 6 leaves of plates: ill.; 17 cm.
Howes no. G77.
Sabin no. 26741
Shaw/Shoemaker no. 25498.

P150   Gibson, Charles Dana, b. 1867.
Sketches in Egypt / written and illustrated by Charles Dana Gibson. New York: Doubleday and McClure Co., 1899.
xv, 114 p., 1 plate: ill.; 26 cm.

P151   Gilpin, William, 1724–1804.
Observations on several parts of the counties of Cambridge, Norfolk, Suffolk, and Essex: also on several parts of North Wales relative chiefly to picturesque beauty, in two tours, the former
made in the year 1769, the latter in the year 1733 / by William
Gilpin. London: Printed for T. Cadell and W. Davies, 1809.
x, 208 p., 20 leaves of plates: ill.; 23 cm.

P152 Gilpin, William, 1724–1804.
Observations on the coasts of Hampshire, Sussex, and Kent relative chiefly to picturesque beauty: made in the summer of the
year 1774 / by William Gilpin. London: Printed for T. Cadell and
W. Davies, 1804.
viii, 135 p., 6 leaves of plates: ill.; 23 cm.

P153 Gilpin, William, 1724–1804.
Observations on the river Wye and several parts of South Wales,
&c. relative chiefly to picturesque beauty: made in the summer
of the year 1770 / by William Gilpin. London: Printed for
R. Blamire, 1792.
xvi, 152, 16 leaves of plates: col. ill.; 23 cm.

P154 Gilpin, William, 1724–1804.
Observations on the western parts of England relative chiefly to
picturesque beauty: to which are added a few remarks on the picturesque beauties of the Isle of Wight / by William Gilpin. London: Printed for T. Cadell, Jun., and W. Davies, 1798.
xvi, 359, p., 18 leaves of plates: ill.; 23 cm.

P155 Gilpin, William, 1724–1804.
Remarks on forest scenery and other woodland views (relative
chiefly to picturesque beauty): illustrated by the scenes of New-
Forest in Hampshire / by William Gilpin. London: Printed for
R. Blamire, 1791.
2 v.: ill., map; 23 cm.

P156 Gillette, Martha Hill, b. 1833.
Overland to Oregon and in the Indian wars of 1853: with an
account of earlier life in rural Tennessee. Ashland, Ore.: Lewis
Osborne, 1971.
77, [3] p.: ill., fold. map.; 27 cm.

P157 Goldie, John, 1793–1886.
Diary of a journey through Upper Canada and some of the
New England states, 1819 / by John Goldie. Toronto: William

Tyrrell, 1897.
56 p., 3 leaves of plates: ill.; 20 cm.

P158   [Goodwin, Nathaniel], 1782–1855.
Memorandum of a journey from Hartford to Niagara Falls and
return in 1828: also Hartford to Mendon in 1821. Vineland, N.J.:
F. D. Andrews, 1909.
12 p.; 19 cm.

P159   Greeley, Horace, 1811–72.
Glances at Europe in a series of letters from Great Britain,
France, Italy, Switzerland, &c., during the summer of 1851. New
York: Dewitt and Davenport, 1851.
viii, 350 p.; 19 cm.

P160   [Greene, Asa], 1789–1838.
Travels in America / by George Fibblton, Esq. [pseud.], ex barber
to his Majesty, the King of Great Britain. New York: William
Pearson, Peter Hill, and others, 1833.
216 p.; 20 cm.
Howes no. G376.
Sabin no. 28585.
Shaw/Shoemaker no. 19100.

P161   Gurney, Joseph John, 1788–1847.
A winter in the West Indies described in familiar letters to Henry
Clay of Kentucky / by Joseph John Gurney. London: John Mur-
ray, 1841.
xvi, 282, 12 p., 2 leaves of plates: ill.; 23 cm.
Sabin no. 29312.

P162   Gustorf, Frederick Julius, 1800–1845.
The uncorrupted heart: journal and letters of Frederick Julius
Gustorf, 1800–1845 / edited, with introductory notes by Fred Gustorf; translated from the German by Fred Gustorf and Gisela Gustorf. Columbia: University of Missouri Press, 1969.
viii, [4], 182 p.; 24 cm.

P163 Hadfield, Joseph, 1759–1851.
An Englishman in America, 1785: being the diary of Joseph Hadfield; edited and annotated by Douglas S. Robertson. Toronto: Hunter-Rose Co., 1933.
ix, 232 p., 1 plate: ill.; 24 cm.

P164 Hall, Basil, 1788–1844.
Travels in North America in the years 1827 and 1828 / by Basil Hall. Edinburgh: Printed for R. Cadell; London: Simpkin and Marshall, 1830.
3 v.: ill.; 20 cm.
Howes no. H47.
Sabin no. 29725.

P165 Hall, Francis, d. 1833.
Travels in Canada and the United States in 1816 and 1817 / by Lieut. Francis Hall. Boston: From the London ed. by Wells and Lilly, 1818.
322 p.; 22 cm.
Howes no. H62.
Sabin no. 29769.
Shaw/Shoemaker no. 44223.

P166 Hall, Margaret (Hunter), "Mrs. Basil Hall," 1799–1876.
The aristocratic journey: being the outspoken letters of Mrs. Basil Hall written during a fourteen months' sojourn in America, 1827–1828; prefaced and edited by Una Pope-Hennessy . . . New York; London: Knickerbocker Press, 1931.
vii, 308 p., 13 leaves of plates: ill.; 23 cm.

P167 Hall, Newman, 1816–1902.
From Liverpool to St. Louis / by Rev. Newman Hall. London: George Routledge and Sons [etc.], 1870.
xxv, 294, p., 1 plate: ill.; 18 cm.
Sabin no. 29834.

P168 Hallam, George.
Narrative of a voyage from Montego Bay in the island of Jamaica

to England . . .: across the island of Cuba to Havana; from
thence to Charles Town, South Carolina, Newcastle on the Delaware, and Baltimore, Maryland; and by land to Washington and
back, thence to Philadelphia, and through the Jerseys to New
York where he embarked and made the voyage to Havre-de-
Grace, in France . . . performed in the autumn, 1809 / by G. Hallam . . . London: Printed for C. J. G. and F. Rivington, 1831.
iv, 116 p., 1 fold. plate: ill.; 24 cm.

P169   Hamerton, Philip Gilbert, 1834–94.
The Saône: a summer voyage / by Philip Gilbert Hamerton; with
a hundred and forty-eight illustrations by Joseph Pennell and the
author and four maps. Boston: Roberts Brothers, 1888.
xix, 386 p.: ill., maps; 24 cm.

P170   Hamilton, Alexander, 1712–65.
Hamilton's itinerarium: being a narrative of a journey from
Annapolis, Maryland, through Delaware, Pennsylvania, New
York, New Jersey, Connecticut, Rhode Island, Massachusetts,
and New Hampshire . . . / by Doctor Alexander Hamilton;
edited by Albert Bushnell Hart. St. Louis: William K. Bixby,
1907.
xxvii, 263, [48] p. of plates, 5 leaves of plates: ill., facsims; 24 cm.
Howes no. H125.

P171   [Hamilton, Thomas], 1789–1842.
Men and manners in America / by the author of Cyril Thornton,
etc. . . . Edinburgh: W. Blackwood; London: T. Cadell, 1833.
2 v.; 19 cm.
Howes no. H138.
Sabin no. 30034.

P172   Hamy, Ernest Théodore, 1842–1908.
The travels of the naturalist Charles A. Lesueur in North
America, 1815–1837 / by E. T. Hamy, Milton Haber, translation,
H. F. Raup, ed. Kent, Ohio: Kent State University Press, 1968.
xiii, 96 p., 10 leaves of plates: ill.; 24 cm.

P173 Hardy, Mary (McDowell) Duffus, lady, 1825?–91.
Through cities and prairie lands: sketches of an American tour /
by Lady Duffus Hardy. New York: R. Worthington, 1890.
xii, 338 p.; 20 cm.

P174 Heap, Gwinn Harris.
Central route to the Pacific from the valley of the Mississippi to
California: journal of the expedition of E. F. Beale . . . and
Gwinn Harris Heap from Missouri to California in 1853 / by
Gwinn Harris Heap. Philadelphia: Lippincott, Grambo, [etc.],
1854.
136, 32 p., 14 leaves of plates (1 fold., col.): ill.; 23 cm.
Howes no. H378.
Sabin no. 31175.

P175 Heine, Wilhelm, 1817–85.
Graphic scenes in the Japan expedition / by William Heine . . .
New York: G. P. Putnam, 1856.
10 plates: ill.; 52 cm.

P176 Hennepin, Louis, seventeenth century.
A new discovery of a vast country in America extending above
four thousand miles between New France & New Mexico . . .:
giving an account of the attempts of the sieur de la Salle upon
the mines of St. Barbe &c., the taking of Quebec by the English,
with the advantages of a shorter cut to China and Japan . . . / by
L. Hennepin, now a resident in Holland. London: Henry Bon
wicke, 1699.
2 v. in 1: ill.; 20 cm.
Howes no. H416.
Sabin no. 31372.

P177 Henry, Alexander, 1739–1824.
Alexander Henry's travels and adventures in the years 1760–
1776 / edited with historical introduction and notes by Milo Milton Quaife. Chicago: R. R. Donnelley and Sons Co., 1921.
xxxii, 340 p., 2 leaves of plates (1 fold.): ill.; 18 cm.

P178   Heriot, George, 1759–1839.
           Travels through the Canadas: containing a description of the pic-
           turesque scenery on some of the rivers and lakes . . . / by
           George Heriot, Esq. London: Richard Phillips, 1807.
           xii, 602 p., 28 leaves of plates (some fold., col.): ill.; 28 cm.
           Sabin no. 31489.

P179   Hillard, George Stillman, 1808–79.
           Six months in Italy / by George Stillman Hillard. Boston: Tick-
           nor, Reed and Fields, 1854.
           2 v.; 19 cm.

P180   Hodges, William, 1744–97.
           Travels in India during the years 1780, 1781, 1782, & 1783 / by
           William Hodges. London: Printed for the author and sold by
           J. Edwards, 1793.
           vi, 156 p., 1 fold. plate: ill.; 30 cm.

P181   Hodgson, Adam.
           Letters from North America written during a tour in the United
           States and Canada . . . / by Adam Hodgson. London: Hurst,
           Robinson, 1824.
           2 v.: ill. (fold. map); 23 cm.
           Sabin no. 32357.

P182   Houel, Jean Pierre Louis Laurent, 1735–1813.
           Voyage pittoresque des isles de Sicile, de Malte et de Lipari, où
           l'on traite des antiquités qui s'y trouvent encore . . . / par Jean
           Houel, peintre du roi. Paris: Imprimerie de Monsieur, 1782–87.
           4 v.: ill., maps, plans; 52 x 34 cm.

P183   Howells, William Dean, 1837–1920.
           Venetian life / by William Dean Howells; with illustrations from
           original water colors. Cambridge: Printed at the Riverside Press,
           1892.
           2 v.: col. ill.; 20 cm.

P184   Huc, Evfariste Régis, 1813–60.
The Chinese empire: forming a sequel to the work entitled "Recollections of a journey through Tartary and Thibet" / by M. Huc. London: Longman, Brown, Green, and Longmans, 1855.
2 v.: map; 23 cm.

P185   Hunter, Robert, 1764–1843.
Quebec to Carolina in 1785–1786: being the travel diary and observations of Robert Hunter, Jr., a young merchant of London / edited by Louis B. Wright and Marion Tinling. San Marino, Calif.: Huntington Library, 1943.
ix, 393 p.; 24 cm.

P186   Huret, Jules, 1864–1915.
En Amérique: New York à la Nouvelle-Orléans. Paris: Bibliothèque-Charpentier, 1904.
420 p.; 19 cm.

P187   James, Edwin, 1797–1861.
Account of an expedition from Pittsburgh to the Rocky Mountains performed in the years 1819 and 20: by order of the Honourable John C. Calhoun, Secretary of War . . . / compiled by Edwin James. Philadelphia: H. C. Carey and I. Lea, 1823.
2 v.: ill.; 31 cm.
Howes no. J41.
Sabin no. 35682.
Shaw/Shoemaker no. 12942.

P188   James, Edwin, 1797–1861.
Account of an expedition from Pittsburgh to the Rocky Mountains performed in the years 1819 and 1820: by order of the Hon. J. C. Calhoun, Secretary of War, under the command of Maj. S. H. Long of the U.S. Top. Engineers / compiled from the notes of Major Long, Mr. T. Say, and other gentlemen of the party by Edwin James . . . London: Printed for Longman, Hurst, Rees, Orme, and Brown, 1823.
3 v.: ill. (some col.); 23 cm.

Howes no. J41.
Sabin no. 35683.

P189   Janin, Jules Gabriel, 1804–74.
        The American in Paris / by M. Jules Janin; illustrations by eigh-
        teen engravings from designs by M. Eugene Lami. London:
        Longman, Brown, Green, and Longmans; New York: Appleton
        and Son, 1843.
        vii, 256 p., 18 leaves of plates: ill.; 23 cm.

P190   Janson, Charles William.
        The stranger in America: containing observations made during
        a long residence in that country . . . London: Printed for
        J. Cundee, 1807.
        499 p., 12 leaves of plates: ill.; 28 cm.
        Howes no. J59.
        Sabin no. 35770.

P191   Jarves, James Jackson, 1820–88.
        Italian rambles: studies of life and manners in new and old
        Italy / by James Jackson Jarves . . . New York: G. P. Putman's
        Sons, 1883.
        iv, 446 p.; 16 cm.

P192   Jonveaux, Emile, 1819–71.
        L'Amérique actuelle / par Emile Jonveaux, précédé d'une intro-
        duction par Edouard Laboulaye. Paris: Charpentier et cie, 1870.
        xvi, 339 p.; 19 cm.
        Sabin no. 36638.

P193   Josselyn, John, w. 1630–75.
        An account of two voyages to New-England made during the
        years 1638, 1663 / by John Josselyn, gent. Boston: William Vea-
        zie, 1865.
        [5], vii, 211 p.; 25 cm.
        Howes no. J254.

P194 Kalm, Pehr, 1716–79.
Travels into North America: containing its natural history and a circumstantial account of its plantations and agriculture in general . . . London: T. Lowndes, 1772.
2 v.: ill.; 22 cm.
Howes no. K5.
Sabin no. 36989.

P195 Kane, Paul, 1810–71.
Wanderings of an artist among the Indians of North America . . . / by Paul Kane. London: Longman, Brown, Green, Longmans, and Roberts, 1859.
xvii, 455, [6] p., 9 leaves of plates (1 fold.): ill.; 23 cm.
Howes no. K7.
Sabin no. 37007.

P196 Keating, William Hypolitus, 1799–1840.
Narrative of an expedition to the source of St. Peter's River, Lake Winnepeek, Lake of the Woods . . .: performed in the year 1823 . . . under the command of Stephen H. Long, major U. S. T. E. / compiled from the notes of Major Long, Messrs. Say, Keating, and Calhoun by William H. Keating . . . Philadelphia: H. C. Carey and I. Lea, 1824.
2 v.: ill.; 23 cm.
Howes no. K20.
Sabin no. 37137.
Shaw/Shoemaker no. 16763.

P197 Kendall, Edward Augustus, 1776?–1842.
Travels through the northern parts of the United States in the years 1807 and 1808 / by Edward Augustus Kendall. New York: I. Riley, 1809.
3 v.; 22 cm.
Howes no. K74.
Sabin no. 37358.
Shaw/Shoemaker no. 17862.

P198   King, Edward, 1848–96.
The great South: a record of journeys in Louisiana, Texas, the
Indian Territory, Missouri, Arkansas, Mississippi, Alabama,
Georgia, Florida, South Carolina, North Carolina, Kentucky, Ten-
nessee, Virginia, West Virginia, and Maryland / by Edward King
. . . Hartford, Conn.: American Publishing Co., 1875.
802, iv p.: ill.; 26 cm.
Clark, *New South*, vol. 1, no. 120.
Howes no. K149.

P199   Kinzie, Juliette Augusta (Magill), "Mrs. John H. Kinzie,"
1806–70.
Wau-bun, the "early day" in the North-west / by Mrs. John H.
Kinzie. New York: Derby and Jackson; Cincinnati, H. W. Derby,
1856.
498 p., 6 leaves of plates: ill.; 23 cm.
Howes no. K171.
Sabin no. 37941.

P200   Kircher, Athanasius, 1602–80.
Athanasii Kircheri e Soc. Jesu China monumentis, quà sacris quà
profanis, nec non variis naturæ & artis spectaculis, aliarumque
rerum memorabilium argumentis illustrata, auspiciis Leopoldi
Primi roman, imper. . . . Amstelodami: apud Joannem Jansson-
ium à Waesberge & Elizeum Weyerstraet, 1667.
[14], 237, [11] p., 29 leaves of plates: ill.; 32 cm.

P201   Klinckowström, Axel Leonhard, friherre, 1775–1837.
Baron Klinkowström's America, 1818–1820 / translated and
edited by Franklin D. Scott from the Swedish ed., Bref om de
Förenta Staterna, författade under en resa till Amerika åren 1818,
1819, 1820 af Friherre Axel Klinkowström. Evanston, Ill.: Northwestern University Press, 1952.
xiv, 262 p., 1 plate: ill.; 24 cm.

P202   Klinckowström, Axel Leonhard, friherre, 1775–1837.
Bref om de Förenta Staterna, författade under en resa till Amerika, åren 1818, 1819, 1820 / af friherre Axel Klinkowström. Stock-

holm: Ecksteinska, 1824.
2 v.: ill.; 21 cm.
Howes no. K201.
Sabin no. 38053.

P203	Knapp, Samuel Lorenzo, 1783–1838.
Extracts from a journal of travels in North America: consisting of
an account of Boston and its vicinity / by Ali Bey [pseud.]. Bos-
ton: Printed by Thomas Badger, Jun., 1818.
124 p.; 19 cm.
Howes no. K210.
Shaw/Shoemaker no. 44525.
Sabin no. 38071.

P204	Knight, Sarah Kemble, 1666–1727.
The journal of Madam Knight / with an introductory note by
George Parker Winship. New York: Peter Smith, 1935.
xiv, 72 p., 1 fold. plate: ill.; 21 cm.

P205	Koch, Albert C., 1804–67.
Journey through a part of the United States of North America in
the years 1844 to 1846 / by Albert C. Koch; translated and edited
by Ernst A. Stadler; foreword by John Francis McDermott. Car-
bondale: Southern Illinois University Press, 1972.
xxxv, 177 p., 26 leaves of plates: ill.; 23 cm.

P206	[Kriebel, Howard Wiegner].
Seeing Lancaster County from a trolley window. Lancaster, Pa.:
Conestoga Traction Co., [1910].
80, [16] p., ill.; 25 cm.

P207	Kurz, Rudolph Friedrich, 1818–71.
Journal of Rudolph Friedrich Kurz: an account of his experiences
among fur traders and American Indians on the Mississippi and
the upper Missouri rivers during the years 1846 to 1852; translated by Myrtis Jarrell, edited by J. N. B. Hewitt. Washington,
D.C.: Government Printing Office, 1937.

ix, 382 p., 48 leaves of plates: ill.; 23 cm.
Howes no. K281.

P208   Laboulaye, Edouard, 1811–83.
        Paris in America / by Dr. René Lefebvre . . . (Edouard Labou-
        laye); translated by Mary L. Booth. New York: Charles Scribner,
        1863.
        373, x p.; 19 cm.
        Sabin no. 38440.

P209   La Farge, John, 1835–1910.
        Reminiscences of the South Seas / by John La Farge . . . with 48
        illustrations from paintings and drawings made by the author in
        1890–91. Garden City, N.Y.: Doubleday, Page, 1912.
        480 p., 48 leaves of plates (some col.): ill.; 25 cm.

P210   Lahontan, Louis Armand de Lom D'Arce, baron de, 1666–1715?
        Nouveaux voyages de mr. le baron de Lahontan dans l'Amer-
        ique Septentrionale: qui contiennent une relation des differens
        peuples qui y habitent, la nature de leur governement, leur com-
        merce, leur coûtume, leur religion, & leur manier de faire la
        guerre . . . A La Haye: chez les Freres l'Honoré, 1704.
        2 v. in 1: ill.; 17 cm.
        Howes no. L25.
        Sabin no. 38639.

P211   Lakier, Aleksandr Borisovich, 1825–70.
        A Russian looks at America: the journey of Aleksandr Borisovich
        Lakier in 1857 / translated from the Russian and edited by
        Arnold Schrier, Joyce Story; foreword by Henry Steele Com-
        mager; introduction by Arnold Schrier. Chicago: University of
        Chicago Press, 1979.
        xli, 272 p., 32 leaves of plates: ill.; 24 cm.

P212   Lamb, Joseph, 1833–98.
        A voyage to the gardens of the Hesperides / by Joseph Lamb;
        being a series of letters written while on a voyage to the Azores,

Portugal, and Spain in the year 1895. New York: Printed privately for F. S. Lamb by H. Roberts Northrop, [1895?].
195 p., 4 leaves of plates: ill.; 28 cm.

P213   Lambert, John, w. 1811.
Travels through Canada and the United States of North America in the years 1806, 1807, & 1808; to which are added biographical notices and anecdotes of some of the leading characters in the United States / by John Lambert. London: Printed for C. Cradock and W. Joy [etc.] 1813.
2 v.: ill.; 22 cm.
Howes no. L40.
Sabin no. 38734.

P214   Lanman, Charles, 1819–95.
Letters from the Alleghany Mountains / by Charles Lanman.
New York: G. P. Putnam, 1849.
198, 31 p.; 20 cm.
Howes no. L89.
Sabin no. 38921.

P215   La Rochefoucauld-Liancourt, François Alexandre Frédéric, duc de, 1747–1827.
Journal de voyage en Amérique et d'un séjour a Philadelphie, 1 octobre 1794–18 avril 1795 / [par] duc de Liancourt (La Rochefoucauld-Liancourt); avec des lettres et des notes sur la Conspiration de Pichegru . . . publié avec une introduction et des notes par Jean Marchand. Baltimore: Johns Hopkins Press, 1940.
157 p., 7 leaves of plates.: ill.; 27 cm.

P216   La Rochefoucauld Liancourt, François Alexandre Frédéric, duc de, 1747–1827.
Travels through the United States of North America, the country of the Iroquois, and Upper Canada in the years 1795, 1796, and 1797 . . . / by the Duke de La Rochefoucauld Liancourt . . . London: R. Phillips, 1799.
2 v., ill.; 28 cm.
Sabin no. 39057.

P217   Latrobe, Charles Joseph, 1801–75.
The rambler in North America / by Charles Joseph Latrobe. London: R. B. Seeley and W. Burnside, 1836.
2 v.; 21 cm.
Howes no. L127.
Sabin no. 39222.

P218   Lawrence, Amos, 1786–1852.
Extracts from the diary and correspondence of the late Amos Lawrence: with a brief account of some incidents in his life / edited by his son, William R. Lawrence. Boston: Gould and Lincoln; New York: Sheldon, Lamport and Blakeman; London: Trubner, 1856.
viii, 369, [8] p., 3 leaves of plates: ill.; 21 cm.
Sabin no. 39384.

P219   Le Comte, Louis, 1655–1728.
Memoirs and observations: topographical, physical, mathematical, mechanical, naval, civil, and ecclesiastical; made in a late journey through the empire of China and published in several letters / by Louis Le Comte; translated from the Paris ed. and illustrated with figures. London: Printed for Benj. Tooke, 1698.
[20], 517, [10] p., 6 leaves of plates (some fold.): ill.; 20 cm.

P220   [Lees, John], w. 1764.
Journal of J. L. of Quebec, merchant. Detroit: Society of Colonial Wars of the State of Michigan, 1911.
55 p., 2 leaves of plates: col. ill.; 24 cm.

P221   Leoni, Pietro.
Les merueilles de la ville de Rome: où est traité des eglises, stations, & reliques des corps saints qui y sont; avec la guide qui enseigne aux estrangers à aysement trouver les choses plus remarquables de Rome . . . Rome: Chez Bernabo, 1725.
[5], 216 p., 1 plate: ill.; 18 cm.

P222   Leslie, Miriam Florence (Folline) Squier, d.1914.
California: a pleasure trip from Gotham to the Golden Gate,

April, May, June 1877 / [by] Mrs. Frank Leslie. Nieuwkoop, Netherlands: B. De Graaf, 1972.
xxiv, 6, 286, [2] p., 23 leaves of plates: ill.; 18 cm.

P223 Lesseps, Jean Baptiste Barthélemy, baron de, 1766–1834.
Journal historique du voyage de M. de Lesseps . . .: dans l'expédition de M. le comte de la Pérouse . . . depuis l'instant où il a quitté les frégates françoises au port Saint-Pierre & Saint-Paul du Kamtschatka, jusqu'à son arrivée en France le 17 octobre 1788 . . . Paris: Imprimerie Royale, 1790.
2 v.: ill., maps; 21 cm.
Howes no. L270.
Sabin no. 40208.

P224 [Letts, John M].
California illustrated: including a description of the Panama and Nicaragua routes / by a returned Californian. New York: W. Holdredge, 1852.
224 p.: ill.; 23 cm.
Howes no. L300.

P225 Lewis, Henry, 1819–1904.
Das illustrirte Mississippithal: dargestellt in 80 nach der Natur aufgenommenen Ansichten vom Wasserfalle zu St. Anthony an bis zum Gulf von Mexico . . . / von H. Lewis . . . Nebst einer historischen und geographischen Beschreibung der den Fluss begränzenden Länder, mit besonderer Rückksicht auf die verschiedenen den obern Mississippi bewohnenden Indianer Stämme. Düsseldorf: Arnz, [1857].
431 p., 80 leaves of plates (1 fold.): col. ill.; 28 cm. Howes no. L312.
Sabin no. 40807.

P226 Lewis, Henry, 1819–1904.
Making a motion picture in 1848 by Henry Lewis' journal of a canoe voyage from the falls of St. Anthony to St. Louis / with an introduction and notes by Bertha L. Heilbron. Saint Paul: Minne-

sota Historical Society, 1936.
4, 58 p., 14 leaves of plates: ill.; 24 cm.

P227   Lewis, Matthew Gregory, 1775–1818.
        Journal of a West-India proprietor: kept during a residence in the
        island of Jamaica / by the late Matthew Gregory Lewis. London:
        J. Murray, 1834.
        [8], 408 p.; 23 cm.
        Sabin no. 40821.

P228   Lewis, Meriwether, 1774–1809.
        Original journals of the Lewis and Clark Expedition, 1804–1806:
        printed from the original manuscripts in the library of the Ameri-
        can Philosophical Society . . . / edited with introduction, notes,
        and index by Reuben Gold Thwaites . . . New York: Antiquarian
        Press, 1959.
        8 v.: ill., maps; 24 cm.

P229   Lieber, Francis, 1800–1872.
        Letters to a gentleman in Germany written after a trip from Phila-
        delphia to Niagara / edited by Francis Lieber. Philadelphia:
        Carey, Lea and Blanchard, 1834.
        356 p.; 26 cm.
        Sabin no. 40978.
        Shaw/Shoemaker no. 25336.

P230   Lieber, Francis, 1800–1872.
        The stranger in America: comprising sketches of the manners,
        society, and national peculiarities of the United States in a series
        of letters to a friend in Europe / by Francis Lieber. London:
        R. Bentley, 1835.
        2 v.; 20 cm.
        Sabin no. 40984.
        Shaw/Shoemaker no. 32607.

P231   Lincklaen, John, 1768–1822.
        Travels in the years 1791 and 1792 in Pennsylvania, New York,
        and Vermont: journals of John Lincklaen, agent of the Holland

Land Company with a biographical sketch and notes. New York;
London: G. P. Putnam's Sons, 1897.
xi, 162, 6 leaves of plates (some fold.): ill.; 22 cm.

P232 Louis Philippe, King of France, 1773–1850.
Diary of my travels in America / Louis-Philippe, King of France,
1830–1848; translated from the French by Stephen Becker. New
York: Delacorte Press, 1977.
202 p., 15 leaves of plates: ill.; 20 x 28 cm.

P233 Luden, Heinrich, 1778–1847.
Reise Sr. Hoheit des Herzogs Bernhard zu Sachsen-Weimar-
Eisenach durch Nord-Amerika in den Jahren 1825 und 1826 /
Herausgegeben von Heinrich Luden . . . Weimar, Ger.: Wilhelm
Hoffman, 1828.
2 v.: ill.; 23 cm.
Sabin no. 4953.

P234 Lyell, Charles, Sir, 1797–1875.
A second visit to the United States of North America / by Sir
Charles Lyell . . . New York: Harper and Brothers; London:
J. Murray, 1849.
2 v.: ill.; 20 cm.
Howes no. L574.
Sabin no. 42763

P235 Lyell, Charles, Sir, 1797–1875.
Travels in North America: with geological observations on the
United States, Canada, and Nova Scotia / by Charles Lyell. Lon-
don: John Murray, 1845.
2 v.: ill., maps; 21 cm.
Howes no. L575.
Sabin no. 42761.

P236 Lynch, Jeremiah, 1849–1917.
Three years in Klondike / by Jeremiah Lynch; edited by Dale L.
Morgan. Chicago: R. R. Donnelley and Sons Co., 1967.
lvi, 375 p., 10 leaves of plates: ill.; 18 cm.

P237   Macdonald, Donald, 1791–1872.
        The diaries of Donald Macdonald, 1824–1826 / with an introduc-
        tion by Caroline Dale Snedeker. Indianapolis: Indiana Historical
        Society, 1942.
        p. 147–379 ; 24 cm.

P238   MacDougall, Sylvia (Borgström)
        A summer tour in Finland / by Paul Waineman [pseud.]; with six-
        teen illustrations in colour by Alexander Federley and sixteen
        other illustrations. London: Methuen, 1908.
        xvi, 318, [30] p., 32 leaves of plates: ill. (some col.); 23 cm.

P239   M'Ilvaine, William, 1813–67.
        Sketches of scenery and notes of personal adventure in Califor-
        nia and Mexico / by William M'Ilvaine, Jr. Philadelphia: Smith
        and Peters, 1850.
        44 p., 16 leaves of plates: ill.; 26 cm.
        Howes no. M112.
        Sabin no. 43328.

P240   MacKay, Alexander, 1808–52.
        The western world; or, Travels in the United States in 1846–47
        . . . / by Alex MacKay. London: R. Bentley, 1851.
        3 v.: ill.; 20 cm.
        Howes no. M117.

P241   Mackay, Charles, 1814–89.
        Life and liberty in America; or, Sketches of a tour in the United
        States and Canada in 1857–8 / by Charles Mackay . . . London:
        Smith, Elder, [1859].
        2 v. in 1: ill.; 20 cm.
        Howes no. M118.
        Sabin no. 43355.

P242   McKenney, Thomas Loraine, 1785–1859.
        History of the Indian tribes of North America: with biographical
        sketches and anecdotes of the principal chiefs . . . / by Thomas

L. M'Kenney and James Hall. Philadelphia: F. W. Greenough [etc.], 1838–44.
3 v.: col. ill.; 52 cm.
Howes no. M129.
Sabin no. 43410a.
Shaw/Shoemaker no. 51414.

P243 McKenney, Thomas Loraine, 1785–1859.
Sketches of a tour to the lakes, of the character and customs of the Chippeway Indians, and of incidents connected with the Treaty of Fond du Lac . . . / by Thomas L. McKenney. Minneapolis: Ross and Haines, 1959.
viii, 493 p.: ill.; 22 cm.

P244 M'Robert, Patrick.
A tour through part of the northern provinces of America: being a series of letters wrote on the spot in the years 1774 & 1775 . . . / by Patrick M'Robert. Philadelphia: Historical Society of Pennsylvania, 1935.
x, 47 p.; 25 cm.

P245 Manning, Samuel, 1822–81.
American pictures drawn with pen and pencil / by the Rev. Samuel Manning. [London]: Religious Tract Society, [1876]
224 p., 24 leaves of plates: ill.; 29 cm.

P246 Marcy, Randolph Barnes, 1812–87.
Exploration of the Red River of Louisiana in the year 1852 / by Randolph B. Marcy . . . Washington, D.C.: Beverly Tucker, 1854.
xv, 310 p., 65 leaves of plates (1 fold.): ill. (1 col.); 24 cm.
Howes no. M276.
Sabin no. 44512.

P247 Marryat, Frank, 1826–55.
Mountains and molehills; or, Recollections of a burnt journal / by Frank Marryat. London: Longman, Brown, Green and Longmans, 1855.
x, 443 p., 8 leaves of plates: ill.(col.); 22 cm.

Howes no. M299.
Sabin no. 44695.

P248   Marryat, Frederick, 1792–1848.
        A diary in America: with remarks on its institutions by Capt.
        Marryat. Philadelphia: Carey and Hart, 1839.
        2 v.; 20 cm.
        Howes no. M300.
        Sabin no. 44696.
        Shaw/Shoemaker no. 57056.

P249   Marryat, Frederick, 1792–1848.
        A diary in America: with remarks on its institutions / [by Frederick Marryat]. London: Longman, Orne, Brown, Green and Longmans, 1839.
        3 v. in 6 pts.; 20 cm.
        Sabin no. 44696.

P250   Marryat, Frederick, 1792–1848.
        A diary in America: with remarks on its institutions / by Capt.
        Marryat. Paris: Baudry, 1840.
        2 v.; 24 cm.
        Sabin no. 44696.

P251   Martineau, Harriet, 1802–76.
        Retrospect of western travel / by Harriet Martineau. London:
        Saunders and Otley; New York: Sold by Harper and Brothers,
        1838.
        2 v.; 21 cm.
        Howes no. M348.
        Sabin no. 44940

P252   Mayer, Frank Blackwell, 1827–99.
        With pen and pencil on the frontier in 1851: the diary and
        sketches of Frank Blackwell Mayer / edited with an introduction
        and notes by Bertha L. Heilbron. Saint Paul: Minnesota Historical Society, 1932.
        xii, 214 p.: ill.; 21 cm.

P253   Mazzei, Filippo, 1730–1816.
Recherches historiques et politiques sur les Etats-Unis de l'Amérique Septentrionale: où l'on traite des établissemens des treize
colonies, de leurs rapports & de leurs dissentions avec la
Grande-Bretagne, de leurs gouvernemens avant & après la révo-
lution &c. / par un citoyen de Virginie; avec quatre lettres d'un
bourgeois de New Heaven [Condorcet] sur l'unité de la législa-
tion . . . A Colle, et se trouve a Paris: chez Froullé, 1788.
4 v. in 2; 21 cm.
Howes no. M456.
Sabin no. 47206.

P254   Meares, John, 1756?–1809.
Voyages made in the years 1788 and 1789 from China to the
north west coast of America: to which are prefixed an introductory narrative of a voyage performed in 1786 from Bengal in the
ship Nootka; observations on the probable existence of a North
West Passage . . . / by John Meares. London: Printed at the Logo-
graphic Press, 1790.
viii, [12], xcv, 372, [108]p.: ill.; 31 cm.
Howes no. M469.
Sabin no. 47260.

P255   Melish, John, 1771–1822.
Travels through the United States of America in the years 1806 &
1807, and 1809, 1810, & 1811: including an account of passages
betwixt America and Britain and travels through various parts of
Britain, Ireland, & Canada . . . / by John Melish. Philadelphia:
John Melish, 1815.
Howes no. M496.
Shaw/Shoemaker no. 35249.

P256   Michaux, François André, 1770–1855.
Travels to the west of the Alleghany Mountains in the states of
Ohio, Kentucky, and Tennessee and back to Charleston by the
upper Carolinas . . . / by François André Michaux. London:
Printed by D. N. Shury, for B. Crosby and J. P. Hughes, 1805.

xii, 294 p.; 23 cm.
Sabin no. 48705.

P257   Michaux, François André, 1770–1855.
        Voyage à l'Ouest des Monts Alléghanys dans les états de l'Ohio,
        du Kentucky, et du Tennessée, et retour à Charleston par les
        Hautes-Carolines / par F. A. Michaux. Paris: Chez Levrault,
        Schoell, v., 312 p., 1 plate: fold. map; 20 cm. 1804.
        Howes no. M579.
        Sabin no. 48703.

P258   Milbert, Jacques Gérard, 1766–1840.
        Picturesque itinerary of the Hudson River and the peripheral
        parts of North America / by J. Milbert. Ridgewood, N.J.: Gregg
        Press, [1968?]
        xxviii, 308 p.: ill.; 27 cm.

P259   Mittelberger, Gottlieb.
        Gottlieb Mittelbergers Reise nach Pennsylvanien im Jahr 1750
        und Rückreise nach Teutschland im Jahr 1754. Stuttgard, Ger.:
        Gedruckt bey Gottlieb Friderich Jenisch, 1756.
        [8], 120 p.; 18 cm.
        Howes no. M705.
        Sabin no. 49761.

P260   Mohr, Nicolaus, 1826–86.
        Excursion through America / by Nicolaus Mohr; edited by Ray
        Allen Billington. Chicago: R. R. Donnelley and Sons Co., 1973.
        lxxvi, 398 p.: ill.; 18 cm.

P261   Möllhausen, Balduin, 1825–1905.
        Diary of a journey from the Mississippi to the coasts of the
        Pacific / by Balduin Möllhausen. New York; London: Johnson
        Reprint Corp., 1969.
        2 v.: ill.; 22 cm.

P262 Möllhausen, Balduin, 1825–1905.
Reisen in die Felsengebirge Nord-Amerikas bis zum Hoch-
Plateau von Neu-Mexico: unternommen als Mitglied der im Auf-
trage der Regierung der Vereinigten Staaten ausgesandten
Colorado-Expedition / von Balduin Möllhausen . . . Eingeführt
durch zwei Briefe Alexander von Humboldt's in facsimile. Leipzig: Hermann Costenoble, Otto Porfürst, [1861].
2 v.: col. ill.; 21 cm.
Howes no. M712.

P263 Möllhausen, Balduin, 1825–1905.
Tagebuch einer Reise vom Mississippi nach den Küsten der
Südsee / von Balduin Möllhausen; Eingeführt von Alexander von
Humboldt . . . Leipzig: Hermann Mendelssohn, 1858.
6, xiv, viii, 494 p., 14 leaves of plates: col. ill.; 31 cm.
Howes no. M713.
Sabin no. 49914.

P264 Montfaucon, Bernard de, 1655–1741.
The travels of the learned Father Montfaucon from Paris thro'
Italy: containing I. an account of many antiquities at Vienna,
Arlels, Nimes, and Marseilles in France.; II. the delights of Italy,
viz. libraries, manuscripts, statues, paintings, monuments,
tombs . . . London: Printed by D. L. for E. Curll [etc.], 1712.
vii, xv, 463 p., 5 leaves of plates: ill.; 20 cm.

P265 Montulé, Edouard de.
Travels in America, 1816–1817 / Edouard de Montulé; translated
from the original French edition of 1821 by Edward D. Seeber.
Bloomington: Indiana University Press, 1951.
197 p., 18 leaves of plates: ill.; 26 cm.

P266 Moore, Nathaniel Fish, 1782–1872.
Diary: a trip from New York to the Falls of St. Anthony in 1845 /
edited by Stanley Pargellis and Ruth Lapham Butler. Chicago:
For the Newberry Library by the University of Chicago Press,
1946.
xviii, 101 p., 8 leaves of plates: ill.; 21 cm.

P267   Moreau, F. Frédéric.
Aux Etats-Unis: notes de voyage . . . / par F. Frédéric Moreau;
avec un croquis de l'auteur. Paris: E. Plon, Nourrit, 1888.
263 p., 1 plate: ill.; 19 cm.

P268   Moreau de Saint-Méry, Frédéric Louis Elie, 1750–1819.
Moreau de St. Méry's American journey [1793–98] / translated
and edited by Kenneth Roberts [and] Anna M. Roberts. Garden
City, N.Y.: Doubleday, 1947.
xxi, 394, [8] p., 1 plate: ill.; 24 cm.

P269   Morley, Frank Vigor, b. 1899.
Travels in East Anglia / by F. V. Morley. New York: Harcourt,
Brace, [1923].
xi, 254 p., 16 leaves of plates: ill. (some col.); 20 cm.

P270   Moss, Fletcher, 1843–1919.
Pilgrimages to old homes / by Fletcher Moss. Didsbury, Eng.: By
the author, 1906.
xii, 392, p., 1 plate: ill.; 27 cm.

P271   Moss, Fletcher, 1843–1919.
Pilgrimages to old homes mostly on the Welsh border / by
Fletcher Moss. Didsbury, Eng.: By the author, 1903.
xx, 405, p., 1 plate: ill.; 27 cm.

P272   Muir, John, 1838–1914.
Travels in Alaska / by John Muir. Boston: Houghton Mifflin Co.,
1915.
xiii, 327 p., 12 leaves of plates: ill.; 21 cm.

P273   Murray, Amelia Matilda, 1795–1884.
Letters from the United States, Cuba and Canada / by the Hon.
Amelia M. Murray. New York: Putnam, 1856.
2 v. in 1; 20 cm.
Howes no. M912.
Sabin no. 51486.

P274 Murray, Charles Augustus, Sir, 1806–95.
Travels in North America during the years 1834, 1835 & 1836
. . . / by the Hon. Charles Augustus Murray. New York: Harper
and Brothers, 1839.
2 v.; 19 cm.
Howes no. M913.
Sabin no. 51491.
Shaw/Shoemaker no. 57387.

P275 Myers, J. C.
Sketches on a tour through the northern and eastern states, the
Canadas, & Nova Scotia / by J. C. Myers. Harrisonburg, Va.:
J. H. Wartmann and Brothers, 1849.
475 p.; 16 cm.
Howes no. M932.

P276 [Nason, Daniel].
A journal of a tour from Boston to Savannah: thence to Havana
in the island of Cuba . . . thence to New Orleans and several
western cities . . . / by a citizen of Cambridgeport. Cambridge:
Printed for the author, 1849.
114 p.; 16 cm.
Sabin no. 51881.

P277 [Nicklin, Philip Holbrook], 1786–1842.
A pleasant peregrination through the prettiest parts of Pennsylva-
nia / performed by Peregrine Prolix [pseud.]. Philadelphia: Grigg
and Elliott, 1836.
148 p.; 16 cm.
Howes no. N149.
Sabin no. 55237.
Shaw/Shoemaker no. 39295.

P278 Nieuhof, Johan, 1618–72.
Atlas Chinensis: being a second part of a relation of remarkable passages in two embassies from the East-India Company of
the United Provinces to the Vice-Roy Singlamong and General
Taising Lipovi, and to Konchi, Emperor of China and East-

Tartary . . . / by A. Montanus; English'd . . . by J. Ogilby, etc.
London: printed by Tho. Johnson for the author, 1671.
2 v.: ill.; 20 cm.
723 p.: ill., fold.map; 42 cm.

P279   Nieuhof, Johan, 1618–72.
An embassy from the East-India Company of the United Provinces to the Grand Tartar Cham, emperour of China: delivered
by their excellcies Peter de Goyer and Jacob de Keyzer at his
Imperial city of Peking; wherein the towns, villages, ports, rivers, &c. in their passages from Canton to Peking are ingeniously
described / by Mr. John Nieuhoff; with an appendix of several
remarks taken out of Father Athanasius Kircher; Englished and
set forth with their several sculptures by John Ogilby. London:
Printed by John Macock for the author, 1669.
327 (i.e. 307), 18, 106 p.: ill.; 42 cm.

P280   Norden, Frederick Ludvig, 1708–41.
Travels in Egypt and Nubia / by Frederick Lewis Norden . . . ;
translated from the original . . . and enlarged with observations
from ancient and modern authors . . . by Dr. Peter Templeman.
London: Printed for Lockyer Davis and Charles Reymers, 1757.
2 v. in 1: ill.; 47 cm.

P281   Norwood, Henry, fl. 1649.
A voyage to Virginia / by Colonel Norwood. [London: s.n., ca.
1732]
50 p.; 25 cm.
Clark, *Old South*, vol. 1, no. 130.
Sabin no. 55933.

P282   Nuttall, Thomas, 1766–1859.
A journal of travels into the Arkansas territory during the year
1819: with occasional observations of the manners of the aborigi-
nes / by Thomas Nuttall. Philadelphia: T. H. Palmer, 1821.
296 p., 6 leaves of plates: ill., fold. map; 23 cm.
Clark, *Old South*, vol. 2, no. 48.
Howes no. N229.

Sabin no. 56348.
Shaw/Shoemaker no. 6319.

P283 O'Donovan, Jeremiah.
A brief account of the author's interview with his countrymen
and of the parts of the Emerald Isle whence they emigrated . . . /
by Jeremiah O'Donovan. Pittsburgh: By the author, 1864.
382 p., 20 cm.
Howes no. O24.

P284 O'Ferrall, Simon Ansley, d. 1844.
A ramble of six thousand miles through the United States of
America / by S. A. Ferrall. London: Effingham Wilson, 1832.
xii, 360, 16 p., 1 plate: ill.; 22 cm.

P285 Oliver, William.
Eight months in Illinois / William Oliver. Ann Arbor, Mich.: University Microfilms, [1966].
iv, 141 p.; 17 cm.

P286 Olliffe, Charles.
American scenes: eighteen months in the New World / translated with introduction and notes by Ernest Falbo [and] Lawrence A. Wilson. Painesville, Ohio: Lake Erie College Press,
1964.
xiii, 143 p.: ill.; 23 cm.

P287 Olmsted, Frederick Law, 1822–1903.
A journey in the back country / by Frederick Law Olmsted. New
York: Burt Franklin, 1970.
xvi, [11], 492 p.; 23 cm.

P288 Olmsted, Frederick Law, 1822–1903.
A journey through Texas; or, A saddle-trip on the south-western
frontier; with a statistical appendix / by Frederick Law Olmsted
. . . New York: Dix, Edwards; London: S. Low, Son, 1857.
xxxiv, 516 p., 2 leaves of plates (1 fold.): ill.; 19 cm.

Howes no. O79.
Sabin no. 57243.

P289 Ossoli, Sarah Margaret (Fuller), marchesa d', 1810–50.
Summer on the lakes in 1843 (1844) / Margaret Fuller. Nieuwkoop: B. De Graaf, 1972.
xxxv, 256 p., 8 leaves of plates: ill.; 18 cm.

P290 Palmer, John, fl. 1818.
Journal of travels in the United States of North America and in
Lower Canada performed in the year 1817 . . . / by John Palmer.
London: Printed for Sherwood, Neely, and Jones, 1818.
vii, 456, 8 p., 1 fold. plate: ill.; 22 cm.
Howes no. P49.
Sabin no. 58360.

P291 Parker, Samuel, 1779–1866.
Journal of an exploring tour beyond the Rocky Mountains under
the direction of the A. B. C. F. M.: performed in the years 1835,
'36, and '37 . . . / by Rev. Samuel Parker. Ithaca, N.Y.: By the
author, 1838.
371 p., 2 leaves of plates (1 fold.): ill.; 20 cm.
Howes no. P89.
Sabin no. 58729.
Shaw/Shoemaker no. 52133.

P292 Parkinson, Richard, 1748–1815.
A tour in America in 1798, 1799, and 1800 . . . / by Richard Par-
kinson. London: Printed for J. Harding [etc.], 1805.
2 v.; 22 cm.
Howes no. P96.
Sabin no. 58786.

P293 Paul Wilhelm, Duke of Württemberg, 1797–1860.
Travels in North America, 1822–1824 / translated by W. Robert
Nitske; edited by Savoie Lottinville. Norman: University of Oklahoma Press, 1973.
xxxiv, 456 p.; ill.; 24 cm.

P294   Pausanius.
An account of the statues, pictures, and temples in Greece /
translated from the Greek of Pausanius by Uvedale Price. London: Printed for T. Evans, 1780.
251 p.; 21 cm.

P295   Pennell, Elizabeth Robins, 1855–1936.
Italy's garden of Eden / by Elizabeth Robins Pennell; with illustrations by Joseph Pennell. [Philadelphia]: Pennell Club, 1927.
[4], 36, [1] p.: ill.; 25 cm.

P296   Pennell, Elizabeth Robins, 1855–1936.
Over the Alps on a bicycle / by Elizabeth Robins Pennell. London: T. Fisher Unwin, 1898.
110 p.: ill.; 21 cm.

P297   Pennell, Elizabeth Robins, 1855–1936.
To gipsyland / written by Elizabeth Robins Pennell and illustrated by Joseph Pennell. New York: Century Co., 1893.
240 p., 28 leaves of plates: ill.; 20 cm.

P298   Pennell, Joseph, 1857–1926.
A Canterbury pilgrimage / ridden, written, and illustrated by
Joseph and Elizabeth Pennell. New York: Charles Scribner's
Sons, 1885.
78 p.: ill.; 22 cm.

P299   Pennell, Joseph, 1857–1926.
Our journey to the Hebrides / by Joseph Pennell and Elizabeth
Robins Pennell. New York: Harper and Brothers, 1889.
xx, 225, [6] p., 30 leaves of plates: ill.; 20 cm.

P300   Pennell, Joseph, 1857–1926.
Our sentimental journey through France and Italy / by Joseph &
Elizabeth Robins Pennell. London; New York: Longmans,
Green, 1888.
xvi, 268, [16] p., 20 leaves of plates: ill.; 20 cm.

P301   Pennell, Joseph, 1857–1926.
Two pilgrims' progress from fair Florence to the eternal city of
Rome / by Joseph and Elizabeth Robins Pennell; with pen drawings by Joseph Pennell. Boston: Little Brown, 1899.
181 p, 19 leaves of plates: ill.; 20 cm.

P302   Phillips, Sir Richard, 1767–1840.
A morning's walk from London to Kew / by Sir Richard Phillips.
London: J. and C. Adlard, 1820.
xvi, 393, [15] p.: ill., map; 20 cm.

P303   Pictet, Charles, 1755–1824.
Tableau de la situation actuelle des Etats-Unis d'Amériques:
d'après Jedidiah Morse et les meilleurs auteurs américains par
C. Pictet, de Genève. Paris: chez Du Pont, L'an III de la
République, 1795.
2 v.: fold. maps, fold. tab.: ill.; 20 cm.
Howes no. P349.
Sabin no. 62679.

P304   Piercy, Frederick Hawkins, 1830–91.
Route from Liverpool to the Great Salt Lake Valley . . . / by Frederick Piercy . . . ; edited by James Linforth. Liverpool: F. D. Richards; London: Latter Day Saints Book Depot, 1855.
viii, 120 p., 30 leaves of plates (1 fold.): ill.; 34 cm.
Howes no. L359.

P305   Piercy, Frederick Hawkins, 1830–91.
Route from Liverpool to Great Salt Lake Valley / by Frederick
Hawkins Piercy; edited by Fawn M. Brodie. Cambridge: Belknap
Press of Harvard University Press, 1962.
xxx, 313 p., 37 leaves of plates: ill; 25 cm.

P306   Pike, Zebulon Montgomery, 1799–1813.
An account of expeditions to the sources of the Mississippi: and
through the western parts of Louisiana to the sources of the
Arkansaw, Kans, La Platte and Pierre Jaun rivers . . . during the
years 1805, 1806, and 1807; and a tour through the interior parts

of New Spain . . . in the year 1807 / by Major Z. M. Pike. Philadelphia: C. and A. Conrad, [etc.], 1810.
5, 277, 65, 53, 87 p., 3 leaves of plates: charts; 26 cm.
Howes no. P373.
Sabin no. 62836.
Shaw/Shoemaker no. 21089.

P307 Pinart, Alphonse Louis, 1852–1911.
Journey to Arizona in 1876 / Alphonse Pinart; translated from the French by George H. Whitney; biography & bibliography of Pinart by Henry R. Wagner . . . Los Angeles: Zamorano Club, 1962.
xi, [4], 47 p., 1 fold. plate: col. ill.; 26 cm.

P308 Pons, François Raymond Joseph de, 1751–1812.
A voyage to the eastern part of Terra Firma or the Spanish Main in South-America: during the years 1801, 1802, and 1804 . . . / by F. Depons . . . translated by an American gentleman. New York: I. Riley, 1806.
3 v.; 23 cm.
Sabin no. 19642.
Shaw/Shoemaker no. 11180.

P309 Porter, Lavinia Honeyman.
By ox team to California: a narrative of crossing the plains in 1860 / by Lavinia Honeyman Porter. Oakland: Oakland Enquirer Publishing Co., 1910.
xi, 139 p.; 25 cm.
Howes no. P488.

P310 Power, Tyrone, 1797–1841.
Impressions of America during the years 1833, 1834, and 1835 / by Tyrone Power. Philadelphia: Carey, Lea and Blanchard, 1836.
2 v.; 19 cm.
Howes no. P533.
Shaw / Shoemaker no. 39694.
Sabin no. 64780.

P311   Prieto, Guillermo, 1818–97.
Viaje á los Estados-Unidos / por Fidel (Guillermo Prieto) (1877).
Mexico: Impr. de Dublan y Chavez, 1877–78.
3 v., ill.; 23 cm.
Howes no. P607.

P312   Pritchard, James Avery, 1816–62.
The overland diary of James A. Pritchard from Kentucky to California in 1849: with a biography of Captain James A. Pritchard by Hugh Pritchard Williamson. Denver: Fred A. Rosenstock, 1959.
221 p., 5 leaves of plates (some fold.): ill.; 27 cm.

P313   Pückler-Muskau, Herman, Fürst von, 1785–1871.
Tour in England, Ireland, and France in the years 1828 and 1829 . . . in a series of letters / by a German prince. Philadelphia: Carey and Lea, 1833.
xx, 571 p.; 23 cm.
Shaw/Shoemaker no. 20878.

P314   The rambles and reveries of an art-student in Europe. Philadelphia: T. T. Watts, 1855.
208 p.; 23 cm.

P315   Reed, Andrew, 1787–1862.
A narrative of the visit to the American churches by the deputation from the Congregation Union of England & Wales / by Andrew Reed and James Matheson. London: Jackson and Walford, 1835.
2 v.: ill.; 24 cm.
Sabin no. 68535.

P316   Remington, Frederic, 1861–1909.
Pony tracks / written and illustrated by Frederic Remington.
New York: Harper and Brothers, 1895.
viii, 269 p.; 23 cm.
Howes no. R207.

P317 Revere, Joseph Warren, 1812–80.
A tour of duty in California including a description of the gold
region and an account of the voyage around Cape Horn: with
notices of Lower California, the Gulf and Pacific coasts, and the
principal events attending the conquest of the California / by
Joseph Warren Revere . . . ; edited by Joseph N. Balestier. New
York: C. S. Francis; Boston: J. H. Francis, 1849.
vi, [6], 305, [6] p., 7 leaves of plates (1 fold.): ill.; 20 cm.
Howes no. R222.
Sabin no. 70182.

P318 Richards, F. De Bourg.
Random sketches; or, What I saw in Europe; from the portfolio
of an artist / by F. De B. Richards. Philadelphia: G. Collins, 1857.
344 p., 4 leaves of plates: ill.; 20 cm.

P319 Robertson, James, of Manchester, Eng.
A few months in America: containing remarks on some of its
industrial and commercial interests / by James Robertson . . .
London: Longman; Manchester, Eng.: James Galt, 1855.
vii, 230, [8] p.; 19 cm.
Howes no. R353.
Sabin no. 71954.

P320 Robin, Charles-César.
Voyage to Louisiana, 1803–1805 / by C. C. Robin; an abridged
translation from the original French by Stuart O. Landry, Jr.
New Orleans: Pelican Publishing Co., 1966.
270, [2] p.; 23 cm.

P321 Robin, Claude.
Nouveau voyage dans l'Amérique Septentrionale en l'année
1781: et campagne de l'armée de m. le comte de Rochambeau /
par m. l'abbé Robin. A Philadelphie; Paris: Chez Moutard, 1782.
ix, 222 p. 20 cm.
Howes no. R361.
Sabin no. 72033.

P322   Rogissart, sieur de, fl. 1706.
Les delices de l'Italie: contenant une description exacte du païs, des principales villes, de toutes les antiquités, & de toutes les raretez es qui s'y trouvent; ouvrage enrichi d'un très-grand nombre de figures en taille-douce . . . Paris: Par la Compagnie des Libraires, 1707.
4 v.: ill., maps; 18 cm.

P323   Rothschild, Salomon de, baron, 1835–64.
A casual view of America: the home letters of Salomon de Rothschild, 1859–1861 / translated and edited by Sigmund Diamond. Stanford, Calif.: Stanford University Press, 1961.
136 p.; 23 cm.

P324   Rousiers, Paul de, 1857–1934.
La vie américaine: ouvrage illustré . . . d'après les photographies faites spécialement pour l'ouvrage par M. Georges Rivière . . . Paris: Firmin-Didot, 1892.
698 p.: ill.; 30 cm.

P325   Roux de Rochelle, Jean Baptiste Gaspard, 1762–1849.
Welt-Gem-älde-Gallerie oder Geschichte und Beschreibung aller Lender und Velker, par Roux de Rochelle, Deutsch von Dr. C. A. Mebold. Stuttgart: E. Schweizerbart, 1838.
1 v. in 2,: ill.; 22 cm.

P326   [Russell, John], w. 1740.
Letters from a young painter abroad to his friends in England: adorned with copper plates. London: W. Russel, 1750.
2 v.: ill.; 20 cm.

P327   Ryan, William Redmond.
Personal adventures in Upper and Lower California in 1848–9: with the author's experience at the mines; illustrated by twenty-three drawings . . . / by William Redmond Ryan . . . London: William Shoberl, 1850.
2 v.: ill.; 19 cm.

Howes no. R558.
Sabin no. 74532.

P328   Saint Non, Jean Claude Richard de, 1727–91.
Voyage pittoresque: ou, Description des royaumes de Naples et
de Sicile. Paris: Imprimerie de Clousier, 1781–86.
4 v. in 5: ill., maps (some fold.); 51 cm.

P329   Sala, George Augustus, 1828–95.
My diary in America in the midst of war / by George Augustus
Sala. London: Tinsley Brothers, 1865.
2 v.; 22 cm.
Howes no. S45.

P330   Sansom, Joseph, 1765 or 1766–1826.
Letters from Europe during a tour through Switzerland and Italy
in the years 1801 and 1802 / written by a native of Pennsylvania.
Philadelphia: Printed for the author by A. Bartram and sold by
T. Dobson, 1805.
2 v.; 24 cm.
Shaw/Shoemaker no. 9311.

P331   Sarmiento, Domingo Faustino, 1811–88.
Travels in the United States in 1847 / translation and introductory essay by Michael Aaron Rockland. Princeton: Princeton University Press, 1970.
xiii, 330 p., 4 leaves of plates: ill.; 23 cm.

P332   Saugrain de Vigni, Antoine François, 1763–1820.
L'odyssée américaine d'une famille française / [par] le docteur
Antoine Saugrain; étude suivie de manuscrits inédits et de la cor-
respondance de Sophie Michau Robinson par H. Fouré Selter.
Baltimore: Johns Hopkins Press, 1936.
ix, 123 p., 12 leaves of plates: ill.; 23 cm.

P333   Schlissel, Lillian.
Women's diaries of the westward journey / Lillian Schlissel; pref.

by Carl N. Degler. New York: Schocken Books, 1982.
viii, 262 p.: ill.; 24 cm.

P334   Schöpf, Johann David, 1752–1800.
Travels in the Confederation [1783–1784] / from the German of
Johann David Schoepf, translated and edited by Alfred J. Mor-
rison . . . Philadelphia: W. J. Campbell, 1911.
2 v.: ill.; 20 cm.
Howes no. S176.

P335   Schoolcraft, Henry Rowe, 1793–1864.
Narrative journal of travels through the northwestern regions of
the United States: extending from Detroit through the great
chain of American lakes to the sources of the Mississippi River;
performed as a member of the expedition under Governor Cass
in the year 1820 / by Henry R. Schoolcraft . . . Albany: E. and
E. Hosford, 1821.
419, [4] p., 7 leaves of plates (1 fold.): ill. (some col.); 23 cm.
Howes no. S186.
Sabin no. 77862.
Shaw/Shoemaker no. 6729.

P336   Schoolcraft, Henry Rowe, 1793–1864.
Narrative of an expedition through the upper Mississippi to
Itasca Lake, the actual source of this river: embracing an explor-
atory trip through the St. Croix and Burntwood (or Broule) Riv-
ers in 1832 / by Henry R. Schoolcraft. New York: Harper and
Brothers, 1834.
307 p., 5 leaves of plates (some fold.): ill.; 22 cm.
Howes no. S187.
Sabin no. 77863.
Shaw/Shoemaker no. 26655.

P337   Schultz, Christian, ca. 1770–ca. 1814.
Travels on an inland voyage through the states of New York,
Pennsylvania, Virginia, Ohio, Kentucky, and Tennessee, and
through the territories of Indiana, Louisiana, Mississippi, and

New-Orleans: performed in the years 1807 and 1808 . . . / by
Christian Schultz, Jun. Ridgewood, N.J.: Gregg Press, [1968]
2 v. in 1: ill.; 24 cm.

P338   Shirreff, Patrick.
A tour through North America: together with a comprehensive
view of the Canadas and United States . . . / by Patrick Shirreff.
Edinburgh: Oliver and Boyd, 1835.
iv, v, 473 p.; 22 cm.
Howes no. S425.
Sabin no. 80554.

P339   Silliman, Benjamin, 1779–1864.
Remarks made on a short tour between Hartford and Quebec in
the autumn of 1819 / by the author of A journal of travels in
England, Holland, and Scotland. New-Haven: S. Converse, 1820.
407 p., 9 leaves of plates: ill.; 1820.
Howes no. S459.
Sabin no. 81041.
Shaw/Shoemaker no. 3225.

P340   Silliman, Benjamin, 1779–1864.
Remarks made on a short tour between Hartford and Quebec in
the autumn of 1819 / by the author of A journal of travels in
England, Holland, and Scotland. New-Haven: S. Converse, 1824.
443 p., 9 leaves of plates: ill.; 19 cm.
Howes no. S459.
Sabin no. 81042.
Shaw/Shoemaker no. 17985.

P341   Smet, Pierre-Jean de, 1801–73.
Missions de l'Orégon et voyages dans les montagnes rocheuses
en 1845 et 1846 / par le père P. J. de Smet . . . ; ouvrage traduit
de l'anglais, par M. Bourlez. Paris: Poussielgue-Rusand, 1848.
408 p., 19 leaves of plates: ill.; 18 cm.
Howes no. D286.
Sabin no. 82266.

P342   Smith, John, 1580–1631.
        The generall historie of Virginia, New England, & the Summer
        Isles: together with the true travels, adventures and observa-
        tions; and a sea grammar / by Capitain Smith. Glasgow: James
        MacLehose and Sons; New York: Macmillan Co., 1907.
        2 v.: ill., maps; 23 cm.

P343   Smith, John, 1580–1631.
        Travels and works of Captain John Smith, President of Virginia
        and Admiral of New England, 1580–1631 / edited by Edward
        Arber. Edinburgh: John Grant, 1910.
        2 v.: ill., maps; 22 cm.

P344   Smith, Joshua Toulmin, 1816–69.
        Journal in America, 1837–1838 / by Joshua Toulmin Smith, edited
        with introduction and notes by Floyd Benjamin Streeter. Me-
        tuchen, N.J.: Printed for C. F. Heartman, 1925.
        54 p.; 25 cm.

P345   Smith, William Loughton, 1758–1812.
        Journal of William Loughton Smith, 1790–1791 / edited by Albert
        Matthews. Cambridge, Eng.: Cambridge University Press, 1917.
        p. 21–88, 2 leaves of plates: ill.; 24 cm.

P346   Smyth, John Ferdinand Dalziel, 1745–1814.
        A tour in the United States of America: containing an account of
        the present situation of that country . . . / by J. F. D. Smyth.
        London: Printed for G. Robinson [etc.], 1784.
        2 v.; 22 cm.
        Howes no. S730.
        Sabin no. 85254.

P347   Sonnini de Manoncour, Charles Nicholas Sigisbert, 1751–1812.
        Travels in upper and lower Egypt / by C. S. Sonnini and by
        Vivant Denon during the campaigns of Buonaparte in that coun-
        try . . . Glasgow: W. Sommerville, A. Fullarton, J. Blackie, 1815.
        [5], 476 p., 6 leaves of plates (some fold.): ill.; 22 cm.

P348 Stansbury, Phillip, 1802?–70.
A pedestrian tour of two thousand three hundred miles in North
America . . . / by P. Stansbury. New York: J. D. Myers and
W. Smith, 1822.
xii, viii, [13]–274, [6] p., 9 leaves of plates: ill.; 19 cm.
Howes no. S885.
Sabin no. 90376.
Shaw/Shoemaker no. 10333.

P349 Staunton, Sir George Leonard, bart., 1737–1801.
An authentic account of an embassy from the King of Great
Britain to the Emperor of China . . .: taken chiefly from the
papers of His Excellency the Earl of Macartney . . . Sir Erasmus
Gower . . . and of other gentlemen in the several departments of
the embassy / by Sir George Staunton. Philadelphia: Printed for
Robert Campbell by John Bioren, 1799.
2 v. in 1: ill.; 22 cm.
Evans no. 36363.
Sabin no. 90843.

P350 Stebbins, William, 1786–1858.
The journal of William Stebbins, Stratford to Washington in
1810 / with an introduction by Leonard W. Labaree and notes by
Pierce W. Gaines. [Hartford, Conn.?]: Acorn Club, 1968.
57, [2] p.; 22 cm.

P351 Steedman, Charles John, b. 1856.
Bucking the sagebrush; or, The Oregon trail in the seventies / by
Charles J. Steedman; illustrated by Charles M. Russell. New
York; London: G. P. Putnam's Sons, 1904.
ix, 270 p., 13 leaves of plates (some fold.): ill. (some col.; 22 cm.
Howes no. S916.

P352 Steele, Edward Dunsha, 1829–65.
Edward Dunsha Steele, 1829–1865: pioneer, schoolteacher, cabinetmaker, and musician; a diary of his journey from Lodi, Wis-
consin, across the plains to Boulder, Colorado in the year 1859 /

edited by Nolie Mumey. Boulder, Colo.: Johnson Publishing
Co., 1960.
90 p., 1 fold. plate: map; 29 cm.

P353   Stephens, John Lloyd, 1805–52.
Incidents of travel in Central America, Chiapas, and Yucatan /
by John L. Stephens. London: John Murray, 1841.
2 v.: ill.; 23 cm.
Sabin no. 91297.

P354   Stephens, John Lloyd, 1805–52.
Incidents of travel in Yucatan / by John L. Stephens . . . illustrated by 120 engravings. New York: Harper and Brothers, 1843.
2 v.: ill.; 23 cm.
Sabin no. 91299.

P355   Stork, William.
A description of East-Florida: with a journal kept by John Bartram of Philadelphia, botanist to His Majesty for the Floridas,
upon a journey from St. Augustine up the river St. John's as far
as the lakes . . . London: Sold by W. Nicoll [etc.], 1769.
[4], viii, 40, xii, 35, [1] p., 3 leaves of fold. plates: ill.; 27 x 21 cm.
Sabin no. 92222.

P356   Strickland, Sir William, bart., 1753–1834.
Journal of a tour in the United States of America, 1794–1795 / by
William Strickland; edited by J. E. Strickland . . . New York:
New-York Historical Society, 1971.
xxiii, [3]–335 p., 17 leaves of plates: ill.; 25 cm.

P357   Strong, William Emerson, 1840–91.
A trip to the Yellowstone National Park in July, August, and September, 1875: from the journal of General W. E. Strong. Washington, D.C., 1876.
143 p., 16 leaves of plates (some fold.): ill.; 30 cm.
Howes no. S1083.

P358   Stuart, James, 1775–1849.
       Three years in North America. / by James Stuart. New York:
       J. and J. Harper, 1833.
       2 v.; 20 cm.
       Howes no. S1099.
       Sabin no. 93170.
       Shaw/Shoemaker no. 21389.

P359   Stuart, James, 1755–1849.
       Three years in North America / by James Stuart. Edinburgh: Rob-
       ert Caldwell; London: Whittaker, 1833.
       2 v.: ill., fold. map; 20 cm.
       Howes no. S1099.
       Sabin no. 93170.

P360   Stuart-Wortley, Lady Emmeline C. E. (Manners), 1806–55.
       Travels in the United States, etc. during 1849 and 1850 / by the
       Lady Emmeline Stuart-Wortley. New York: Harper and Brothers,
       1851.
       463, 4, 7, [5] p.; 20 cm.
       Howes no. W687.
       Sabin no. 93220.

P361   Stukeley, William, 1687–1765.
       Itinerarium curiosum; or, An account of the antiquitys, and
       remarkable curiositys in nature or art observed in travels thro'
       Great Britain / by William Stukeley. London: Printed for the
       author, 1724.
       [10], 198, [6] p., 100 leaves of plates (some fold).: ill.; 36 cm.

P362   Sutcliff, Robert, d. 1811.
       Travels in some parts of North America in the years 1804, 1805,
       & 1806 / by Robert Sutcliff. York, Eng.: Printed by C. Peacock for
       W. Alexander [etc.], 1811.
       xi, 293 p. 6 leaves of plates: ill.; 18 cm.
       Howes no. S1145.
       Sabin no. 93943.

P363   Sutcliff, Robert, d. 1811.
Travels in some parts of North America in the years 1804, 1805,
& 1806 / by Robert Sutcliff. Philadelphia: B. and T. Kite, 1812.
xi, 289 p.; 21 cm.
Howes no. S1145
Sabin no. 93943.
Shaw/Shoemaker no. 26833.

P364   Svin'in, Pavel Petrovich, 1788–1839.
Opyt zhyvopisnavo puteshestviya po severnoi Amerike. St.
Petersburg, Russia: Printshop, 1815.
[5], 219 p., 6 leaves of plates (some fold.): ill.; 18 cm.
Howes no. S1159.
Sabin no. 93992.

P365   Swan, John Alfred, 1817–96.
A trip to the gold mines of California in 1848 / by John A. Swan;
edited with introduction and notes by John A. Hussey. San Francisco: Book Club of California, 1960.
xxxv, 51 p., 1 plate: ill.; 25 cm.

P366   Tait, John Robinson, 1834–1909.
European life, legend, and landscape / by an artist. Philadelphia:
James Challen and Son, 1859.
154, [8] p.; 22 cm.

P367   Tardieu, André, 1876–1945.
Notes sur les Etats-Unis: la société, la politique, la diplomatie.
Paris: Calmann-Lévy 1908.
iii, 381 p.; 19 cm.

P368   Taylor, Bayard, 1825–78.
Eldorado; or, Adventures in the path of empire comprising a voyage to California via Panama, life in San Francisco and Monterey, pictures of the gold region, and experiences of Mexican
travel / by Bayard Taylor. New York: George P. Putman; London: R. Bentley, 1850.
2 v.: ill.; 19 cm.

Howes no. T43.
Sabin no. 94440.

P369   Taylor, Bayard, 1825–78.
Eldorado; or, Adventures in the path of empire comprising a voyage to California via Panama, life in San Francisco and Monterey, pictures of the gold region, and experiences of Mexican travel / by Bayard Taylor. New York: George P. Putnam, 1856.
xiv, 444 p., 7 leaves of plates: ill. (some col.); 19 cm.
Sabin no. 94440.

P370   Taylor, Bayard, 1825–78.
The lands of the Saracen; or, Pictures of Palestine, Asia Minor, Sicily, and Spain / by Bayard Taylor. New York: George P. Putnam; London: Sampson Low, Son, 1856.
451 p., 3 leaves of plates: ill., fold. map; 19 cm.

P371   Taylor, Bayard, 1825–78.
Picturesque Europe: a delineation by pen and pencil of the natural features and the picturesque and historical places of Great Britain and the continent. New York: D. Appleton, [1875–79].
3 v.: ill.; 33 cm.

P372   Taylor, Bayard, 1825–78.
A visit to India, China, and Japan in the year 1853 / by Bayard Taylor. New York: George P. Putnam, London: Sampson Low, Son, 1855.
xvii, [13]–539 p., 1 plate: ill.; 19 cm.

P373   Thornton, Jessy Quinn, 1810–88.
Oregon and California in 1848: with an appendix including recent and authentic information on the subject of the gold mines of California and other valuable matter of interest to the emigrant, etc. . . . / by J. Quinn Thornton . . . New York: Harper and Brothers, 1849.
2 v.: ill.; 21 cm.
Howes no. T224.
Sabin no. 95630.

P374   Torrington, John Byng, fifth viscount, 1742?–1813.
The Torrington diaries: containing the tours through England
and Wales of the Hon. John Byng (later fifth viscount Torrington) between the years 1781 and 1794 / edited with an introduction by C. Bruyn Andrew and with a general introduction by
John Beresford. London: Eyre and Spottiswoode, 1934–38.
4 v.: ill.; 22 cm.

P375   Townsend, John Kirk, 1809–51.
Narrative of a journey across the Rocky Mountains to the Colum-
bia River and a visit to the Sandwich Islands, Chili, &c.: with a
scientific appendix / by John K. Townsend. Philadelphia: Henry
Perkins; Boston: Perkins and Marvin, 1839.
352 p.; 24 cm.
Howes no. T319.
Sabin no. 96381.
Shaw/Shoemaker no. 58926.

P376   Trollope, Anthony, 1815–82.
North America / by Anthony Trollope. Philadelphia: J. B. Lippincott, 1862.
2 v. in 1; 22 cm.

P377   Tuckerman, Henry Theodore, 1813–71.
The Italian sketch book / by an American. Philadelphia: Key and
Biddle, 1835.
216 p.; 19 cm.
Shaw/Shoemaker no. 34620.

P378   Tuckerman, Henry Theodore, 1813–71.
The Italian sketch book. Boston: Sight and Stearns, 1837.
272 p.; 20 cm.
Shaw/Shoemaker no. 47130.

P379   Tudor, Henry.
Narrative of a tour in North America: comprising Mexico, the
mines of Real de Monte, the United States, and the British colonies . . . / by Henry Tudor. London: James Duncan, 1834.

2 v.; 19 cm.
Howes no. T404.

P380 Tudor, William, 1779–1830.
Letters on the eastern states / by William Tudor. Boston: Wells
and Lilly, 1821.
423 p.; 23 cm.
Howes no. T405.
Sabin no. 97407.
Shaw/Shoemaker no. 7016.

P381 Upham, Samuel Curtis, 1819–85.
Notes of a voyage to California via Cape Horn: together with
scenes in El Dorado in the years 1849–50; with an appendix containing reminiscences / by Samuel C. Upham. Philadelphia: By
the author, 1878.
594 p.: ill.; 24 cm.
Howes no. U23.

P382 Voyages au Kentoukey, et sur les bords du Genesée, précédé de
conseils aux liberaux, et à tous ceux qui se proposent de passer
aux Etats-Unis / par M**** . . . ; ouvrage accompagné d'une carte
géographique, levée sur les lieux par l'auteur en 1820. Paris:
M. Sollier, 1821.
243 p., 1 fold. plate: ill.; 22 cm.
Sabin no. 42898.

P383 Waldo, Samuel Putnam, 1780–1826.
The tour of James Monroe, President of the United States,
through the northern and eastern states in 1817: his tour in the
year 1818; together with a sketch of his life; with descriptive and
historical notices of the principal places through which he
passed / by S. Putnam Waldo. Hartford, Conn.: Silas Andrus,
1819.
348 p., 1 plate: ill.; 18 cm.
Howes no. W29.
Sabin no. 101012.
Shaw/Shoemaker no. 50014.

P384 Waller, John Augustine.
A voyage in the West Indies: containing various observations
made during a residence in Barbadoes and several of the Lee-
ward Islands / by John Augustine Waller. London: Printed for
Sir Richard Phillips, 1820.
[4], 106 p., 6 leaves of plates: ill.; 24 cm.
Sabin no. 101114.

P385 Waln, Robert, 1794–1825.
The hermit in America on a visit to Philadelphia: containing
some account of the human leeches, belles, beaux, coquettes,
dandies, cotillion poets, and painters of America / edited by
Peter Atall. Philadelphia: M. Thomas, 1819.
215 p.; 19 cm.
Howes no. W60.
Sabin no. 101137.
Shaw/Shoemaker no. 50022.

P386 Wansey, Henry, 1752?–1827.
An excursion to the United States of North America in the summer of 1794 . . . / by Henry Wansey. Salisbury: J. Easton [etc.],
1798.
xi, 270, [14] p., 2 leaves of fold. plates: ill.; 18 cm.
Sabin no. 101240.

P387 Waterton, Charles, 1782–1865.
Wanderings in South America, the North-west of the United
States, and the Antilles in the years 1812, 1816, 1820, & 1824
. . . / by Charles Waterton . . . New York: Sturgis and Walton
Co., 1909.
xxvi, 338 p., 16 leaves of plates: col. ill.; 22 cm.

P388 Welby, Adlard.
A visit to North America and the English settlements in Illinois:
with a winter residence at Philadelphia . . . / by Adlard Welby.
London: Printed for J. Drury [etc.], 1821.
xii, 224 p., 14 leaves of plates: ill.; 21 cm.

Howes no. W229.
Sabin no. 102514.

P389   Weld, Isaac, 1774–1856.
Travels through the states of North America and the provinces
of Upper and Lower Canada, during the years 1765, 1796, and
1797 / by Isaac Weld. London: John Stockdale, 1800.
2 v.: ill.; 22 cm.
Howes no. W235.
Sabin no. 102541.

P390   Weston, Richard.
A visit to the United States and Canada in 1833 . . . / by Richard
Weston. Edinburgh: Richard Weston and Sons [etc.], 1836.
ii, 312 p.; 18 cm.
Howes no. W291.
Sabin no. 103052.

P391   Wheler, Sir George, 1650–1723.
A journey into Greece . . .: a voyage from Venice to Constantinople; an account of Constantinople and the adjacent places; a voyage through the Lesser Asia; a voyage from Zant through several
parts of Greece to Athens; an account of Athens; several journey's from Athens into Attica, Corinth, Boeotia, &c. / by George
Wheler. London: Printed for W. Cademan [etc.], 1682.
483 p., 8 leaves of plates (some fold.): ill.; 31 cm.

P392   White, John, d. 1840.
History of a voyage to the China Sea / by John White. Boston:
Wells and Lilly, 1826.
ix, 327 p., 6 leaves of plates (1 fold.): ill.; 24 cm.
Sabin no. 103411.
Shaw/Shoemaker no. 27634.

P393   Wied, Maximilian, Prinz von, 1782–1867.
Reise in das innere Nord-America in den Jahren 1832 bis 1834 /
von Maximilian Prinz zu Wied. Coblenz, Ger.: J. Hoelscher,
1839–41.

4 v.: ill.; 32–46 cm.
Howes no. M443a.

P394   Wied, Maximilian, Prinz von, 1782–1867.
Travels in the interior of North America / by Maximilian, prince
of Wied . . . Leipzig: Schmidt and Guenther, [192–].
2 v.: ill.; 34 x 42 cm.
Howes no. M443a.
Sabin no. 47017.

P395   Wilson, Charles Henry.
The wanderer in America; or, truth at home . . . / by C. H. Wilson. Thirsk, Eng.: Printed for the author by Henry Masterman,
1824.
120 p.; 20 cm.
Howes no. W517.
Sabin no. 104611.

P396   Wilson, Ernest Henry, 1876–1930.
China, mother of gardens / by Ernest H. Wilson . . . Boston:
Stratford Co., 1929.
x, 408 p., 61 leaves of plates: ill., fold. map; 27 cm.

P397   Wilson, Henri.
Relation des iles Pelew, situées dans la partie occidentale de
l'océan Pacifique: composée sur les journaux et les commuinic-
ations du capitaine Henri Wilson . . . / traduit de l'Anglois de
George Keate. Paris: Le Jay fils, Maradan, 1788.
xiv, 384 p., 17 leaves of plates (some fold.): ill.; 26 cm.

P398   Wilson, Rufus Rockwell, 1865–1949.
Rambles in colonial byways / by Rufus Rockwell Wilson; illustrated from drawings by William Lincoln Hudson and from photographs . . . Philadelphia and London: J. B. Lippincott Co.,
1901.
2 v.: ill.; 19 cm.

P399   Wines, Enoch Cobb, 1806–79.
A trip to Boston: in a series of letters to the editor of the United
States Gazette / by the author of "Two years and a half in the
navy." Boston: C. C. Little and J. Brown, 1838.
224 p.; 17 cm.
Howes no. W560.
Sabin no. 104774.
Shaw/Shoemaker no. 53696.

P400   Winthrop, Theodore, 1828–61.
Life in the open air and other papers / by Theodore Winthrop.
Boston: Ticknor and Fields, 1863.
iv, 374 p.: 1 plate: ill.; 19 cm.

P401   Wollenweber, Louis August, 1807–88.
Gemälde aus dem Pennsylvanischen Volksleben . . . / von L. A.
Wollenweber. Philadelphia und Leipzig: Schäfer und Koradi,
1869.
143 p.; 16 cm.

P402   Wollstonecraft, Mary, 1759–97.
Letters written during a short residence in Sweden, Norway,
and Denmark / by Mary Wollstonecraft. Wilmington, Del.:
Printed for and sold by J. Wilson, and J. Johnson, 1796.
218, [5], 12, p.; 17 cm.
Evans no. 31653.

P403   Wood, W. W.
Sketches of China: with illustrations from original drawings / by
W. W. Wood. Philadelphia: Carey and Lea, 1830.
7, 250 p., 6 leaves of plates: ill.; 21 cm.
Shaw/Shoemaker no. 5533.

P404   Woods, John, d. 1829.
Two years' residence on the English prairie of Illinois / edited by
Paul A. Angle. Chicago: R. R. Donnelley and Sons Co., 1968.
xxxv, 242 p.: ill.; 18 cm.

P405   Wright, Edward.
Some observations made in travelling through France, Italy, &c.
in the years 1720, 1721, and 1722 / by Edward Wright. London:
Tho. Ward and E. Wicksteed, 1730.
2 v.: ill.; 26 cm.

P406   Wright, W. W.
Doré / by a stroller in Europe. New York: Harper and Brothers,
1857.
vi, 386, [2] p.; 20 cm.

Short-Title Bibliography

Clark, Thomas D. *Travels in the New South: A Bibliography*. Norman: University of Oklahoma Press, 1962.

Clark, Thomas D. *Travels in the Old South: A Bibliography*. Norman: University of Oklahoma Press, 1962.

Evans, Charles. *American Bibliography: A Chronological Dictionary of All Books, Pamphlets, and Periodical Publications Printed in the United States of America from the Genesis of Printing in 1639 Down to and Including the Year 1800, with Bibliographical and Biographical Notes*. Chicago: Printed for the author, 1903–59.

Howes, Wright. *U.S.iana (1650–1950): A Selective Bibliography in which Are Described 11,620 Uncommon and Significant Books Relating to the Continental Portion of the United States*. New York: R. R. Bowker for the Newberry Library, 1962.

Sabin, Joseph. *Bibliotheca Americana: A Dictionary of Books Relating to America from Its Discovery to the Present Time*. New York: J. Sabin, 1868–1936.

Shaw, Ralph R., and Richard Shoemaker. *American Bibliography . . .* New York: Scarecrow Press, 1958–89. (Authors record entire series that was also compiled by others and, from 1964, entitled *A Checklist of American Imprints . . .*)

Chronological Index to Manuscripts

Comprehensive Index to Manuscripts

222

Comprehensive Index

Lafayette, Marquis de, M55
Lake Erie, M81
Landis, Solomon, M78
Laurens, Henry, M19
Lawrence, Charles B., M19
Lawrence, James, M63
Lawyers, M19, M42, M44, M56, M74,
  M83
Lear in the Storm (painting), M19
Lebanon Co., Pa., M37, M78
Lee, Miss, M24
Lee, Robert E., M15
Leeds, Eng., M39
Lehman, George, M4
Leicester Academy, M44
Leipzig, Ger., M69
Leitner, Edward A., M4
Lengerts Wagon Shop, Philadelphia,
  M16
Leopold II, emperor of Austria, M28
Leslie, Charles Robert, M55
Libbey glass, M71
Life of Benjamin Franklin, The, M45
Life of Napoleon Bonaparte, M67
Life of Richard Savage, The, M67
Lincoln, Abraham, M13, M15, M34,
  M65, M68, M74
Linguists, M50, M56
Little, Arthur, M1
Little Egg Harbor, N.J., M91
Liverpool, Eng., M5, M28, M39,
  M40, M45, M57, M80. *See also*
  individual entries for specific
  sites, organizations, etc.
Liverpool Hero (ship), M63
London, M2, M5, M27, M28, M45,
  M47, M55, M57, M65, M68, M69.
  See also individual entries for spe-
  cific sites, organizations, etc.
London Bolt and Nut Company, Lon-
  don, M89
London Tract Society, London, M68
Long Branch, N.J., M90
Long Island, N.Y., M29, M90
Long Island Sound, M58
Loret, Victor, M57

Loring-Emmerton House, Salem,
  Mass., M1
Lossing, Benson J., M63
Louisiana, M74
Louvre, Paris, M27, M47, M68
Lovell, Albert A., M44
Lowell, Mass., M48. *See also* individ-
  ual entries for specific sites, orga-
  nizations, etc.
Lowell Institute, Lowell, Mass., M14
Lubeck, Ger., M47
Ludlow, R., M67
Luggage makers, M13
Lumbering, M66
Lutherans, M4, M45, M50, M52
Luxor, Egypt, M57
Lyons, Fr., M35, M45, M89
Lytton, Lord, M67

Mabie, Charles A., M51
Macao, China, M76
McClellan, George B., general, M74,
  M82
Madame Tussaud's Gallery, London,
  M27, M28, M68
Madison Co., N.Y., M24
Madonna of the Apostles, The (paint-
  ing), M14
Magdeburg, Ger., M45
*Maiden: A Story for My Young Coun-
  trywomen, The*, M80
Maine, M52, M66
Mainz, Ger., M28
Malden, Mass., M14, M65
Male diarists, M1-M3, M6, M9, M10,
  M13, M14, M16-M21, M23-M29,
  M31, M37, M39, M41, M43-M53,
  M55, M56, M58, M60, M62, M63,
  M65-M67, M90
Manahawkin, N.J., M90
Manchester, Eng., M39, M40
Manila, the Philippines, M76
Mansfield, La., M74
Mansion of Health, Manahawkin,
  N.J., M90
Marble Faun, The, M57

Retrospect of Western Travel, M36
Revolution. *See* United States Revo-
lution
Rhine River, Ger., M28, M89
Rhone River, Switz., M68
Rice plantations, M52
Richardson, J., M48
Richardson, Joseph G., M72
Richardson, Ruth Hoskins, M73
Richardson family, M26
Richmond, Maine, M23
Richmond, Va., M13, M65, M82
Richter, Mr., M45
Rikers Island, N.Y., M38
Rimmer, William, M14
Rinehart, W. G., M86
Robertson, Harry, M85
Rochester, N.Y., M8
Rockville, Md., M82
Rogers, Daniel, M54
Rogers, Elizabeth, M54
Rogers, Elizabeth Bromfield, M54
Rogers, Henry, M54
Rogers, John, M89
Rogers family, M54
Rome, It., M27, M35, M57, M68,
M88, M89. *See also* individual
entries for specific sites, organiza-
tions, etc.
Roosevelt, Theodore, M85
Rosemary Lane, London, M45
Rotterdam, Holland, M45
Rotunda, New York City, M67
Rouen, Fr., M35
Royal Gallery, Madrid, M88
Royal Palace, Berlin, M28
Royal Palace, Dresden, M28
Rumford, Charles G., M74
Rumford, Jonathan, M75
Rumford, Samuel Canby, M75
Rumford family, M75
Rush, Benjamin, M46, M87
Ruskin, John, M44
Russia, M47
Ruxer, J., M58

Sachs, Hans, M57
Sacketts Harbor, N.Y., M60
*Sailors and Saints; or, Matrimonial
Manoeuvers*, M67
St. Augustine, Fla., M30, M52. *See
also* individual entries for specific
sites, organizations, etc.
Saint George's Chapel, Windsor Cas-
tle, Eng., M68
Saint Helena, M27
Saint James Church, Bristol, Pa.,
M62
Saint John's Church, New York City,
M19
Saint Johns River, Fla., M5
Saint Laurent (steamboat), M89
Saint Matthew's Church, M17
Saint Paul's Cathedral, London,
M28, M68
Saint Peter's Cathedral, Rome, M27,
M68
St. Petersburg, M47, M69. *See also*
individual entries for specific
sites, organizations, etc.
Salem, Mass., M1. *See also* individual
entries for specific sites, organiza-
tions, etc.
Salem, N.H., M20
Salisbury, Md., M86
Salisbury, N.H., M32
San Francisco, Calif., M6
Sanitary Fairs, M13, M34
Saratoga, N.Y., M80
Sass Gallery, London, M55
Savage, Edward, M19
Sawmills, M58, M83
Saws, M21
Saxony, Ger., M50
Scattergood, Thomas, M26
Scholars' Club, Boston, M20
School students. *See* Students
Schoolteachers. *See* Teachers
Schuylkill River, Pa., M89
Scientific American, M21, M88
Scotland, M39, M57, M68

Geographical Index to Published Travel Accounts